W9-AUN-742

WARPLANES
OF THE WORLD
1918-1939

WARPLANES
OF THE WORLD
1918-1939

Michael J.H. Taylor

Charles Scribner's Sons
NEW YORK

Contents

Copyright © Ian Allan Ltd 1981

U.S. edition published by Charles Scribner's Sons 1981

Copyright under the Berne Convention

All rights reserved. No part of this book
may be reproduced in any form without the
permission of Charles Scribner's Sons.

1 3 5 7 9 11 13 15 17 19 I/C 20 18 16 14 12 10 8 6 4 2

Printed in Great Britain
Library of Congress Catalog Number: 81-50925
ISBN: 0-684-16984-3

Introduction

To the uninformed casual observer, the interwar years might seem to have been dull, uneventful and without any real significance, compared with the years of World War 1 and 2. He might well assume them to have been a time of relief from the massive slaughter of 1914-18, of peace and of slow technical advance. How wrong he would be. It was a time of continuous strife somewhere in the world, a time of trial and error in new methods of aerial warfare, a time when the beaten nations of World War 1 re-emerged as new aggressive powers and a time which moulded the events that led up to the greatest aerial battle in history, World War 2.

Technically, it was during the 1919-39 'peaceful era' that most of the major changes in aircraft construction and configuration took place. It heralded the almost total supersedence of the biplane by the low-wing monoplane, the change from wood to metal construction, from open to enclosed cockpits and from fixed to retractable undercarriages. However, with the start of hostilities by Nazi Germany in 1939, there were still many first line aircraft in service around the world that had been built before or had not adhered to the latest trends. Poland was one country that paid the ultimate price for its outdated open-cockpit high-wing fighters. However, there are always exceptions to any rule, and aircraft like the Gloster Gladiator biplane fighter and the German Junkers Ju87 dive bomber with its fixed undercarriage were examples of modern technology in old guises. It should always be remembered that it was during this period that the first jet aircraft flew, in the form of the German Heinkel He178.

From an historical viewpoint, the interwar years started in November 1918 when Germany surrendered to the Allies. The Versailles Treaty was signed in June 1919 and this made Germany surrender its World War 1 aircraft and aero-engines, banned the further construction or sponsorship of military aircraft and, most important, forbade the existence of a German Air Force. It was not long before German aircraft manufacturers got round this by setting up factories in other countries including Russia, Sweden and Switzerland. There, they built military types for other nations as well as later, in the guise of harmless transport aircraft, producing bomber prototypes ready for the re-emergence of the Luftwaffe in 1933.

Another view of things to come was the launching of the first US aircraft carrier, the USS *Langley,* in September 1922 and the first Japanese carrier, the *Hosho*, in December of the same year, both following Britain's lead. Ironically, it was Britain who taught Japan the techniques of carrier operations and methods of torpedo attack, and an ex-Sopwith employee who designed some of the first military aircraft to be home-produced in Japan. It was a small and non-aggressive gesture, but the lessons were put to practical use when, in 1942, carrier forces of America and Japan met in the Battle of the Coral Sea and the Battle of Midway. Luckily, America triumphed and the latter battle turned the tide of events against Japan.

Meanwhile, in post World War 1 Britain both the RAF and the Naval air service had been dramatically reduced in size, leaving only a small number of squadrons and flights to 'carry on' as best they could. At the end of the war the RAF had an impressive inventory of 22,650 aircraft and no less than 188 operational squadrons. By the close of 1919 the number of operational squadrons had been cut to 12 and the Naval air service had been reduced still further. As so often seen today, the need for economy caused the near-strangulation of both services and they were kept alive mainly by Britain's overseas commitments. Operations by mixed British forces against the 'Mad Mullah' in 1920, the policing of countries like Germany, Iraq and India, all helped the air services in those early, difficult, postwar years to prove themselves being worthwhile, even in a time of peace. In fact, such was the importance of the overseas commitments that all but two RAF squadrons were stationed away from home. Needless to say, this also reflected the relatively safe position, in terms of possible hostilities, in which postwar Britain found itself. It was not until the early 1920s that the first new fighters, in the form of Gloster Grebes for the RAF and Nieuport Nightjars for the Navy, went into service.

Some reference has already been made to American and Japanese aircraft carriers, but it was Britain who commissioned the first carriers with a flush-deck and the first off-set island structure — HMS *Argus* and HMS *Eagle* respectively. The rapid development of carriers by Britain reflects the seriousness in which such operations were held. Aircraft arrester techniques went through many stages of development both in Britain and abroad, and the British insistence on armoured metal landing decks held the Royal Navy in very good stead when, during World War 2, Japanese suicide aircraft did relatively little harm compared with that done to the wooden-deck carriers of America.

The 1930s started with the RAF receiving its first new Hawker Hart light bombers and, in the tradition of the Fairey Fox and in the same way as the later Bristol Blenheim I, they proved faster than the contemporary fighters. The Hart was an outstanding aircraft, with very clean lines, and developed from it was a whole line of fighter, army co-operation and bomber aircraft. On a wider historical front, it was in September 1931 that Japan attacked China. For the peace-loving nations, all hopes for the future were pinned on the 1932 International Disarmament Conference held under the authority of the League of Nations. However, Japan withdrew in March 1933 and Germany followed in October. It was also in 1933 that Winston Churchill gave the first warnings about the growth of military aviation in Germany; but it took another two years for Hitler to announce the existence of the Luftwaffe.

That year of 1935 was an important one for Britain, as the first moves were made to provide radar cover, and the first flight took place of the great Hawker Hurricane fighter (and incidentally the German Bf109). Also in 1935, widespread hostilities started. Italy invaded Abyssinia in October, and in the following March Germany occupied the Rhineland. Within a few months, German forces were fighting in the Spanish Civil War, and soon began testing their most modern combat aircraft under battle conditions.

The final chapter of the interwar years started in 1938 with the German occupation of Austria and the signing of the Munich Agreement. Had the war started at the time of the Munich Crisis, the Battle of Britain might well have been fought by a collection of Gloster Gauntlets, Gladiators and a small number of Hurricanes then in service. The extra year gave the RAF time to add the famous Spitfire to its inventory.

The story ends with the invasion of Czechoslovakia and Poland in 1939. This brought the so-called 'interwar' period to an abrupt end, and the military aircraft of the following years are fully covered in a companion book of this series, *Aircraft of World War 2* by Kenneth Munson.

The author wishes to acknowledge the valuable help given by Malcolm Passingham in respect of several French, Italian, Japanese and Soviet entries, and expresses gratitude to the many companies from around the world that supplied material from their archives.

Errata

In a reference book of this nature, first started in 1974, production exigencies and the discovery of new information often leads to inaccuracies. The following were found at a late stage in production:

p8 **Aichi D1A** The dive bomber prototype was a modification of the *2nd* German prototype.

p12 **Arado Ar65** Photo: Ar68A prototype.

p14 **Armstrong Whitworth Whitley** Photo: Mk II.

p27 **Boeing PW-9** Max speed: 163mph.

p33 **Caproni Ca133** Length: 50ft 4.25in.

p41 **Dewoitine D27C1** The D1 began life in *1922*.

p49 **Fairey Swordfish** Span: 45ft 6in, Length: 36ft 4in.

p72 **Hawker Nimrod** Max speed: 181mph.

p75 **Heinkel He51** The He51B models fitted out as seaplanes were designated *He51B-2*.

p85 **Latécoère 298** The 298 had a *three*-man crew.

p90 **Martin B-10** The US Army ordered *seven* Douglas YB-7s.

p92 **Martin T3M/T4M** Max speed: 121mph.

p96 **Mitsubishi 2MR** Armament: *Four* 7.7mm MGs.

p103 **Ni-D62C1** The Ni-D622 engine was an H-S 12Md.

p127 **Vickers Wellesley** Range: 1,100-2,590 miles.

p146 **Grumman JF/J2F Duck** Engine: 750hp.

p149 **Junkers Ju86** The very high altitude reconnaissance versions were designated Ju86P/Ju86R.

p163 **Potez 63** Photo: Romanian Potez 633.

p170 **Nakajima E4N1** This was the predecessor of the E8N.

p173 **Norway** Marines *Flyverbatfabrikk*.

p174 **Avro 504** Photo: Avro 504N.

Part One

Aero A11   Czechoslovakia

Purpose: General purpose
Makers: Aero Tovàrna Letadel
In service: From 1928
Photo: Finnish Aero A11

Engine: One 240hp Walter W-IV
Span: 41ft 11.25in
Length: 26ft 11in
Height: 10ft 2in
Weight loaded: 3,381lb
Crew: Two
Max speed: 133.5mph
Service ceiling: 25,000ft
Range: 465.5 miles
Armament: One forward-firing Vickers machine gun and two rear-mounted Lewis guns

Developed from the heavier and slightly larger Aero A12, the A11 first flew in 1923. It was a second generation aircraft, destined to supersede the early Letov types that had been built soon after the inauguration of the Czech aircraft industry during 1918-19. However, unlike the Letovs which had bulky but streamlined round-section fuselages, the A11 followed much more closely the general configuration already established by Aero in its earlier products. With a fuselage of steel-tube construction and wooden wings, all fabric covered, the A11 was powered by a 240hp Walter W-IV engine (a virtual copy of a German BMW inline) and, unlike the A12, had a frontal radiator. A large number of variants were produced through the 1920s, made possible by the fact that different engines of greatly varying power could be fitted in the aircraft. Major variants found in the total of 440

aircraft built included the basic A11 (with standard equipment including photographic and wireless apparatus) and A11N day and night reconnaissance biplanes respectively, and Ab11 and Ab11N day and night light bombers respectively. The bombers were powered by Breitfeld Danek Perun II six-cylinder engines, each producing 240hp at normal rating (although of original design, the Perun was largely based on German engines). Other important variants included the A11H-S, which was a modification of the A11 — although often stated to be a modification of the Ab11 — with a 300hp Hispano-Suiza 8Fb engine, deeper fuselage and other structural changes, removable observer/trainee dual controls and only one rear gun. A number were built for Finland and, although general performance was lower than that of the A11, the type proved highly manoeuvrable. Day and night advanced flying trainer versions of the A11 were also built, powered by 180hp Perun I engines, as was the Perun II-powered A29 twin-float seaplane, nine of which were produced and flown by the Czech Army Air Force as target tugs. Maximum speed was 121mph. The latter were the first seaplanes to be designed and built in Czechoslovakia. Subsequent derivatives of the A11 included the larger A30 long-range reconnaissance bomber which had an endurance of 6hr (powered by a 500hp Skoda L engine) and the A32 (qv).

As well as setting many duration records in 1925 (including a 13.25hr flight on 13 September 1925 and flights made to Cracow and Warsaw in October of the same year), an Ab11, crewed by Captain Stanovsky and M. Simek, was flown in 1926 on a 9,320-mile journey which encompassed many countries in Europe, North Africa and Turkey.

Aero A32

Purpose: Close support
Makers: Aero Továrna Letadel
In service: From 1928
Photo: Ap32

Engine: One 420hp Walter-built Jupiter IV radial
Span: 40ft 9.5in
Length: 26ft 11in
Height: 10ft 2in
Weight loaded: 4,248lb
Crew: Two
Max speed: 143mph
Service ceiling: 18,000ft
Range: over 495 miles
Armament: Two forward-firing Vickers machine guns and two Lewis machine guns in rear cockpit. Underwing racks for 12 22lb bombs

In the first half of the 1920s a firm named J. Walter & Co of Prague received a licence to build the powerful Jupiter radial engine from the Bristol Aircraft Co of England. Aero planned to use the Czech-built Jupiter engine in two new aircraft, the A27 twin-engined night bomber and the Aero A32. The latter was basically another derivative of the excellent A11, and the prototype was no more than an Ab11 installed with the new engine and designated A11J (J for Jupiter). However, because of the modifications incorporated into production A11Js, the type was redesignated A32. 31 were delivered to the Czech Army Air Force for close support work, bombing and reconnaissance duties. Two other refined variants were produced from 1930, the Ap32 and Apb32. These differed from the earlier type in having revised undercarriages and other improvements including neater engine cowlings. These, together with 16 A32s ordered for the Finnish Air Force and powered by Gnome-Rhône Jupiter engines licence-built in France, raised the total of A32s and variants built to 116 aircraft.

Aero A100 and A101

Purpose: Reconnaissance/Bomber
Makers: Aero Továrna Letadel Dr Kabes
In service: From 1934
Photo: Aero A101
Data: Aero A100

Engine: One 650hp Avia Vr36
Span: 48ft 3in
Length: 34ft 9in
Height: 11ft 6in
Weight loaded: 7,100lb
Crew: Two
Max speed: 168mph
Service ceiling: 21,325ft
Range: 590 miles
Armament: Two forward-firing Vickers machine guns and two Lewis guns in rear cockpit. Up to 1,320lb of bombs

Originating as a variant of the Aero A30, the A100 was first designated A430. Compared with the earlier aircraft it was considerably modernised and supported several features that it shared with Aero's new two-seat trainer, the A46. Both were far more streamlined, the rear-mounted Lewis guns of the A100 being fitted to a flexible mounting to allow stowage when not required, to reduce drag. Both aircraft were given divided-type undercarriages, while their engines, although of different type, were neatly cowled. Beneath the engine of each was situated a radiator in a tunnel with controllable shutters. The A100 took part in, and won, a competition held by the Czech Defence Ministry in 1933, after which production of the aircraft was initiated. 44 examples were built in 1933-5, and these served as long-range armed reconnaissance aircraft, although they actually had a shorter endurance than the A30. However, compared with the types that were then operational in reconnaissance or general purpose roles with other air forces, the A100 had favourable performance. Two bomber variants of the A100 were also built, the A101 and Ab101. The 29 A101s, built at the same time as the A100s, were generally similar externally, differing mainly in having a re-shaped vertical tail of greater area, a modified rear cockpit and a new undercarriage. Power was provided by an 800hp Praga-built Isotta-Fraschini Asso-1000 engine (Praga being the former Breitfeld Danek company). The last variant of the design, and last Czech-built biplane bomber, was the larger Ab101. More than 60 examples were produced from 1936 as a stop-gap measure, powered by 860hp Praga-built Hispano-Suiza 12Y engines. These were not only unsuccessful in terms of performance but were of such outdated design that when production ceased in 1938 they were withdrawn from service. The bomber variants of the design carried bombs vertically in the forward fuselage, these being released pneumatically, and externally beneath the fuselage.

Aichi D1A

Japan

Purpose: Dive bomber/Reconnaissance
Makers: Aichi Tokei Denki KK (Aichi Clock and Electric Co Ltd)
In service: 1934-39
Photo: D1A1
Data: D1A2

Engine: One 610hp Nakajima Hikari radial
Span: 37ft 5in
Length: 30ft 6in
Height: 11ft 2.25in
Weight loaded: 5,755lb
Crew: Two
Max speed: 193mph
Range: 575 miles
Armament: Two forward-firing 7.7mm machine guns and one in rear cockpit. 835lb of bombs (682lb in D1A1 version)

Although the Imperial Japanese Navy had operated aircraft carriers since the early 1920s — one of only four countries that had taken seriously this new type of fighting ship — it at first had to rely heavily on foreign expertise in the field of shipboard aircraft design. In 1933, a competition was held between Aichi Tokei Denki and the Nakajima Aircraft Works for a carrier-borne dive bomber. The Aichi-produced D1A1 won and was ordered into production as the Type 94 Model 1, powered by the 580hp Nakajima Kotobuki II-Kai 1 radial engine; and 162 examples were produced for the Naval Air Service. However, the design was far from being totally original. In 1931 the Japanese Navy had ordered a twin-float reconnaissance-bomber from Ernst Heinkel Flugzeugwerke of Germany suitable for shipboard operations. The resulting aircraft was designated He50 and, following development and modification of the design, a few aircraft were delivered to the Aichi company in 1933 as He66 export reconnaissance aircraft, plus a dive bomber prototype (He50B). (Interestingly, a number of He50s were also taken into service by the German Luftwaffe, and a small number were bought by and eventually operated in China.) The Aichi dive bomber prototype was in fact the re-engined and modified German prototype; after further modification to the wings, undercarriage and tail surfaces, the D1A1 entered production and first went on board the Japanese aircraft carrier *Ryujo* in 1934 — Japan's fourth carrier, commissioned in 1933 and destined to be sunk in 1942. Also in 1934, the JNAF issued new requirements for a dive bomber. By strengthening and refining the D1A1, Aichi produced the D1A2, the first of which flew in October 1936. Although external differences were few, the D1A2 had wheel spats fitted to the improved undercarriage. The wing structure was also improved and a Nakajima Hikari radial engine was installed, fitted with a longer-chord cowling. Entering production as the Type 96 bomber, no fewer than

428 examples were produced. Aircraft of the type attacked and sunk, in 1937, the USS *Panay* in the Yangtse incident and were used during the second Sino-Japanese conflict (as were the Chinese He50s). A limited number of Hikari 1-powered D1A2-K trainers were used by the JNAF and these continued to fly during the early part of World War 2.

Amiot 140 and 143 France

Purpose: Bomber/Reconnaissance
Makers: Amiot (SECM)
In service: From 1935
Photo and Data: Amiot 143

Engines: Two 870hp Gnome-Rhône 14K radials
Span: 80ft 6.5in
Length: 59ft 10.5in
Height: 16ft 9.75in
Weight loaded: 21,385lb
Crew: Five
Max speed: 192.5mph
Service ceiling: over 26,250ft
Max range: 807 miles
Armament: Four 7.5mm machine guns in nose turret, dorsal turret and ventral position.
Up to 1,984lb of bombs carried internally, plus bombs carried externally

To meet an Armée de l'Air requirement for a multi-seat combat aircraft (taken to mean a bomber suited

to day and night operations and heavily armed with machine guns) several French companies produced, in 1930, fairly large twin-engined prototypes for evaluation. Although all the prototypes had some unconventional design features, all but one were of roughly similar configuration. The odd man out was the Breguet 41 which had sesquiplane wings, a very deep forward fuselage containing the internal bomb compartment and positions for the pilots, nose and rear gunners, and a tapering boom-type rear fuselage. However, in the autumn of 1933 the specification was changed to bring in the additional roles of fighting and reconnaissance. Having evaluated the aircraft, the Amiot 140M was chosen for production and an order for 40 was placed. In a continuing programme of development the Amiot 141M was designed, differing from the earlier model only in having 700hp Lorraine Orion engines (instead of 650hp Lorraine 12Fas) and in being re-stressed to allow a heavier bomb load to be carried. This model, like the following Amiot 142 with 650hp Hispano-

9

Suiza 12Ybrs engines, was not adopted for service. However, in August 1943 the first flight took place of an improved version, the Amiot 143M. A total of 138 were eventually built, and were delivered to the Armée de l'Air from mid-1935. By the end of the year no less than 40 had been accepted into service. The last production versions of the basic design were five-seat Amiot 143B5s and four-seat 143BN4s, for day and night duties respectively, and were delivered from the end of 1937. The 143 version featured an enclosed cockpit for the pilot and turrets for the nose and upper rear gunners (all of which were open positions in the Amiot 140M), while a similar type of deep balcony under the forward fuselage to that of the 140M, although less streamlined, housed the bomb aimer, ventral rear gunner and bomb bay. Despite being obsolete 91 were still in service, including six in storage and 29 set apart for training, in late 1939. The aircraft's most famous action of the war was performed on 14 May 1940 when 13 Amiot 143s of Groupement 9 and 10 made a daylight attack on the bridges over the River Meuse at Sedan, and the area nearby, in a vain attempt to halt the invading German armies.

ANF Les Mureaux 113, 114, 115 and 117   France

Purpose: Reconnaissance/Bomber/Fighter
Makers: Les Ateliers de Constructions du Nord de la France et des Mureaux
In service: From 1933
Photo: 115 prototype
Data: ANF 113

Engine: One 650hp Hispano-Suiza 12Ybrs
Span: 50ft 6in
Length: 32ft 9.5in
Height: 11ft 9in
Weight loaded: 5,525lb
Crew: Two
Max speed: 199mph
Service ceiling: 34,750ft
Range: 620 miles
Armament: See below

In the early 1930s the French aircraft industry had a predilection for designing its smaller aircraft with parasol wings. No exception to this was the Mureaux 113 reconnaissance aircraft, which had been developed from the 650hp Hispano-Suiza-powered Mureaux 110. It was of all-metal construction, the outer wing surfaces being supported by a pair of struts from each side of the fuselage. The deep rectangular-section fuselage accommodated the pilot in the front cockpit and the observer in the rear, the latter having a foldable seat and removable dual controls. A divided undercarriage was fitted, with faired wheels. The radiator, installed inside a tunnel with controllable shutters, was prominently placed below the engine. Under a modernisation and expansion programme for the air force, a total of 49 entered service in 1934. However, four years later only about one-third remained in service, these being operated as two-seat night fighters together with four Mureaux 114 experimental night fighters. The Mureaux 115 was also ordered under the original modernisation programme, and subsequent programmes, and 97 Mureaux 115R2s (delivered from mid-1930s) and 22 115R2-B2s were built. Both Mureaux 115 versions featured a new flat frontal radiator, replacing the earlier-described underslung type, while equipment changes could also be found. The fighter-bomber version was armed with one 20mm forward-firing cannon, by virtue of its Hispano-Suiza 12Ycrs 'moteur canon' engine, two rear-mounted machine guns and up to 661lb of bombs. However, the 'moteur canon' installation did not prove a success and the forward armament was subsequently changed to one 7.5mm MAC gun firing through the propeller shaft and two more guns. In 1935 the Mureaux 117R2 reconnaissance aircraft was produced, featuring strengthened wings. 105 examples were eventually built, along with 12 Mureaux 117R2-B2 fighter-bombers, powered by the 'moteur canon' engine. Additional armament consisted of two machine guns fore and aft and up to 441lb of bombs. Mureaux 115/117s were gradually, from 1939, replaced by Potez 63/11s. Nevertheless more than 200 Moreaux types were available in May 1940, reduced to 62 by the end of June.

Ansaldo A300 Series　　　　　　　　　　Italy

Purpose: General purpose
Makers: Società Anonima Aeronautica Ansaldo
In service: From 1921
Photo and Data: A300-4

Engine: One 300hp Fiat A12bis
Span: 36ft 10.25in
Length: 28ft 8.5in
Height: 9ft 9in
Weight loaded: 3,750lb
Crew: Two
Max speed: 124mph
Service ceiling: 21,325ft
Armament: Three machine guns, two fixed
forward-firing and one in rear cockpit

Up to 1923, the Italian Air Force had not been independent of the Army and Navy and, as a result, had been badly neglected after the end of World War 1. Without a firm governmental air policy and with demobilisation of its units, the air force had become virtually non-existent as a viable fighting force. This situation was aggravated further by the lack of financial support for the aircraft manufacturers to build new prototype aircraft. However, with the forming of the Air Force proper as the Regia Aeronautica, pride was quickly restored and the number of fully operational squadrons rapidly increased, flying mostly newly built aircraft, all under the watchful eye of Italy's head of state, Sig Mussolini. One of the few new aircraft built during the difficult period was the Ansaldo A300, the prototype of which appeared in 1919 and heralded the start of a series of aircraft that were built in very large numbers for the Regia Aeronautica. The original A300 was modified in 1920 into the A300-2, and a limited number were produced as two-seat reconnaissance aircraft (reconnaissance squadrons making up the largest section of the air force). These were followed by the A300-3 three-seater, of which nearly 90 were constructed. Like the earlier aircraft, these were powered by 300hp Fiat A12bis engines. However, it was with the A300-4 version that quantity production really got underway. The prototype made its maiden flight in 1922 and was soon ordered into production. About 700 two-seat A300-4s were built and were used for reconnaissance and light attack duties, powered by a developed version of the A12bis. It is probable that A300-4s took part in the occupation of Corfu in 1923. A300-4s played an ever-increasing role in the air force during the expansion years, when the 1924-5 figure of some 60 squadrons was raised to 84 (not including training) by 1926. The only other military version to enter production was the A300-6. Interestingly, a civil passenger version of the A300 was also produced, with the fuselage extended over the upper biplane wing (and many other structural changes) and with enclosed accommodation for four passengers. In 1925 the aircraft division of Ansaldo was taken over by Fiat, and in the following year was renamed Aeronautica d'Italia.

Arado Ar65, Ar68 and Ar197   Germany

Purpose: Fighter
Makers: Arado Flugzeugwerke GmbH
In service: 1936-40 (Ar68)
Data: Ar68E

Engine: One 690hp Junkers Jumo 210Da
Span: 36ft 1in
Length: 31ft 2in
Height: 10ft 10in
Weight loaded: 4,450lb
Crew: One
Max speed: 208mph
Service ceiling: 26,600ft
Range: over 300 miles
Armament: Two 7.9mm MG17 machine guns.
Provision for six underwing bombs

Despite the fact that Germany did not officially announce the existence of the Luftwaffe until 9 March 1935, the air service had, in fact, been reborn several years earlier. Under a series of partially disguised names, all used so as not to evoke action from other nations rather than just to adhere to the Treaty of Versailles, the basis for an air force had been formed by the turn of the decade and German aircraft manufacturers were busy designing military aircraft accordingly. With several unsuccessful but nevertheless important prototype fighters under its belt, Arado produced the Ar65 in 1931. Powered by a BMW VI engine with a continuous rating of about 500hp, the type entered production as the Arado Ar65E, and deliveries began in 1933. With a maximum speed of 186mph, the Ar65 was unspectacular, but it was a start. During production, the Ar65E gave way to the Ar65F, which differed little, and these remained operational as fighters until 1935, when they began to be transferred to training units. Meanwhile, the Ar68 had appeared in 1933. Five prototypes were built, the first and fourth with BMW VI engines, the others with Junkers Jumo 210s. Following production of a small number of Ar68Fs, with the BMW powerplant, the Ar68E entered production with the Jumo engine and became the major version. The Luftwaffe received its first Ar68Fs in 1936, supplemented soon after by 'Es'. Although an improvement over the Heinkel He51, the biplane fighter had had its day and these were gradually replaced by more modern types. However, a few remaining Ar68s were used as night fighters during the first winter of the war. Following development of the Ar68G and 'H' versions — the 'H' fitted with an 850hp BMW132 radial engine and having an enclosed cockpit — three prototypes of a similar type to the latter were built as Ar197s. The second and third prototypes were powered by 815hp and 880hp BMW engines respectively, while the first had a Junkers Jumo 210. All three flew in 1937. The type was to have been used as a fighter and light bomber operating from German aircraft carriers. In the event, no production was undertaken. However, it is interesting to note that although Germany planned to have six carriers in service during World War 2, none were completed. The largest of these would have been the *Graf Zeppelin*, which was launched in 1938 but was never finished. The *Seydlitz* was a converted cruiser and was scuttled uncompleted in 1945.

Armstrong Whitworth Atlas

UK

Purpose: Army co-operation
Makers: Sir W. G. Armstrong Whitworth Aircraft Ltd
In service: From 1927

Engine: One 450hp Armstrong Siddeley Jaguar IVC radial
Span: 39ft 6in
Length: 28ft 6in
Height: 10ft 6in
Weight loaded: 4,000lb
Crew: Two
Max speed: 143mph
Service ceiling: 17,300ft
Range: 480 miles
Armament: One fixed forward-firing Vickers machine gun and one Lewis machine gun in rear cockpit. Four 112lb bombs could be carried on racks under wings

During World War 1 the Armstrong Whitworth company built a number of military aircraft for use in the reconnaissance, light bombing and fighter roles. Designs, understandably, varied considerably. However, after the war the company designed the Siskin fighter and then retained the same basic configuration for a number of later aircraft, including the Starling and AW16 fighters and the Atlas. The Atlas typified the RAF's main activity in the 1920s, that of policing and trouble-shooting in the Middle East and India. It was designed as a 'maid of all work', enabling the one aircraft type to carry out the many tasks required of a small policing force, often in hostile territory. It had a long range, which could be extended further by the use of auxiliary underwing

tanks, and was equipped with wireless apparatus, message retrieving gear (attached to the undercarriage and hooked beneath the fuselage when not being used) and a camera for its main role as an army co-operation aircraft. Forward and rear-mounted machine guns and underwing bomb racks gave it the muscle required to deal with unruly natives. The prototype Atlas made its maiden flight on 10 May 1925, powered by a 450hp Jaguar radial engine. Production started in the following year as a replacement for the ageing Bristol Fighter (which had been in service since 1917, latterly as a general purpose aircraft). Atlas Is could be powered by one of a number of Armstrong Siddeley Jaguar or Jaguar/Major radial engines. When the Atlas entered service in the autumn of 1927, it became the first RAF aircraft designed specifically for army co-operation work. It was, in fact, another first for Britain, as had been the Vickers Vernon in the troop transport role. In addition to being stationed in the UK, it was operated in the Middle East, based at Heliopolis, where it was also used for communications work, alongside a squadron of Bristol Fighters based at Ismailia. A dual-control training version was also built and entered training schools in 1931, remaining active for a number of years. Also produced were a limited number of Atlas seaplanes, identical to the landplane version except for their two long single-step metal floats. A total of nearly 470 Atlas were built, of which 23 were supplied to other countries, including Canada, China (very modified Atlas IIs powered by Jaguar-Major engines), Greece and Japan. With the RAF, the Atlas based in the UK were replaced by Audax from 1931, but the type remained operational in the Middle East for several more years.

Armstrong Whitworth Siskin III   UK

Purpose: Fighter
Makers: Sir W. G. Armstrong Whitworth Aircraft Ltd
In service: 1924-32
Data: Siskin IIIA

Engine: See below
Span: 33ft 2in
Length: 25ft 4in
Height: 10ft 2in
Weight loaded: 3,040lb
Crew: One
Max speed: 156mph
Service ceiling: 27,100ft
Armament: Two fixed Vickers machine guns. Four 20lb bombs could be carried

The Siskin was one of the first new aircraft to be received by the RAF after the end of World War 1. Up to the time it entered service, the much reduced RAF was mostly operating war-built machines. It was also important for helping to put on a sound footing the new Armstrong Whitworth company, formed in 1921. Preceded by the prototype Siskin, with a 330hp ABC (Walton Motors) Dragonfly nine-cylinder radial engine, and the Siskin II — also of wood construction with a 350hp Armstrong Siddeley

Jaguar radial — the Siskin III entered production in 1923. It was unusual for a British aircraft in having sesquiplane-type wings and was of mixed construction. Some 64 Siskin IIIs were produced for the RAF, first entering service in 1924 as Snipe replacements, and serving until the arrival of the improved IIIA version. The standard engine was the 325hp Armstrong Siddeley Jaguar III radial. As already mentioned, the Siskin III was followed into service by the developed Siskin IIIA, which first flew on 20 October 1925. This differed from the earlier model in being normally fitted with a 385/450hp Armstrong Siddeley Jaguar IV supercharged engine, having a redesigned vertical tail and slight changes to the rear fuselage and upper wing dihedral. Some 340 Siskin IIIA fighters were built for the RAF, plus nearly 50 two-seat dual-control trainers. Delivery of the IIIA to the RAF began in 1927. Small numbers of Siskins were also supplied to other air forces, including IIIA fighters and trainers to Canada and two-seat trainers to Estonia, the latter known as Siskin IIIDCs and operated alongside Avro 504, 626 and Avian trainers right up to the end of the 1930s. Two other versions of the Siskin were built, the Siskin IIIB, powered by a Jaguar VIII engine and featuring an engine ring cowl, and the Siskin V, ordered by the Romanian Government but subsequently abandoned.

Armstrong Whitworth Whitley   UK

Purpose: Night bomber
Makers: Sir W. G. Armstrong Whitworth Aircraft Ltd
In service: 1937-44
Photo: Mk I
Data: Mk V

Engine: Two 1,075hp Rolls-Royce Merlin X inlines
Span: 84ft 0in

Length: 72ft 6in
Height: 15ft 0in
Weight loaded: 28,200lb
Crew: Five
Max speed: 228mph at 16,750ft
Service ceiling: 17,600ft
Normal range: 1,500 miles
Armament: Five .303in machine guns. Up to 7,000lb of bombs

With the introduction of the Whitley into Bomber Command, the RAF was provided with one of its main types of bomber to be used during the early war years. Although overshadowed to some degree by its compatriot, the Vickers Wellington, and then by later four-engined bombers, it nevertheless achieved notable wartime success and many RAF 'firsts' (see *Aircraft of World War II*). The first prototype AW38 flew on 17 March 1936 and the first of 34 production Mk Is, with 795hp Armstrong Siddeley Tiger IX radial engines, entered service with the RAF in March 1937. There followed 46 Mk IIs, powered by 920hp Tiger VIII engines and 80 Mk IIIs, which were similar except for a retractable ventral 'dustbin' turret (creating a good deal of drag). Next

came 33 Mk IVs and seven Mk IVAs of 1938, with 1,030hp Rolls-Royce Merlin IV and 1,075hp Merlin X engines respectively, and the Mk V of 1939 which introduced a power-operated four-gun rear turret in a lengthened rear fuselage. Deliveries of the Mk V continued until mid-1943, bringing the total production of this version to 1,476. After the projected Mk VI came the definitive version, the Mk VII. These were built for Coastal Command as reconnaissance and anti-submarine aircraft and were the first Coastal Command aircraft to carry the long range ASV Mk II radar. By the outbreak of war, the RAF had between 190 and 200 Whitleys on strength, the main force entering service in 1940.

Avia B-534   Czechoslovakia

Purpose: Fighter
Makers: Avia
In service: From 1934
Photo: Bk-534

Engine: One 850hp Avia-built Hispano-Suiza 12Ydrs inline
Span: 30ft 10in
Length: 26ft 10.75in
Height: 10ft 2in
Weight loaded: 4,365lb
Crew: One
Max speed: 245mph at 14,425ft
Service ceiling: 34,875ft
Range: 373 miles
Armament: Four fuselage-mounted 7.7mm machine guns.

In the early 1930s Avia produced the B-34 single-seat fighter, evidently as a possible BH-33 replacement. No production was undertaken and instead the aircraft was used for development purposes. In 1932 the type appeared in its latest form, having been re-engined with a closely-cowled 650hp Hispano-Suiza, with which it achieved approximately 195mph. The fighter featured an underslung radiator in a tunnel with controllable shutters, and was armed with four machine guns, two firing through troughs in the engine cowling and two in the lower wings. The main wheels were enclosed in large fairings. Following further refinement of the design, it made its maiden flight in August 1933 as the B-534 prototype. No time was wasted in putting the B-534 in production for the Czech Air Force and a total of 445 were eventually

completed. Of metal construction, partially fabric covered, B-534s were produced with both open and enclosed cockpits, and later models were fitted with streamlined wheel fairings (the single-strut cantilever undercarriage originally planned never being fitted). Of the total number produced, 35 were converted to carry an engine-mounted machine gun and were redesignated Bk-534. The Czech Air Force was understandably proud of its fighter but the first signs that it was becoming outdated appeared in 1937 when, at the Zurich Air Meeting, the B-534 was beaten in three contests in the military aircraft competitions by the German Bf109. Nevertheless, compared with the German biplane fighter equivalent, the Arado Ar68, it was faster by nearly 40mph. Following the invasion of Czechoslovakia, large numbers of B-534s were operated in passive roles by the Luftwaffe, although some were employed as fighters on the Russian Front.

Avia BH-17, BH-21 and BH-22   Czechoslovakia

Purpose: Fighter
Makers: Avia
In service: From 1924
Photo and Data: BH-21

Engine: One 300hp Skoda-built Hispano-Suiza 8Fb
Span: 29ft 2.5in
Length: 22ft 6.5in
Height: 8ft 11.75in
Weight loaded: 2,392lb
Crew: One
Max speed: 153mph
Service ceiling: 25,300ft
Range: 342 miles
Armament: Two fixed .303in Vickers machine guns

The BH-17 was a biplane fighter with a maximum speed of 146mph, powered by a 300hp Skoda-built Hispano-Suiza 8Fb engine. It had been designed to compete in a fighter competition organised by the Czech Defence Ministry and was matched against aircraft designed by both of the other Czech aircraft manufacturers, Aero (A20 biplane, displayed at the 1924 Prague Aero Show) and Letov, as well as with other Avia prototypes. One of the latter was of particular interest, the Avia BH-7. It was a parasol monoplane of extremely clean appearance. The wing, braced by N-type struts, had a very thick centre-section and was built up of two box section main spars, with ribs and webs, and mostly covered with plywood, the whole then fabric covered. This construction gave it immense strength and rigidity. The axle of the divided undercarriage had an aerofoil-section fairing, and two thin radiators were mounted between the Vee-struts. It was reported that this aircraft was capable of 162mph. Two orders were placed with Avia for BH-17s in 1924, but only the first was completed. On receiving the latter order, Avia decided to modify the design, partly to improve the pilot's forward view, by removing the fairing around the cabane structure in which the oil and water tanks were positioned, changing the I-type interplane struts for N-type and by removing the undercarriage-mounted radiators and replacing them with a retractable honeycomb radiator fitted under the fuselage. The result was the BH-21, which appeared at the close of 1924. Some 120 examples of the BH-21 were produced and proved highly successful. 50 were also licence-built in Belgium following a competition held in Brussels in 1926 against both French and Italian aircraft. Avia also produced 30 examples of a single-seat unarmed lightweight version for advanced flying and tactics training, designated BH-22, and powered by the 180hp Skoda-built Hispano-Suiza 8Aa engine, with which it achieved 134mph. Another variant, for night fighter training, was built as the BH-23.

Avia BH-33

Czechoslovakia

Purpose: Fighter
Makers: Avia
In service: From 1927
Data: BH-33L

Engine: One 500hp Skoda L
Span: 31ft 2in
Length: 23ft 8.25in
Height: 10ft 3in
Weight loaded: 3,589lb
Crew: One
Max speed: 185mph
Service ceiling: 28,550ft
Range: 280 miles
Armament: Two fixed (modified Vickers) Mk 28 machine guns

The BH-33, first flown in 1927, became a first-line single-seat fighter with the Czech Army Air Force and also achieved considerable export success in the face of very stiff foreign opposition. It was of all-wood construction and was developed from a BH-21 that had been installed with a 450hp Jupiter VI engine. Although of generally similar appearance to previous Avia designs, such as the BH-21 and the larger Jupiter-powered BH-26 two-seat fighter, it differed mainly in being fitted with a tail-fin and unbalanced rudder. In an effort to further develop the design, the BH-33E appeared in 1929. This was a much improved version, in terms of structure and performance, and had a fuselage constructed of steel tubes, a new top wing of similar span to the lower, a new cabane structure, a split-axle Vee undercarriage and either a Walter-built Jupiter VI or VII (480hp) engine (the latter giving the aircraft better performance at altitude). The last version of the type was the larger and heavier 500hp Skoda L-engined BH-33L, distinguished most easily by its new streamlined engine cowling. BH-33Es and Ls served with the Czech Army Air Force well into the 1930s; many were exported and licence-built. The standard BH-33 was licence-built by Podlaska Wytwórnia Samolotów SA of Poland and BH-33Es were ordered by Yugoslavia and Russia. BH-33Ls were also licence-built in Yugoslavia (where it followed the licence-production of the Potez 25). Interestingly, the BH-33 was entered into a competition for fighters organised by the Romanian Government at Bucharest in 1927. Other aircraft competing included another Czech fighter, the Letov S20, the Italian CR20 and the French Loire-Gourdou-Leseurre 32. Despite the BH-33 putting up the best performance in terms of maximum speed the climb, and LGL32 was ordered for Romanian service.

Avions Fairey Firefly

UK

Purpose: Fighter
Makers: Fairey Aviation Co Ltd and Société Anonyme Belge Avions Fairey
In service: From 1932
Photo and Data: Firefly IIM

Engine: One supercharged 480hp Rolls-Royce Kestrel IIS
Span: 31ft 6in
Length: 24ft 8in
Height: 9ft 4.25in
Weight loaded: 3,290lb
Crew: One

Max speed: 223mph
Armament: Two Vickers machine guns

Sharing only its name and parent company with the later Firefly F Mk 1 two-seat naval monoplane fighter of World War 2, the original Firefly I biplane was built at Fairey's expense and first flown in November 1925. This was powered by the Fairey Felix engine — a licence-built 430hp Curtiss D12 — and although it reached a maximum speed of well over 180mph, it did not go into production. Fairey then built an improved Firefly to take part in a 1929 Air Ministry fighter competition. The new aircraft was of mixed construction with single-bay wings, the lower having a much smaller span and chord than the upper. The original interplane struts were exchanged for N-type, the upper deck fairing aft of the pilot's cockpit was extended (a feature that had been added to the Firefly I), and other refinements included a new tail-fin and rudder which reversed the layout of the original Firefly by having a fin of greater area than the rudder. With the replacement of the Felix engine with a Rolls-Royce Kestrel, which allowed a much cleaner cowling, the aircraft was named Firefly II. This aircraft took part in the competition but, despite its excellent performance, lost to a Hawker fighter. Again the Firefly was modified, this time taking in metal construction. Noticeable changes to configuration included much neater interplane struts, a new cockpit shape which did away with the upper deck fairing, much more rounded vertical tail, and a modified undercarriage, the forward struts of which met the new underslung radiator. The Firefly in this form was renamed IIM. Fairey now had a truly world-class fighter on its hands, but no orders. However, the IIM entered another competition, this time in Belgium, against stiff opposition from aircraft of other countries. Following a flying display, which was subsequently crowned by a terminal velocity dive, the superiority of the Firefly was obvious and an order was placed on behalf of the Belgian Aéronautique Militaire. With further Belgian orders, it was stipulated that construction of the majority of the fighters had to be carried out in Belgium. A final total of about 60 IIMs was built by the Société Anonyme Belge Avions Fairey up to 1933 and these became standard fighters in Belgium right through the remaining years of peace. During their career they served alongside other British types like the Fairey Fox, Gloster Gladiator, Hawker Hurricane, Fairey Battle and Avro 504N, and the indigenous Renard R-31 army co-operation high-wing monoplane.

Avions Fairey Fox

Belgium

Purpose: Fighter/Reconnaissance
Makers: Fairey Aviation Co Ltd and Société Anonyme Belge Avions Fairey
In service: From 1935

Engine: See below
Span: 38ft 0in
Length: 30ft 1in
Height: 11ft 0in
Weight loaded: 5,170lb
Crew: Two
Max speed: 227mph
Service ceiling: 32,800ft
Armament: Three 7.62mm FN Browning machine guns, two in fuselage firing forward and one in rear cockpit

As described under the Fairey Fox entry, the early Fox I/IAs of the RAF were an outstanding success. As a follow-on to meet the latest RAF requirements, Fairey built the Fox IIM, a metal structure successor powered by a Kestrel IB engine. This failed to attract Air Ministry orders but, undeterred, Fairey offered the light bomber to Belgium, which ordered enough aircraft to equip a single squadron (powered by Kestrel IIS supercharged engines). Production was also undertaken by the Société Anonyme Belge Avions Fairey in Belgium, an associated company. Altogether, the Belgian air force received 40 Fox IIs. Further production in Belgium produced Fox IIIs, initially with similar engines to those of the Fox II. The majority were built as Fox IIICs and, like the earlier IIIs, had two forward-firing machine guns. However, the IIIC also had the first enclosed cockpit of a Belgian aircraft, in the form of a transparent covering over the pilot's cockpit and a hinged hood over part of the observer's cockpit (the latter enabled the observer to stand when required). These were operated as fighter-reconnaissance aircraft. In a further attempt to increase performance and thereby enable more indigenous aircraft to be taken into military service, Avions Fairey produced the Fox VI. An 860hp Hispano-Suiza 12Ydrs 12-cylinder engine was installed, together with streamlined wheel fairings and the enclosed hood described above. Including the prototype, at least 80 Fox VIRs and Fox VICs were built as reconnaissance and fighter aircraft

respectively for the Aéronautique Militaire, which adopted the type for service in 1935. A small number of Belgian Foxes were also built as dual-control trainers and two combat Fox VIs found their way to the Swiss Air Force, but further examples were not ordered. The final version of the Fox to be produced was the VIII, of which enough for one squadron were built in 1938-9 in order to strengthen the air force in view of the real threat of invasion. A total of 176 two-seat Foxes of all versions was built in Belgium, a small number seeing action against the Germans in 1940.

Beriev MBR-2 USSR

Purpose: General purpose
In service: From 1934
Photo: MBR-2
Data: MBR-2*bis*

Engine: See below
Span: 62ft 4in
Length: 44ft 3.5in
Weight loaded: about 9,500lb
Max speed: 136mph
Service ceiling: 16,400ft
Range: 930 miles
Armament: Three 7.62mm machine guns.
Underwing racks for 660lb of bombs, depth charges or mines

The name Beriev has been synonymous with Soviet flying-boats since the early 1930s, and present-day M-12s (Be-12s) still operate in the maritime patrol role with the Soviet Naval Air Force. Georgi Mikhailovich Beriev began designing seaplanes in 1928 and two years later became principal designer of maritime aircraft at a design bureau. The MBR-2, sometimes mistakenly called the Be-2 (which was also known as the KOR-1 and was a twin-float biplane), first appeared in 1931 as a short-range coastal reconnaissance flying-boat. It was of very modern appearance, all contemporary British 'boats having biplane wings until the late 1930s. With a wooden hull and metal constructed wings, the first MBR-2s produced were powered by 680hp M-17B

(BMW VI) inline engines and were armed with machine guns in open bow and dorsal emplacements. The dorsal position was later modified by the installation of a manually-operated turret (with a fairly restricted field of fire because of the aircraft's configuration). An 860hp AM-34N engine was fitted in the much improved MBR-2*bis*

version. A total of over 1,300 examples of the flying-boat were built before and during World War 2 and these could also be converted to become ski or landplanes. The MBR-2 was one of the few indigenous flying-boat designs to equip the Soviet forces during World War 2.

Blackburn Baffin   UK

Purpose: Carrier-borne torpedo bomber
Makers: Blackburn Aeroplane and Motor Co Ltd
In service: 1934-36
Photo: First production Baffin

Engine: One 565hp Bristol Pegasus IM3 radial
Span: 45ft 6in
Length: 38ft 4in
Height: 12ft 10in
Weight loaded: 7,610lb
Crew: Two
Max speed: 136mph
Service ceiling: 15,000ft
Range: 450 miles
Armament: One Vickers forward and one Lewis machine gun in rear cockpit. Up to 1,730lb of bombs (carried on Blackburn universal bomb carriers) or one larger bomb or torpedo.

Between production of the Ripon and Shark, Blackburn produced only four successful aircraft (in terms of numbers built) and a whole host of failures, including the Sprat two-seat trainer, Turcock, Nautilus and F3 single and two-seat fighters, Beagle and B3 torpedo bombers, Sydney three-engined flying-boat and several civil aircraft in both biplane and monoplane forms. One of the successes was the Baffin. Derived from the Ripon, which it replaced as

the Fleet Air Arm's first-line torpedo bomber, the Baffin first entered service in early 1934. Two prototypes had been produced, one with a Pegasus engine and one with an Armstrong Siddeley Tiger I engine. The Pegasus-engined version first flew in 1932 and, following tests, was chosen for production. However, overall performance had been disappointing. For although the Ripon and Baffin were virtually identical except for their engine installations, the lighter and neater radial engine of the latter was confidently expected to allow a higher degree of improvement than was achieved. Like the later Ripons, the Baffin had foldable wings and carried air bags inside the fuselage to enable the aircraft to remain buoyant in an emergency. As well as the prototypes and 33 aircraft (incl Boffins K2884-7, the last few with 580hp Pegasus IIM3 engines) more than 60 Ripons were converted into Baffins, entailing installation of the new engine and a complete structural check-up. These served with FAA squadrons on board three of the seven British aircraft carriers (three of which were in reserve in 1935), HMS *Courageous*, HMS *Furious* and HMS *Glorious*, alongside IIIFs, Nimrods, Ospreys and Seals. (Interestingly, of these only *Furious*, the first real carrier, survived World War 2.) A number of ex-RAF Baffins served with the Royal New Zealand Air Force from 1938, and were operated during the first years of the war as reconnaissance aircraft, although of totally obsolete design.

Blackburn Ripon

Purpose: Torpedo bomber/Reconnaissance
Makers: Blackburn Aeroplane & Motor Co Ltd
In service: 1929-34
Photo and Data: Mk IIA

Engine: One 570hp Napier Lion XIA
Span: 44ft 10in
Length: 36ft 9in
Height: 12ft 10in
Weight loaded: 7,866lb
Crew: Two
Max speed: 126mph at sea level
Service ceiling: 10,000ft
Range: 380-1,060 miles
Armament: One forward-firing Vickers machine gun and one Lewis gun in rear cockpit. One Mk VIII or Mk X torpedo, or up to 1,650lb of bombs

The Ripon was designed to supplement and then replace the Blackburn Dart, which had been in service since 1923. The first prototype made its maiden flight on 17 April 1926, powered by a Napier Lion V engine and configured as a landplane. It had been designed for torpedo, bombing and reconnaissance missions and for these it was designed with easily interchangeable wheel or float undercarriages. However, only a small number of aircraft were flown as twin-float seaplanes. Chosen in preference to the Harrow or Buffalo, built by Handley Page and Avro respectively, the latter possessing much the cleanest lines in its Mk I version, the Ripon Mk I was followed by the refined Mk II prototype. Modifications included larger vertical tail surfaces, a new rear gun arrangement to reduce drag, new side-mounted radiators and a Napier Lion XI engine. The new radiators allowed the original frontal radiator to be removed, bringing the frontal area in line with those of the Buffalo and Harrow Mk II and thus losing the last of its Dart-type features. Of the 91 aircraft built for British military service, in Mk II, Mk IIA and Mk IIC versions, the original standard version for the FAA was the composite-construction Ripon Mk IIA. However, the Mk IIC of 1931 introduced a number of important changes (including all-metal wing structure, fabric covered) and surviving examples of earlier versions were subsequently converted to Mk IICs. Capable of being catapulted, the Ripon could carry an extra 120gal fuel tank in place of the underfuselage torpedo when operated on long-range reconnaissance missions. Three British aircraft carriers were equipped with Ripons. Although HMS *Eagle* had previously flown Darts and had sailed on non-active duty with Ripons on board, this carrier lost its torpedo bomber element following a refit, after which it accommodated Fairey IIIFs and Hawker Ospreys. For service on board the other carriers, the Ripons had folding wings to aid storage. The Ripon's service life as such ended in 1934, although more than 60 were subsequently overhauled and converted into Baffins. A licence to build a radial-engined (Armstrong Siddeley Panther, French-built Bristol Jupiter VI or Pegasus IIM3) variant of the Ripon, designated IIF, was acquired by Finland (along with one for the Letov S-18). Finnish production was undertaken by the Government Aircraft Works at Helsinki and the type, powered by Panther engines, subsequently entered service with the Finnish Air Force, bearing the usual swastika symbol (an ancient symbol and nothing to do with the German Nazi Party). Some of these, alongside other outdated British types such as the Bristol Bulldog and Gloster Gamecock, were in service when Russia invaded Finland on 30 November 1939.

Blackburn Shark   UK

Purpose: Torpedo bomber/Spotter-reconnaissance
Makers: Blackburn Aeroplane and Motor Co Ltd/
Blackburn Aircraft Ltd
In service: 1935-38
Photo: Mk III seaplane
Data: Mk II

Engine: See below
Span: 46ft 0in
Length: 35ft 2.75in
Height: 12ft 1in
Weight loaded: 7,870-8,050lb
Crew: Two/three
Max speed: 153mph at 5,500ft
Service ceiling: 16,400ft
Range: 550-1,130 miles
Armament: One .303in Vickers machine gun
forward and one .303in Vickers-Berthier machine
gun in rear cockpit. One 1,500lb torpedo or bombs

The Blackburn Shark was the immediate predecessor
to the famous Fairey Swordfish with the FAA, and
although its span of service in the designed role was
only to last a few years, Sharks remained as aircrew
trainers and target tugs for a further period. The
prototype, originally designated B-6 and featuring a
metal semi-monocoque buoyant fuselage, was built
as a private venture and first flew in May 1934. The
crew of two or three were seated in tandem cockpits,
with a bomb aimer's position (prone) under the
pilot's floor which incorporated a bombing hatch. A
camera could alternatively be fitted in this position.
An initial order for 16 Shark Mk Is was placed three
months after the first flight and was followed by
orders for a total of 123 strengthened Mk II
production aircraft and 95 Mk IIIs, the latter featuring

a glazed cockpit hood with an open aft section for
the rear gunner. The Shark Mk Is were fitted with
Armstrong Siddeley Tiger IV engines, like the
prototype; but the Mk II and III versions had 700hp
Armstrong Siddeley Tiger VI radial engines. Capable
of being operated with a land or float undercarriage
(the floatplanes being catapult-launched from
warships — a method of naval aircraft deployment
first used during World War 1 and which reached its
peak during the interwar years), Sharks first entered
service in the spring of 1935, stationed on board the
aircraft carrier HMS *Courageous,* a 26,500ton
converted light battlecruiser. However, by 1938,
Sharks were being replaced by Swordfish. In
retrospect, it was not a moment too soon for the
Shark, as HMS *Courageous* was the first of the
famous interwar Royal Navy carriers lost in World
War 2, sunk by a German U-boat in 1939. With
regard to export, Blackburn never had the kind of
successes achieved by other British companies like
Bristol and Hawker. However, in 1938, six Shark IIA
seaplanes were exported to Portugal, with de-rated
Tiger engines and Alclad-constructed floats; and in
1937 Boeing Aircraft of Canada was awarded a
contract by the Canadian Department of National
Defence to build Sharks under licence. (The company
had been formed in the summer of 1929 by Boeing
Airplane Company of the USA and Hoffar-Beeching
Shipyards of Vancouver, and in the following year
had built several six-seat Thunderbird flying-boats.
These were followed by small numbers of mail/
passenger-carrying biplanes and the Totem four-seat
flying-boat, while repair of military aircraft was also
undertaken.) A total of 17 Mk IIIs was constructed
for the Royal Canadian Air Force, powered by 840hp
Bristol Pegasus IX engines, and these were operated
with a small number of Mk IIs previously purchased.

Bloch 200   France

Purpose: Night bomber
Makers: Avions Marcel Bloch
In service: From 1934

Engines: Two 870hp Gnome-Rhône 14Kirs/Kjrs
radials

Span: 73ft 7.5in
Length: 52ft 6in
Height: 12ft 10in
Weight loaded: 15,730-16,050lb
Crew: Four
Max speed: 143mph

Service ceiling: 26,300ft
Normal range: 620 miles
Armament: Three 7.5mm machine guns in nose, ventral and dorsal turrets. 2,970-5,500lb of bombs

In service about the same time as the British Heyford biplane, the French Bloch 200 should have been far advanced of the British bomber in terms of performance because of its more modern design, lighter weight and more powerful engines. Indeed, this was expected of it. Designed to a French specification of 1932 for a multi-seat night bomber, the Bloch 200 had high-mounted cantilever metal wings, a metal rectangular-section fuselage, a divided undercarriage with streamlined wheel fairings and an enclosed cockpit for the flight crew. From several aircraft produced for the ensuing bomber competition, the Bloch 200 and the larger Farman 221 (somewhat similar in overall appearance) were subsequently chosen for service.

Following three prototype Bloch 200 BN4s, the first of which made its maiden flight in mid-1933, production was initiated. A total of just over 200 aircraft was eventually produced by Bloch, Potez and Hanriot, the Armée de l'Air first receiving the type during the latter part of 1934. By the close of 1935, 156 were in service and the rest were delivered in the following year. At the height of their service, Bloch 200s equipped 12 squadrons and a naval base. By September 1938, 161 were still serving with five Régions Aériennes, but by the outbreak of war only about one-third of those built remained operational with two home Escadres and overseas. Within a short period even these were withdrawn. The Bloch 200's downfall had been caused mainly by lack of speed; production aircraft falling short of even the designed maximum speed of around 175mph and so were hopelessly outdated by 1939. The Czech Aero and Avia companies built about 124 under licence, these using 750hp Walter K14 engines.

Bloch 210

France

Purpose: Night bomber
Makers: Avions Marcel Bloch
In service: From 1937

Engines: Two 870hp Gnome-Rhône 14Kirs/Kjrs radials
Span: 74ft 10in
Length: 62ft 0in
Height: 15ft 9in
Crew: Five

Weight loaded: 22,487lb
Max speed: 186mph
Service ceiling: 30,000ft
Normal range: 680 miles
Armament: Three machine guns in nose, ventral and dorsal turrets. Up to 4,340lb of bombs in internal horizontal and vertical bomb cells

Although the Bloch 210 was a development of the earlier Bloch 200 and was in service at the beginning

of World War 2, it was another example of an outdated aircraft in French service at a time when modern designs were needed. The Bloch 210 (sometimes named Verdun) was a twin-engined low-wing bomber with retractable undercarriage. It also differed from the earlier model in having a new fuselage with a smooth Vedal metal skin, although it retained the rectangular section, and a new tail assembly. Performance was about that expected by the disappointing Bloch 200. The prototype, powered by 760hp Gnome-Rhône 14Kdrs radials, made its maiden flight in November 1934, and in the next year was converted for testing in seaplane form.

Following nationalisation of the aircraft industry in France in 1936, Bloch became part of the Société Nationale de Constructions Aéronautiques de Sud-Ouest (SNCASO), and as such began manufacturing Bloch 210s for the Armée de l'Air. Nearly 300 Bloch 210s were built, 35 of which were sent to the Republican Air Force in Spain (joining SPAD, Dewoitine and Loire-Nieuport fighters) and 10 exported to Romania. By the outbreak of World War 2, the Armée de l'Air had, in first-line service, around half of the total number of Bloch 210s that were built, and the type remained with several bomber groups until the capitulation of France.

Boeing F2B-1 and F3B-1

USA

Purpose: Fighter/Fighter-bomber
Makers: Boeing Aircraft Company
In service: 1928-32
Photo and Data: F3B-1

Engine: One 425hp Pratt & Whitney R-1340B Wasp radial
Span: 33ft 0in
Length: 24ft 10in
Height: 9ft 2in
Weight loaded: 2,945lb
Crew: One
Max speed: 156mph
Service ceiling: over 21,000ft
Range: 340 miles
Armament: Two fixed forward-firing .30in and/or .50in Browning machine guns. Up to 125lb of bombs

1926 was a busy year for the Boeing company — it had the PW-9/FB fighters in production, and its new experimental aircraft included the Type 66 fighter, Type 64 trainer, Type 69 naval fighter and various commercial aircraft including a four-seat cabin transport and a mailplane to be operated by Boeing between Chicago and San Francisco. The Type 69 was designed especially as a carrier fighter, despite the inherent low orders if accepted for service as the Navy had only three aircraft carriers at that date, and was developed from the earlier PW-9/FB series of biplanes. The prototype first flew on 3 November 1926 and, following tests, the US Navy ordered 32 production aircraft, designated F2B-1s. These biplanes had unequal span wooden wings which tapered in chord. The fuselage and tail unit were of

duralumin and steel construction, fabric covered, and power was provided by a 425hp Wasp radial engine (fed by one 50 US gallon fuel tank in the fuselage and an optional tank of similar capacity which could be carried under the fuselage and dropped in an emergency). The production aircraft were slightly heavier than the prototype, and were used as fighters and fighter-bombers on the USS *Saratoga*. Two similar aircraft were sold for evaluation to Japan and Brazil, but no further orders followed from these countries. Indeed, several times during the latter 1920s and early 1930s American manufacturers sent single examples of their fighters to Japan, where they were used solely by Japanese technicians to see what features could be copied for their own indigenous aircraft. As a follow-on to the successful F2B-1, Boeing built a new and refined prototype, which could be fitted with a single central duralumin float and two wingtip floats, specially designed for launching from standard US Navy catapults. However, the Navy rejected it and so it was modified to have a new swept-back upper wing of greater span. It is usually recorded that the reworked aircraft emerged from the Boeing factory as a landplane. This was not the case. Still with the original floats fitted, the newly winged aircraft was tested and, following the appreciable improvement in performance, was then given a wheeled undercarriage. The US Navy ordered 73 production aircraft as fighter-bombers, designated F3B-1s, and these incorporated further refinements. F3B-1s were delivered to the Navy from the Autumn of 1928 and these served on the USS *Langley, Lexington* and *Saratoga,* alongside T4M-1 torpedo bombers and O2U-1 observation aircraft.

Boeing P-12 and F4B

Purpose: Land or carrier-based fighter
Makers: Boeing Aircraft Company
In service: 1929-37
Photo: F4B-1
Data: P-12C

Engine: One 450hp Pratt & Whitney R-1340-9
Wasp radial.
Span: 30ft 0in
Length: 20ft 1in
Height: 8ft 10in
Weight loaded: 2,629lb
Crew: One
Max speed: 178mph
Service ceiling: 26,200ft
Range: 675 miles
Armament: Two forward-firing .30in and .50in
machine guns. One 500lb or two 116lb bombs on
some naval versions

The service life of the P-12/F4B series of biplane
fighters covered the most potentially dangerous
years of the interwar period, eclipsed only by the
actual outbreak of World War 2, by which time they
were out of front-line use. Dramatic events of the
time included Japan's first attack against China in
1931 and subsequent occupation of Manchuria,
Japan and Germany's departure from the League of
Nations and the International Disarmament
Conference in 1933, Germany's confirmation of the
Luftwaffe (which contravened the Treaty of
Versailles) in 1935, Italy's invasion of Abyssinia in
the same year, the German occupation of the
Rhineland in 1936, and the outbreak of the Spanish
Civil War (which involved directly or indirectly Spain,
Germany, Italy, Russia, Morocco, France, the UK, the
Netherlands, Czechoslovakia and other nations that
sent volunteers and/or equipment to the battle
areas).

In 1928, Boeing produced prototype fighters for
possible naval use as follow-ons to the earlier
F2B/F3B aircraft. They were generally similar except
for their undercarriages and each was powered by a
Pratt & Whitney Wasp engine. Designated XF4B-1s
by the Navy, indicating experimental aircraft, they
marked the beginning of a production programme
under which 551 aircraft were built for the US Navy
as F4Bs and the US Army Air Corps as P-12s, plus
25 for export (some 23 going to Brazil). The success
of the design in satisfying the needs of both US
services was not something that Boeing had
originally expected, as land and naval fighters had
always been too different to make a common design
desirable. The prototypes first flew in 1928 and the
first production aircraft for the Navy, in the form of
27 F4B-1s, were delivered from June 1929. These
incorporated the arrester hook of one prototype and
the divided undercarriage of the other, the latter
feature allowing a 500lb bomb to be carried.
Meanwhile, the Army had briefly tested a prototype
and ordered a small number of production P-12s.
These were followed by orders for 221 P-12Bs,
P-12Cs and P-12Ds, the latter with 525hp Wasp
engines. The Navy also ordered 46 unrated F4B-2s.
A change to all-metal fuselages brought about the
production of P-12Es, P-12Fs, F4B-3s and F4B-4s.
Later production F4B-4s had new headrests that
contained emergency rafts. These were the last US
Navy biplane fighters to have a fixed undercarriage,
and a small number also served with the Marine
Corps. It is believed that a few of these Boeing
fighters may have become operational again for a
very short time from 1941, having been used as
trainers since retirement. With the end of the
production run, Boeing changed to monoplane
configuration for its subsequent military aircraft,
producing next its first and only monoplane fighter,
the P-26.

Boeing P-26

USA

Purpose: Fighter
Makers: Boeing Aircraft Company
In service: 1933-40
Photo and Data: P-26A

Engine: See below
Span: 28ft 0in
Length: 23ft 7.25in
Height: 10ft 0in
Weight loaded: 2,995lb
Crew: One
Max speed: 234mph
Service ceiling: 27,400ft
Range: 350-630 miles
Armament: Two fixed forward-firing .30in and/or .50in machine guns. As fighter bomber could carry five 30lb or two 112lb bombs

Designed at a time when monoplane fighters generally meant aircraft of parasol or gull-wing layout, the P-26 featured a low-wing configuration, although external bracing remained in evidence. It became the first monoplane fighter to serve with the USAAC and, although experimental developments of the basic design were built by Boeing without external wing bracing and with enclosed cockpits, it was the company's only production all-metal low-wing fighter. The first of three prototypes flew on 20 March 1932 and all were subsequently flown on an experimental and evaluation basis by the Army. In the following year the Army ordered 111 production Model 266s, each powered by a Pratt & Whitney R-1340-27 Wasp radial engine (rated at 550hp at 2,200rpm) and differing from the prototypes in having revised wing structure and wheel fairings, larger headrest and other changes. Production

aircraft were designated P-26As. Satisfied with these, the Army ordered a further 25 aircraft and, although most received P-26C designations, all subsequently became P-26Bs when fitted with 600hp Pratt & Whitney R-1340-33 engines with fuel injection. These were the last production fighters from the Boeing company, which now directed its immense talents towards the production of bombers. In 1938, the majority of all combat aircraft in American service were outdated by modern foreign types. This situation, and the prospect of another war, soon brought about a rapid expansion programme. However, the P-26s or 'Peashooters' remained in service until replaced by types like the Seversky P-35, which had modern features missing in the P-26, such as an enclosed cockpit and retractable undercarriage. The only other country to receive new P-26s for service was China, which purchased 11. This Chinese or export version had a maximum take-off weight of 3,380lb as a fighter with maximum fuel and a range of between 555 and 1,115 miles, according to contemporary reports. These saw action against invading Japanese forces from 1937. Their exact fate is not known because of the general chaos of the situation, made worse by the fact that although Japanese forces penetrated well inside China there was no official declaration of war. The P-26s must have served alongside other British, French and American aircraft supplied to the Chinese government via Hong Kong, Burma or French Indo-China, as well as many Russian aircraft flown by Russian pilots. In 1940 ex-American P-26As were used to help form the Philippine Army Air Force, and the dozen aircraft also fought the Japanese. The only other country to receive ex-American P-26As was Guatemala.

Boeing PW-9 and FB Series   USA

Purpose: Fighter
Makers: Boeing Aircraft Company
In service: From 1924
Photo: PW-9D
Data: PW-9C

Engine: One 435hp Curtiss D-12C
Span: 32ft 0in
Length: 23ft 5in
Height: 8ft 8in
Weight loaded: 3,170lb
Crew: One
Max speed: 158mph
Service ceiling: 21,000ft
Range: about 390 miles
Armament: One .30in and one .50in
forward-firing machine guns

The PW-9 has a special place in history as the first Boeing-designed fighter to enter production for the US Army Air Corps, starting a series of fighters which proved lucrative to Boeing throughout the interwar period until the company's equally successful change to multi-engined bombers. This is not to say that Boeing lacked previous experience in producing military aircraft, indeed the company had already produced a number of twin-float naval trainers, Thomas Morse fighters, a dozen large multi- and single-engined ground attack aircraft, and refurbished de Havilland DH4s. Designed and built as a private venture, the first of three prototype PW-9s

made its maiden flight on 29 April 1923. The wooden wings were of sesquiplane type, the fuselage was constructed of metal and the radiator was located under the 435hp Curtiss D12 engine. Following flight trials against other types, production aircraft were ordered, and these were delivered in late 1925. At the same time the Army ordered modified PW-9As, and when these were delivered it brought the total number of PW-9s and PW-9As in service to 55. Next came PW-9Cs and PW-9Ds, the latter delivered from the spring of 1928. The main differences between the 'D' and earlier models were a redesigned radiator, a large balanced rudder and wheel brakes, although earlier PW-9s were subsequently given a balanced rudder. Aircraft of the same basic design were also produced for the US Navy from 1924. The first 10 were built as FB-1s (bringing the total of PW-9 types to 123) and two as FB-2s, the latter being of greater significance despite their numbers as they were fitted with arrester gear for carrier operations from America's first aircraft carrier, the USS *Langley*. Following experimental FB aircraft, with various radial engines installed, came the only other version of the series to go into operational service, the FB-5. Twenty-seven of these were produced, powered by 525hp Packard 2A-1500 engines, and were capable of over 170mph. These subsequently flew from the USS *Lexington*, America's second and largest interwar carrier (40,000 tons), completed in 1927 and sunk by Japan in 1942.

Breda Ba65   Italy

Purpose: Ground attack/Reconnaissance
Makers: Societa Italiana Ernesto Breda
In service: From 1937
Photo and Data: Single-seat Ba65

Engine: One 1,000hp Fiat A80 RC41 or 900hp Isotta-Fraschini-built Gnome-Rhône 14Krsd.

Piaggio PXI RC40 used experimentally
Span: 39ft 8.5in
Length: 31ft 6.25in
Height: 10ft 6in
Weight loaded: 6,503lb (single-seater) 7,716lb (two-seater)
Crew: One, two

27

Max speed: 267mph at 16,400ft (single-seater) 225mph (two-seater)
Service ceiling: 27,225ft (single-seater) 25,910ft (two-seater)
Range: 341 miles (single-seater) 684 miles (two-seater)
Armament: Two 7.7mm and two 12.7mm machine guns in wings. One extra 7.7mm machine gun in turret in rear cockpit of two-seat version. 12.7mm gun in rear turret of Ba65*bis*. Bomb load of up to 2,000lb

The Breda Ba65 was Italy's first single-engined combat aircraft with a low monoplane wing and retractable undercarriage to go into quantity production. The main wheels of the landing gear remained semi-exposed when retracted to avoid serious damage in the event of a wheels-up emergency landing. It was first tested in action during the Spanish Civil War when it served with the Italian Aviacion del Terio in Spain, forming part of the 730 Italian aircraft sent to that country. It was developed from the Breda Ba64 monoplane, that had been powered by an Alfa-Romeo-built Pegasus engine and was capable of speeds around 224mph; and Ba65s were subsequently built as single- and two-seat aircraft. Iraq ordered the first production aircraft which were delivered in 1938 (serving alongside Italian SM79s) and were followed by large orders from the Regia Aeronautica, Portugal, Paraguay and Hungary. When Italy entered World War 2, Ba65s were still operational, employed mainly on reconnaissance and light bombing duties in North Africa, although some saw combat in the Balkans. A developed version of the design with a hydraulically-operated dorsal turret was the Ba65*bis*, of which a smaller number were built.

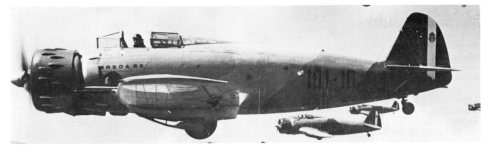

Breguet 19   France

Purpose: Bomber/Reconnaissance
Makers: Société Anonyme des Ateliers d'Aviation Louis Breguet
In service: 1925-40
Photo: Breguet 19A2
Data: Breguet 19B2

Engine: One of several engines, including 400-550hp Hispano-Suiza, Farman, Salmson, Renault, Lorraine-Dietrich and Gnome-Rhône-built Bristol Jupiter engines
Span: 48ft 8in

Length: 31ft 2in
Height: 10ft 11.5in
Weight loaded: 5,174lb
Crew: Two
Max speed: 141mph with a 450hp Hispano-Suiza 12Ha engine
Service ceiling: 22,000ft
Range: c. 500 miles
Armament: One forward-firing machine gun, one or two machine guns in rear cockpit and provision for one gun firing through the floor. Bomb load of about 920lb

The Breguet 19 was one of the most widely used military aircraft of the later 1920s and early 1930s. It was first exhibited at the 1921 Paris Air Show, and the metal-constructed prototype made its maiden flight in May of the following year. To enhance its reputation, the Breguet 19 made a number of long-distance flights, starting with the flight by Lt Peltier Doisy from Paris to Hong Kong in the spring of 1924. Production in both land and seaplane forms began in 1925, and by the close of the following year about 1,100 of the B2 bomber and A2 reconnaissance versions had been built for 10 countries, including Argentina, Bolivia, China, France, Persia, Poland, Romania and Russia. Manufacturing licences were also acquired by Belgium, Greece, Japan, Spain and Yugoslavia. Britain also received a single example as J7507, and this aircraft was used for evaluation trials at the Royal Aircraft Establishment. Several variants of the basic design were also produced for export, but the only one sold in reasonable numbers

was the 650hp Hispano-Suiza-engined Breguet 197, acquired by Greece, Turkey (serving as a reconnaissance-bomber alongside the small force of Supermarine Southampton flying-boats, Curtiss Hawk fighters and subsequently PZL P24 fighters) and Yugoslavia. During 1926, special Breguet 19s broke three world records for distance in a straight line, the longest of which was the Paris-Jask flight of some 3,353 miles. In the following years flights were made across the North and South Atlantic (the former using a Breguet 19 Grand Raid carrying 4,100 litres of fuel instead of the normal 400 litres), round the world (with the exception of the Pacific), and across America, Europe and Asia. At the beginning of 1936, the Armée de l'Air still had more than 100 Breguet 19s in service. It is also interesting to note that among the four aircraft destroyed on the first day of operations by two Nationalist-flown Heinkel He51s during the Spanish Civil War, one was a Breguet 19.

Bristol Bulldog

UK

Purpose: Fighter
Makers: Bristol Aeroplane Co Ltd
In service: 1929-37
Data: Mk IIA

Engine: One 490hp Bristol Jupiter VIIF radial
Span: 33ft 10in
Length: 25ft 2in
Weight loaded: 3,490lb
Crew: One
Max speed: 177mph
Service ceiling: Over 29,000ft
Range: c. 275 miles
Armament: Two forward-firing .303in Vickers machine guns. Provision for four 20lb bombs

To most, the Bulldog represents the typical interwar fighter and is the best known of all RAF fighters of the period, with the exception of the two latecomers, the Hurricane and Spitfire. It was designed in the usual World War 1 tradition of biplane wings, a fixed cross-axle undercarriage and two forward-firing machine guns, while the pilot still occupied an open cockpit. However, it had a turn of speed that was made possible only by the installation of a well

developed and powerful engine, and also supported such modern equipment as a Marconi wireless transmitter and receiver and oxygen apparatus. Designed as a possible replacement for both the Siskin and Gamecock — the former having been (with the Grebe) one of the RAF's first new fighters since the end of World War 1 and the latter the last RAF biplane fighter of wooden construction — the original Bristol Type 105, or Bulldog Mk I, made its maiden flight on 17 May 1927. The design had been partly based on a Bristol-built racing and record-breaking aircraft known as the Badminton, and was followed at the beginning of 1928 by the lengthened Bulldog Mk II. After an Air Ministry competition against other fighters, the Bulldog entered production. Including demonstration and export models, a total of about 90 Mk IIs and 253 Mk IIAs was produced (not including 10 used as instructional airframes), mostly for the RAF. The latter version incorporated several refinements, including a stronger airframe, modified wing spars and ailerons, and a revised undercarriage. Later production Mk IIAs were also fitted with a tailwheel. Some Bulldogs were given experimental ring cowls round their engines, but these did not become standard on

RAF aircraft, although many export fighters had these fitted. The Bulldog eventually equipped 10 RAF squadrons, the first in mid-1929. Its heyday was in 1931-32 when it formed the bulk of the British fighter force, flying alongside three squadrons of Furys and a small number of early Demons, and Bulldogs were operational until the last were withdrawn in 1937, replaced with Hurricanes. The RAF also received more than 50 unarmed two-seat dual-control trainer variants of the Mk IIA, and these were designed to be easily convertible into fighters by changing the rear fuselage and adding the

required armament. Exports of Bulldog Mk II/IIAs were made to Australia, Denmark, Estonia, Latvia, Siam and Sweden. Following the Bulldog IIIA and IV came the last fighter version, the Mk IVA. Seventeen were supplied to Finland, with the Bristol Mercury VIS2 engine and many refinements. These were used during the Winter War against the Russian forces from the end of November 1939, some fitted with ski undercarriages. The Bulldog was the last single-engined fighter of Bristol origin to enter RAF service and was that company's final fighter design with only two machine guns.

Bristol F2B Fighter   UK

Purpose: Army co-operation
Makers: Bristol Aeroplane Co Ltd
In service: 1917-32
Photo and Data: F2B Mk II

Engine: 280hp Rolls-Royce Falcon III
Span: 39ft 3in
Length: 25ft 10in
Height: 9ft 9in
Weight loaded: over 2,850lb
Crew: Two
Max speed: 122mph at 5,000ft (125mph maximum at low level)
Service ceiling: 20,000ft
Armament: One fixed forward-firing Vickers machine gun and one Lewis machine gun in rear cockpit. Up to 240lb of bombs

The Bristol Fighter was one of the immortal aircraft of the RAF, and its name is synonymous with postwar British military aviation. The only other combat aircraft of World War 1 design to serve as long into the 1919-39 period was the DH9A. In fact, such reliance was put on the Bristol Fighter that at least one was tested for possible use on aircraft carriers. First used operationally on the Western Front on 5 April 1917, some 3,800 examples of the Bristol Fighter were built before the end of World War 1, powered by Falcon, Sunbeam Arab, Hispano-Suiza and Siddeley Puma engines. Production of the type continued until 1927, the first version produced

after the war being the F2B Mk II, with provision for tropical equipment. The Mk II version was followed by the Mk III in which the structure of the aircraft was redesigned and strengthened and the new features of the earlier version fitted as standard. Following the completion of production of all new combat models in 1926, the final aircraft built were a small number of dual-control trainers. However, there was one other variant, the F2B Mk IV. This was the designation given to Fighters fitted in 1928 with Handley Page wing slots, a redesigned higher vertical tail, strengthened undercarriage and other refinements. Aircraft with tropical equipment were used to patrol the North-West Frontier of India and, along with DH9As and Vernons, for policing in Iraq from 1922. Others were stationed in Egypt, Palestine, Syria and Turkey. F2Bs were also operated by the RAF in Germany until July 1922. With the arrival in late 1927 of the Armstrong Whitworth Atlas, which was specifically designed for army co-operation work, home-based F2Bs were withdrawn from service. Atlas aircraft replaced the first overseas F2B squadron in 1930, the type finally being withdrawn in 1932. Bristol F2Bs were exported to Belgium, Spain, Canada, Honduras, the Irish Free State (partitioned as such in 1921, later Eire), Mexico, Peru, Greece, New Zealand (remaining in service until 1936) and Norway, and were licence-built in Sweden and other countries. Interestingly, an all-metal development of the Fighter was built as the MR1, for use in countries of extreme temperatures. This did not go into production.

CANT Z501 Gabbiano (Gull)   Italy

Purpose: Reconnaissance
Makers: Cantieri Riuniti dell'Adriatico
In service: 1936-45

Engine: See below
Span: 73ft 9.83in
Length: 49ft 0.6in
Height: 14ft 6.4in
Weight loaded: 13,117lb
Crew: Five
Max speed: 179mph
Service ceiling: 22,966ft
Normal range: 1,616 miles
Armament: Three 7.7mm machine guns. 1,411lb
of bombs

Some eight months after its maiden flight with Mario
Stoppani at the controls on 7 February 1934, the
prototype Z501, military serial MM247, established
a world non-stop distance record. After losing the
title to France, Stoppani won it back with a flight of
3,063.17 miles from the CANT company's factory at
Monfalcone (Trieste) to Berbera (British Somaliland)
during 16-17 July 1935. Designed as a maritime
reconnaissance flying-boat and named Gabbiano
(Gull) because of its distinctive curved, tapering
parasol wing, the Z501 went into service with the
Italian Aviazine Legionaria supporting Franco in the
Spanish Civil War, operating out of Palma (Majorca)
from May 1937. By the time Italy entered World

War 2 202 Z501s were flying with the Italian
Squadriglie da Ricognizione Marittima. Others
exported to Romania were based at Constanza on
the Black Sea. Designed by Filippo Zappata, the
Gabbiano had a slim two-step hull above which was
the parasol wing supported on a complexity of struts.
The strut-braced horizontal tailplane was carried
halfway up the curved single fin and rudder
assembly. The liquid-cooled engine — a 750hp Asso
or 900hp Asso XI RC15 — had a frontal radiator and
was set on the wing centre section in a long tapering
nacelle containing the flight engineer's cockpit. Pilot
and co-pilot were seated side-by-side under an
enclosed canopy. There were semi-enclosed
manually operated gun turrets in the bow and
amidships, each with a single machine gun. A third
weapon was operated by the flight engineer. The
radio operator's cabin was in the hull behind the
pilots' cabin. The structure was wood, the wing and
upper hull being fabric covered. Bomb racks attached
to the wing supporting struts inboard of the
stabilising floats could carry up to 1,102lb of bombs.
The Z501 became well-known in the Mediterranean
during World War 2, where it flew many thousands of
miles on reconnaissance and patrol duties,
protecting convoys and searching for submarines
and mines. Its true claim to affection, however, was
in the air-sea rescue role, in which it saved hundreds
of lives. It earned the affectionate nickname 'Mamm'
aiuto', literally: 'Mummy! Help!', the traditional cry of
Italian children in trouble.

Caproni AP1   Italy

Purpose: Attack
Makers: Caproni Aeronautica Bergamasca
In service: 1936-38

Engine: See below
Span: 39ft 4.44in
Length: 28ft 6.125in
Height: 9ft 11.6in
Weight loaded: 4,916lb
Crew: Two
Max speed: 220.6mph
Service ceiling: 24,606ft

Normal range: 683 miles
Armament: Three 7.7mm machine guns plus anti-
personnel bombs (see below)

Cesar Pallavicino's first design after joining the CAB
company, the AP1, was also the first Italian aircraft
built exclusively for the 'Assalto' ground attack role
following the views expounded by Ten-Col Amedeo
Mecozzi. The AP1 was of mixed construction with
cantilever low wings of wood and tailplane and
rounded-section fuselage built up of steel tubes with

plywood and metal covering. Flaps were fitted and the ailerons were of balanced type. In its original form the first prototype (designation Ca301) had a strut-braced divided undercarriage and was later fitted with a Townend ring for its radial engine. The definitive prototype (serial MM242) had a trousered undercarriage with a single 7.7mm machine gun in each wheel fairing. Each gun could be traversed downwards through a 6° arc. There was internal and external provision for up to 1,102lb of bombs. Power was provided by a 600hp Piaggio Stella IX RC2 air-cooled engine in a long-chord cowling driving a three-bladed propeller. The original tailskid was replaced by a tailwheel. The pilot was located well forward in an open cockpit and immediately behind him was a second cockpit which was faired over so that tests were carried out exclusively in single-seat configuration. The original prototype was first flown by Marazanni on 27 April 1934 and the second prototype (later modified as the AP1bis with retractable undercarriage) flew on 18 May. A batch of 12 series aircraft was ordered in April 1935. They were greatly modified compared with the prototypes. Power was provided by a 680hp Alfa-Romeo 125 RC35 engine. Wing dihedral, span and area were all slightly increased. The tailplane was redesigned and

the main undercarriage legs had straight fairings and slim streamlined wheel spats. Pilot and observer/gunner were housed under a raised glazed canopy. The order was increased to 39 machines (company designation Ca307), all delivered by late 1936. The AP1s were stationed at Ciampino Sud (Rome) with the 5° and 50° Stormi of the 5 Brigata Aerea d'Assalto, serving alongside Breda 64s and Ansaldo AC3s. They participated in the flypast for Hitler on his visit to Italy in May 1938. Towards the end of 1938 AP1s were relegated to flying schools for training. One AP1, registered I-ABHW, was used as an overseas demonstrator. As a result, despite the fact that Italian pilots found the AP1 over-sensitive and dangerously unstable, Paraguay ordered 22 machines (four of them twin-float seaplanes) and El Salvador ordered four. Only seven of the Paraguayan AP1s were delivered, 10 of the order being despatched to Nationalist Spain in October-December 1938. Little was heard of them in the Spanish Civil War. The four seaplanes were converted for land undercarriages and used from 1941 as trainers by the Italians. Series aircraft had two wing-mounted fixed 7.7mm Scotti or SAFAT machine guns plus another 7.7mm weapon on a flexible mounting operated by the observer.

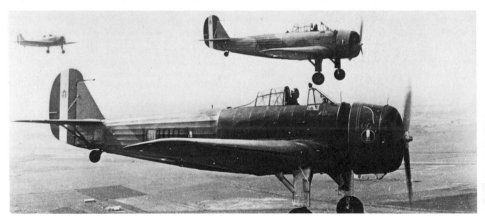

Caproni Ca73   Italy

Purpose: Bomber
Makers: Societa per lo Sviluppo dell'Aviazione in Italia 'Caproni'/Societa Aeroplani Caproni
In service: 1926-1934
Data: Ca73

Engines: See below
Span: 82ft 0.25in
Length: 49ft 6.5in
Height: 18ft 4.75in
Weight loaded: 11,023lb
Crew: Four
Max speed: 108.75mph
Service ceiling: 15,092ft
Normal range: 404 miles
Armament: Three 7.7mm machine guns plus bombs

The Ca73 appeared in 1925 and was the much-needed replacement for the ageing Caproni Ca36M three-engined bomber of World War 1 vintage which still equipped Italian first-line units. Indeed, the elderly Capronis were still seeing action against rebellious tribesmen in Italy's African colonies. The Regia Aeronautica needed the new bomber to pay more than lip service to the doctrine of strategic bombing currently being expounded so lucidly by the famous Italian military aviation theorist Generale Giulio Douhet. Evolved from the experimental four-engine Ca66 by Rudolfo Verduzio in 1924, the Ca73 had been selected by a Military Commission over Breda and Piaggio designs to equip the night bomber Squadriglie. It was a two-bay biplane of inverted sesquiplane type with ailerons fitted to the lower wing only. Between the wings were mounted two 410hp water-cooled Lorraine engines in tandem driving two-bladed propellers, one as a tractor, the other as a pusher. The struts of the divided undercarriage were attached to the lower wing and to the fuselage. Open nose and dorsal gunners' cockpits and a ventral tunnel post each had a single 7.7mm machine gun. Bombs were originally carried on external racks located one below the other on the fuselage sides beneath the wings. Developments of the basic design included the Ca73bis with 450hp Lorraine engines, the Ca73ter (later redesignated Ca82) with 510hp Isotta Fraschini Assos, and the Ca80 with 400hp Jupiters. The Ca88 and Ca89 (the latter formerly known as the Ca73QuaterG) had manually operated dorsal turrets and the ventral gun

located in a retractable turret. Bombs were carried on underwing racks. The Ca79 had a glazed bomb aimer's position in the extreme nose. Ca82Co was a colonial bomber-transport, while the Ca80S, produced in limited quantities, doubled as a paratroop transport as well as an air ambulance. Despite its unprepossessing appearance the Ca73 was a stable yet manoeuvrable aircraft, thanks largely to the considerable care which its designer had taken to ensure even weight distribution. The series saw large-scale service in the Squadriglie di Bombardamento Notturno until 1934 and operated against rebel tribesmen in Libya from the air base at Blida from 1926. The variety of designations led to the whole family being known as Ca74s.

Caproni Ca133 (and Ca148) Italy

Purpose: Bomber/Transport
Makers: Societa Italiana Caproni
In service: 1935-43
Photo and Data: Ca133

Engine: See below
Span: 69ft 7.5in
Length: 50ft 8.25in
Height: 13ft 1.5in
Weight loaded: 14,771lb
Crew: Four
Max speed: 174mph
Service ceiling: 18,135ft
Range: 839 miles

Armament: Four 7.7mm machine guns, one in a retractable manually operated dorsal turret and one in ventral, port and starboard positions

The Ca133 was a typical refinement of the concept of a 'Colonial' aircraft shared by a number of Imperial powers in the period between World Wars 1 and 2. It was intended for general purpose duties in overseas territories where air opposition was weak or non-existent. The first of two prototypes was flown by Mario De Bernardi in December 1934. Resembling an enlarged Ca101 and powered by three 430hp Piaggio PVII C16 Stella radial engines in long-chord

cowlings, the Ca133 was in fact more closely related to the single-engined Ca111, with which it shared a number of components. First production machines were shipped to Ethiopia to support the Italian invasion of that country. A Ca133 made the first photographic reconnaissance sortie over Ethiopian capital Addis Ababa on 6 March 1936. By the time the Haile Selassie regime collapsed in spring 1937, 196 Ca133s had gone into service in what was thereafter known as AOI (Italian East Africa). During the campaign the Ca133 had been used frequently in the bombing role in which it was capable of carrying 2,866lb of bombs. As a military transport the high-wing Ca133 carried 16 fully-equipped troops or the equivalent in stores. Apart from service in East and North Africa up to the early stages of World War 2, the Ca133 operated widely in specialised transport and ambulance roles. Out of 419 produced for the

Regia Aeronautica, 329 were Ca133T transports and 21 Ca133S ambulance aircraft. They operated in the support role in all theatres of war where the Italians were engaged including the short-lived Corpo Aereo Italiano, sent to Belgium in October 1940 to support the German air assault on Britain, and the campaign on the Russian Front. Italian records indicate that two Soviet fighter pilots chivalrously allowed a Ca133S ambulance they had intercepted to continue unmolested — an isolated incident in a bloody war. The Italian national airline Ala Littoria operated a dozen Ca133s in East Africa from 1937 to 1940. A small batch of military Ca133s was exported to Austria. 106 Ca148s were built from 1937. Closely resembling the Ca133, apart from structural strengthening and minor modifications, they were intended largely for civil colonial use. Two survived until 1954.

Curtiss A-3, F8C and O-1 Falcon   USA

Purpose: Attack bomber
Makers: Curtiss Aeroplane and Motor Co Inc
In service: From 1927
Photo: F8C-4 prototype
Data: F8C-5

Engine: One 450hp Pratt & Whitney R-1340-4 Wasp radial
Span: 32ft 0in
Length: 25ft 8in
Height: 10ft 2in
Weight loaded: 4,020lb
Crew: Two
Max speed: 146mph
Service ceiling: 16,250ft
Range: 720 miles
Armament: Two/three 0.30in machine guns. One 500lb bomb under fuselage or four 116lb bombs under wings

Curtiss A-3s and F8Cs had the distinction of being the first aircraft designed after World War 1 to serve with the US forces as standard light attack aircraft. In 1926 the US Army Air Service issued a requirement for a new attack bomber to replace the DH-4s then in

service. An easy and cheap solution was available in the form of a modified version of the V-1150-powered Curtiss O-1 Falcon two-seat armed/unarmed observation aircraft, of which over 100 were built for the US Army Air Corps (plus an additional 76 similar O-11/O-39 observation aircraft powered by Liberty and Conqueror engines respectively. This was selected for production and many 435hp Curtiss V-1150-3-engined aircraft were built as A-3s. These were delivered from late 1927. Subsequent orders resulted in the completion of further modified aircraft for the Army, designated A-3Bs, bringing the total number of A-3/A-3Bs built to around 150. Meanwhile, in 1927, the US Marine Corps had also decided to re-equip with a new fighter/light bomber/observation aircraft. Because of this, four production F8C-1s were built, followed by more than 20 F8C-3s, fitted with 450hp Pratt & Whitney Wasp engines and designated OC-1 and OC-2 by the Corps. The next aircraft built were dive bombers for the Marines and Navy. 27 shipboard F8C-4 Helldivers were produced, which remained in service for only a short time but were capable of diving at full power. These were followed by more than 60 F8C-5 Helldivers (redesignated O2C-1s),

built as landplanes only and not for carrier operations. The last aircraft produced were four F8C-7/8s, one as a transport and two for operational shipboard use. Each had a 575hp Wright Cyclone radial engine and an enclosed cockpit for the pilot which extended aft to protect the rear gunner. These were bought by the Navy under the designation O2C-2.

Curtiss F11C Goshawk USA

Purpose: Fighter/Bomber
Makers: Curtiss Aeroplane and Motor Co Inc
In service: 1933-38
Photo: F11C-2
Data: BFC-2

Engine: One 715hp Wright SR-1820-78 Cyclone radial
Span: 31ft 6in
Length: 25ft 0in
Height: 10ft 7in
Weight loaded: 4,640lb
Crew: One
Max speed: 205mph
225mph (BF2C-1)
Service ceiling: 24,300ft
Range: 570 miles
Armament: Two .30in machine guns. Up to 474lb of bombs, which could be released at any angle of dive

Following its success with the JN 'Jenny' biplane trainer of World War 1, the Curtiss company enhanced its reputation with a series of sleek racing aircraft for the US Navy. But, more importantly for the company, the 1920s saw production contracts covering operational aircraft for the Navy and Army, including land and carrier-based fighters, observation and attack aircraft and trainers. The turn of the decade heralded the unique and beautiful Sparrowhawk parasite fighter, which preceded the much larger F11C-2 fighter and bomber. The prototype of the new aircraft appeared in 1932 and made its first flight on 25 March of that year. Because it was a sea-going aircraft, and the US Navy had only three aircraft carriers at the time, the production order was small, just 27 aircraft. These were delivered to the Navy in early 1933 for operation on board USS *Saratoga* (a 40,000ton aircraft carrier that had been laid down in 1920 as a battle cruiser but completed as an aircraft carrier in 1927). In a bid to keep pace with the modern ideas being incorporated into aircraft by other US manufacturers, Curtiss produced the XF11C-3 prototype with a deeper forward fuselage to accept an undercarriage that retracted into the sides of the fuselage in typical Grumman fashion (whereas the earlier F11C-2s had streamlined fixed undercarriages with spatted wheels). The Navy received 28 examples in 1934 and these formed a fighting and bombing group for a very short time on the recently completed fourth aircraft carrier, the 14,500ton USS *Ranger*. Like *Saratoga* and its sister ship the USS *Lexington*, *Ranger* accommodated a maximum of 80 mixed aircraft. In the spring the designations of both versions were changed to BFC-2 and BF2C-1 respectively. Goshawks were also exported in four versions, known as Hawk I-IV, the first two with fixed undercarriages and the latter two with retractable types. Hawks I and II were powered by 715hp Wright SR-1820F-3 Cyclones, Hawk III by a 745hp R-1820F-53 and Hawk IV by a similarly rated R-1820F-56. There were also differences in fuel capacity — 50 US gallons (Hawk I), 94 (Hawk II), and 110 (Hawk III and IV) — and fuselage lengths. As with the US Navy aircraft, Hawks carried liferafts and had emergency flotation bags in the wings. Just over 250 Hawks were exported, China being the largest purchaser and also acquired a licence to manufacture the type. Reports of 1938 indicate that China then had examples of the first three Hawk versions in service, and these served alongside such modern aircraft as Northrop 2Es, Vought Corsairs, Boeing P-12s, Martin and Vultee bombers, Douglas observation aircraft and various other Italian and German aircraft. Others were sold to Argentina, Bolivia, Columbia, Cuba, Germany, Peru, Siam (see Martin B-10), Spain and Turkey. By 1938 all Goshawks of the US Navy had been withdrawn from service, although many operating abroad remained in service until the outbreak of war.

Curtiss P-1, P-6 and F6C Hawk   USA

Purpose: Fighter
Makers: Curtiss Aeroplane and Motor Co Inc
In service: From 1926
Photo: P-6D
Data: P-6E

Engine: One 675hp Curtiss V-1570-23 Conqueror
Span: 31ft 6in
Length: 23ft 2in
Height: 8ft 11in
Weight loaded: 3,390lb
Crew: One
Max speed: 198mph
Absolute ceiling: 25,800ft
Range: 285-570 miles
Armament: Two fixed forward-firing ·30in Browning machine guns. Up to 240lb of bombs could be carried

During the period covered by this book, two aircraft manufacturers supplied the US forces with most of their fighters — Curtiss and Boeing. The series of Hawk biplane fighters followed into service the small number of Curtiss PW-8s and, indeed, owed much to the earlier design. In the spring of 1925, both the USAAC and US Navy placed orders for the new Curtiss fighter. The Army aircraft were delivered as 10 P-1s, with 435hp Curtiss engines, and five 500hp-engined P-2s. Both had been the result of four years intensive development by Curtiss in co-operation with the military. Unlike the PW-8, the P-1 and P-2 had tapered wings of conventional two-spar type, fabric covered. The upper wing had greater span and chord than the lower. The installation of the different engines in the P-1 and P-2 was made easy by the usual Curtiss practice of making a common mounting structure, which was detachable. Another important feature of the aircraft was the revised water and oil systems, which allowed take-off in half the time usually required in freezing weather. In 1925-28 the USAAC received further aircraft of the series in the form of fighters and advanced trainers, most of which were powered by Curtiss engines. They started with 83 lengthened P-1A, P-1B and P-1C fighters. In addition, over 70 advanced trainers were built as AT-4s, 5s and 5As, powered by Wright engines ranging from 180-220hp. These were designed for easy conversion into fighters, and eventually this was done by giving them Curtiss engines. In this guise they were designated P-1Ds, 'Es' and 'Fs'. Further conversions produced four P-3As, P-1As fitted with Pratt & Whitney R-1340 radials. The next aircraft built for Army service were five supercharged P-5 high-altitude fighters and eight P-6As. These were fitted initially with 625hp Conqueror engines. Deliveries started in October 1929 but, in 1932, they were redesignated P-6Ds when given superchargers. The definitive production version for the Army was the P-6E. The most important change was the use of a 675hp engine, while the most noticeable changes were the faired single-strut undercarriage legs, faired wheels, a slimmer forward fuselage and use of a tailwheel. 46 were ordered, deliveries starting in 1932. Meanwhile, following the nine aircraft originally ordered as F6C-1 and F6C-2s — and often reported at the time as Sea Hawks — the Navy purchased 66 F6C-3s and 4s, powered by 435hp Curtiss and 425hp Pratt & Whitney Wasp engines respectively. Exports of the series included P-1A/P-6s to Japan, P-1A/Bs to China, F6C-4s to Cuba and P-6s to the Netherlands East Indies (in addition to any that may have been licence-built by the Aviolanda Company, which also held a licence for the Dornier Wal).

De Havilland (Airco) DH4 UK

Purpose: Day bomber
Makers: The Aircraft Manufacturing Co
In service: 1917-28
Photo: DH-4B

Engine: One 420hp Liberty 12A
Span: 42ft 4.625in
Length: 29ft 11in
Height: 9ft 8in
Weight loaded: 4,600lb
Crew: Two
Max speed: 118mph
Service ceiling: nearly 13,000ft
Range: 550 miles
Armament: Two fixed forward-firing and one rear-mounted machine guns. Up to 400lb of bombs

Acclaimed as the best single-engined day bomber of World War 1, mostly due to its excellent flying qualities, and high speed, the de Havilland (Airco) DH4 prototype first flew in 1916. Production aircraft were fitted with a variety of engines, the last to power British machines being the 375hp Rolls-Royce Eagle VIII. By the end of World War 1, Britain had produced 1,449 examples. In America, the DH4 had been chosen for production in late 1917. By the end

of production in 1919, a total of nearly 5,000 American aircraft had been built, of which nearly two-fifths had reached France for service with the American Expeditionary Force, mainly built by the Dayton-Wright Airplane Company (3,100 aircraft). After the war, American DH4s were extensively modified and the first major new version was the DH4B, in which the front and rear cockpits were brought closer together and the size of the main fuel tank increased. In 1919-24 well over 1,500 DH4s were modified to 'B' standard. A large number of other variants of the DH4s was produced from 1919, and were used for many roles including attack, communications, night-flying, photographic survey, training, ambulance and co-operation work. The type was also used as a mail-carrying aircraft, modified to accommodate up to 850lb of mail and operated on transcontinental routes. From 1923 new aircraft were also built by Boeing and the short-lived Atlantic Aircraft Corporation, with steel-tube fuselages as the DH-4M. DH-4s served with the US Army Air Corps, Navy and Marines until 1928, aircraft of the DH-4B type being used in June and August 1923 for flight refuelling experiments. DH4s were operated in other countries after the war, including Australia, Canada, Cuba, Greece, Japan, New Guinea, Nicaragua, South Africa, Spain and some South American countries.

De Havilland (Airco) DH9A UK

Purpose: Day bomber
Makers: Westland Aircraft Ltd and others
In service: 1918-31

Engine: See below
Span: 45ft 11in
Length: 30ft 3in
Height: 11ft 4in
Weight loaded: 4,645lb
Crew: Two
Max speed: 123mph
Service ceiling: 16,750ft

Range: 621 miles
Armament: One fixed forward-firing Vickers machine gun and one or two aft mounted Lewis machine guns. Up to 660lb of bombs

Built as a replacement for the disappointing Puma-engined DH9, the DH9A was in service with the RAF from mid-1918 to 1931. The only other wartime designed aircraft to serve for so many years after the end of hostilities was the Bristol Fighter. The prototype DH9A was a converted DH9 fitted with a 375hp Rolls-Royce Eagle VIII, the engine that had proved so successful on the earlier DH4. Production aircraft had either an Eagle or a 400hp Liberty 12 engine, although the Liberty was selected as the standard plant and several thousand had been ordered from America. A total of 885 'Nine-Acks' were built by Westland Aircraft Ltd and other manufacturers by the end of the war (the Aircraft Manufacturing Company being unable to work on the DH9A because of pressure to produce the twin-engined DH10 heavy bomber). The first production DH9As were delivered to No 110 Squadron RAF in June 1918, and these arrived in France a few weeks later to see the tail-end of the action prior to the Armistice. In terms of performance, the DH9A was far superior to the DH9 and carried nearly a 50% increase in bomb load; compared with the DH4, the DH9A had equally impressive increases in warload and in range, but, because of its heavier weight, was inferior in speed and service ceiling. Nevertheless, the fortunes of war had dictated the new importance of long range and heavy warload for bombers to encompass strategic targets well behind the confines of the front lines and the DH9A fitted the task. This was indeed a lucky turn for the RAF and set up the 'Nine-Ack' as an obvious choice for peacetime service abroad. Following the Armistice, some 300 more DH9As were built for the RAF, Auxiliary Air Force and Flying Training Schools. Two RAF squadrons with this aircraft also fought against the Bolsheviks in Russia in 1919 until a change in policy saw the withdrawal of forces. During the 1920s, DH9As were operated as general purpose aircraft for policing and air control duties in Iraq, Aden and India, the latter along the famous North-West Frontier, until they were replaced by purpose-built Westland Wapitis (which incorporated DH9A components). These DH9As were modified to contend with overseas conditions by adding an extra radiator and fuel tank, and sometimes carried a spare wheel, crew survival rations and other equipment. The rations were considered expedient for although the sight of an aircraft was usually enough to scatter irate tribesmen, if 'downed' by rifle fire the crew would need every assistance to survive. The first air control operation began in October 1922, when the RAF became responsible for the entire national security of Iraq, replacing troops, while equipped with just eight squadrons of DH9As, Bristol Fighters, Vickers Vernon transports and Sopwith Snipes. Others were involved in the Kabul airlift of 1928-9 (see Vickers Victoria). Of the DH9As built abroad, a number were produced in Russia as R-1s from 1923, powered by M-5 (Liberty) engines, and a small number of USA-9As were built in America, four later being converted into a USA-9B, an experimental aircraft with pressurised cockpit and two Ordnance IL-1 infantry liaison aircraft. 11 ex-British aircraft were given to Canada and others to Australia in 1920.

De Havilland DH10 Amiens   UK

Purpose: Bomber
Makers: The Aircraft Manufacturing Co
In service: 1918-23
Data: Mk III

Engines: See below
Span: 65ft 6in
Length: 39ft 7.5in
Height: 14ft 6in
Weight loaded: 9,000lb
Crew: Three
Max speed: 113.5mph
Service ceiling: 16,500ft
Endurance: 5hr 45min

Armament: Two or four Lewis machine guns in forward and aft cockpits. Up to 900lb of bombs

It is a sobering thought that the DH10 would not have materialised had it not been for reversal of the Air Board decision, made in 1917, to cancel all heavy bomber projects. More importantly, if these projects had been abandoned, it is probable that little peacetime development of heavy bombers would have followed until the rearmament of the latter 1930s and then, perhaps, without prior knowledge of their worth, the larger bombers of 1939-45 might have been generally overlooked as with Germany. So the importance of aircraft like the DH10 has to be stressed, despite the small number completed during World War 1, coupled with its postwar service. The Amiens, the DH10s unofficial name, was developed from the smaller Beardmore-engined DH3 of 1916 to which it looked remarkably similar. Of mixed construction, the first prototype, often stated to be C8658 but thought to be C4283 and later modified into a DH10C, flew initially in early 1918 with its two 220hp BHP engines mounted as pushers. Unfortunately, performance was considerably below that expected and the Mk II and III prototypes (the latter two of three further prototypes built) were given more powerful tractor-mounted engines. The third prototype first flew on 20 April 1918 (the day before the death of the most famous fighter pilot of World War 1 — Baron Manfred von Richthofen). It was powered by 360hp Rolls-Royce Eagle VIII engines and retained the nosewheels of the Mk I. The next prototype, however, was powered by 400hp Liberty 12 engines and had the nosewheels removed. Production aircraft were based on the Mk III; 1,291 were ordered from seven manufacturers, starting with an order for 200 to be built by Airco, followed by 100 by the Birmingham Carriage Company, one of which was given a twin fin and rudder tail unit. However, only 223 are believed to have been built before cancellation of the type. The

designation of production aircraft changed to DH10A or Amiens Mk IIIA when the engines were mounted on the lower wings. The last production aircraft had 375hp Eagle VIII engines and were accordingly designated DH10C or Amiens Mk IIIC. It is probable that no DH10s were used operationally during World War 1 as only about eight were in service, although it was planned that no less than 15 RAF squadrons would be equipped with the type in 1919 had the war continued. Instead, in 1919, Amiens were used for British Army mail carrying from Britain to Germany, the very first night mail flight being made on 14 May. Others were operational in India and performed bombing raids against hostiles on more than one occasion, alongside DH9As, and were one of the rarer types on mail flights between Cairo and Baghdad. Although a civil version of the DH10 was also expected to appear after the war, no aircraft of this type ever carried a 'G' registration. It is interesting to note that a new twin-engined long-range bomber had already been designed by Airco before the Armistice and a prototype ordered as the DH11. Of exceptionally clean appearance, the aircraft did not fly until 1920 and was never ordered into production. However, with a warload of about 1,780lb, it shows the importance attached to the rapid development of the bomber during the late stage of the war.

De Havilland (Soviet-built) R1M5 USSR

Purpose: Bomber
In service: From 1923

Engine: See below
Span: 45ft 8.5in
Length: 30ft 0.5in
Height: 11ft 4in
Max speed: 110mph
Service ceiling: 13,125ft
Armament: One forward-firing PV-1 machine gun (Vickers) and two DA-2 machine guns (Lewis) in rear cockpit. Small bombs carried on underwing racks

The R1M5 merits a separate entry in this book, although it was basically a Russian-built version of the DH9A, because of the large number produced and its long service with the Soviet Air Force. Its

story began when, in a bid to update the equipment of the Soviet Air Force, Nikolai Polikarpov (later famed for his I-3, I-5, I-15 and I-16 fighters) took charge of the development of an improved version of the DH9A, designated R1M5. By the autumn of 1923 prototypes had been constructed. Production started immediately, early examples being powered by imported engines although later machines were fitted with the M-5, the Soviet-manufactured version of the American Liberty engine constructed at the Ikar works. Production R1M5s were similar in appearance to DH9As but had a slightly better payload-weight ratio; a total of more than 2,800 was produced. In 1927, 15 a month were coming off the production line at the 10 Sawod factory at Taganrog alone, when about 2,000 R1M5s were operational. This total had risen to 2,500 by 1931 when 25

machines a month were coming off the lines at Dux. Meanwhile, in 1924 the Red Air Force became the VVS, and in the following year the first long-distance flight by R1M5s was carried out between Moscow and Peking.

Dewoitine D1 and D9

France

Purpose: Fighter
Makers: Société de Constructions Aéronautiques E. Dewoitine
In service: 1925-33
Photo: D-9
Data: D-1

Engine: See below
Span: 37ft 8.75in
Length: 24ft 7.25in
Height: 9ft 0.25in
Weight loaded: 2,734lb
Crew: One
Max speed: 155.3mph at 12,124ft
Service ceiling: 30,512ft
Range: 373 miles
Armament: Two fixed forward-firing 7.62mm machine guns

Designed to meet a French Aéronautique Militaire requirement of 1922, the D1 was adjudged joint winner with the SPAD 81. The Dewoitine was however, a much more advanced aircraft. Its oval 'shell' fuselage was of metal construction and had a covering of riveted metal panels. The metal wing and all movable control surfaces were fabric covered. The prototype of this parasol wing monoplane flew for the first time on 18 November 1922. Series aircraft retained the angular wings and tailplane of the first machine, but their 300hp Hispano-Suiza 8Fb liquid-cooled engines each had twin radiators attached to the forward undercarriage legs in place of the original Lamblin type fitted under the fuselage. The original faired cabane strut supporting the wing above the fuselage was replaced by two pairs of conventional struts. Orders for France and Greece were cancelled, but the D1 was popular abroad after being extensively demonstrated by Dewoitine pilots Barbot and Doret. Italy bought a single example and then the Ansaldo company constructed a further 126 for the Aeronautica Militare under the designation AC-2. Yugoslavia purchased 24 D1s and Japan a single example. Two D1s went to the Swiss Flugwaffe in 1925. In October 1924 Doret established four world speed-over-distance records in a D1 and piloted a modified D1*ter* at many air

shows until 1933, demonstrating the manoeuvrability of Dewoitine's first aircraft design. Finally, the French Aéronautique Maritime purchased at least 30 modified aircraft for carrier operations on the *Béarn*. These equipped Escadrilles 7C1 and 6C1, the latter land-based at Sidi-Ahmed, Tunisia.

The D-9 of 1924 was powered by a 420hp Gnome-Rhône 9Ab radial engine. It resembled the D1, but had a redesigned vertical tail. Like the D1 it was rejected by France but was used by the Italian Regia Aeronautica, 150 being built by Ansaldo as AC-3s. They flew with the pioneering 5° Gruppo Assalto (Ground Attack Group) after serving with the fighter Squadriglie. The Italian machines had two fixed synchronised Vickers 7.62mm fuselage guns plus a third 7.5mm Darne gun set at an angle over the wing. Yugoslavia also used a batch of D9s and Switzerland had three examples.

Dewoitine D27C1   France

Purpose: Fighter
Makers: Société de Constructions Aéronautiques E. Dewoitine
In service: 1931-1944

Engine: See below
Span: 33ft 9.5in
Length: 21ft 6.25in
Height: 9ft 1.5in
Weight loaded: 3,110lb
Crew: One
Max speed: 185.2mph
Service ceiling: 27,231ft
Normal range: 264 miles
Armament: Two 7.5mm forward-firing machine guns

A logical development in a series of parasol monoplane single-seat fighters which had begun in 1921 with the D1, the prototype D27 was taken over by the Swiss Flugwaffe and flown in 1928. It had a monocoque fuselage of light alloy and the metal spars and ribs of the wing were fabric-covered. The pilot's open cockpit was located just below the cut-out in the trailing edge of the wing. A split-axle undercarriage was fitted. Power was provided by a 500hp Hispano-Suiza 57 12Mb liquid-cooled engine with a chin-type radiator. The wings were braced very close to the centre-section and were cantilevered for two-thirds of the span. Series aircraft built for the Swiss Flugwaffe retained the rounded wing tips and horizontal tailplane of the prototype, but had a new fin and rudder assembly in place of the original angular structure which had been a hitherto regular feature of Dewoitine designs. 66 D27s equipped fighter units in Switzerland until 1940 and proved robust and manoeuvrable. Dewoitine test pilot Marcel Doret established a world speed record at an average of 177.7mph over a 621.4-mile (1,000km) distance course in a D27 on 30 November 1930. As a result of brilliant demonstrations in many countries, D27s were licence-built in Romania (which had already purchased three machines) and Yugoslavia for service with their respective air arms. A small number of D27s and the structurally strengthened D53 version were tested in France, some with different power plants. Seven were used experimentally by naval Escadrille 7C1 operating from the carrier *Béarn*. Marcel Doret's personal D53 became a familiar sight at European air displays throughout the 1930s with virtuoso aerobatic demonstrations.

Dewoitine D500 Series

France

Purpose: Fighter
Makers: Société Aéronautique Française-Avions
Dewoitine
In service: 1935-1940
Photo: D501C1
Data: D500

Engine: See below
Span: 39ft 8in
Length: 25ft 4.75in
Weight loaded: 3,770lb
Crew: One
Max speed: 223mph
Service ceiling: 34,449ft
Range: 528 miles
Armament: One engine-mounted 20mm HS9
cannon plus two wing-mounted 7.5mm MAC 1934
machine guns

The prototype D500 was first flown by test pilot
Marcel Doret on 18 June 1932. While retaining an
open cockpit (albeit with a faired headrest) and strut-
braced undercarriage, it introduced features which
marked it as an epoch-making French fighter.
Construction was all-metal, with the oval-section
monocoque fuselage using flush-riveted stressed
metal skinning. The low cantilever wing was a
single-spar structure with trailing edge 'cut-outs' to
provide good downward visibility. The wide-track
divided undercarriage incorporated Messier oleo-
pneumatic shock absorbers, and the wheels had
'spat'-type fairings and were provided with brakes.
Power was provided by a 600hp Hispano-Suiza
12Xbrs liquid-cooled engine which had its ventral
radiator in a carefully faired bath. The concept
represented a radical advance over the Nieuport-
Delage 62 series which formed the backbone of
France's Escadrilles de Chasse. Tests indicated top
speed of 230.5mph at 16,405ft, 13mph better than
the revised figure demanded by the STAé (Service
Technique Aérienne) official specification.

Production was shared between Dewoitine, Lioré
et Olivier and Loire. Series D500s had twin
synchronised 7.7mm Vickers machine guns plus two
7.5mm Darne guns in small underwing gondolas.
The D501 version was developed to utilise the then
revolutionary 'moteur canon' — a 690hp H-S 12Xrs
engine incorporating a 20mm Hispano-Suiza HS9
cannon between the cylinder blocks, firing through a
hollow propeller shaft. Externally the D501 differed
from the D500 by having no propeller spinner. Both
types had a two-bladed wooden Chauvière propeller.
The full span ailerons were modified as a result of
serious flutter problems. D500 No 48 was tested as
the prototype of a new version with the more
powerful 860hp Hispano-Suiza 12Ycrs engine, the
D510. This machine reached 250mph at 16,405ft.
The only other modifications incorporated were a
larger radiator bath, enlarged vertical tail surfaces
and mass-balanced ailerons. A Ratier 1239 three-
bladed metal propeller was standard. France
received 99 D500s, 143 D501s and 88 D510s. 24
D510Cs equipped squadrons 41 and 42 of the
Chinese Nationalist air force, seeing action against
the Japanese from the summer of 1938. 14 D501Ls
went to Lithuania, three D500Vs to Venezuela, two
D510Js to Japan, a D510A to Britain and a D510R
to the Soviet Union (the major powers were really
only interested in the 'moteur canon'). Two
D510THs, originally for Turkey, found their way to
the Spanish Republicans during the Civil War, but
achieved little in combat. The first D500s and D501s
for France went to the 3ᵉ Escadre at Villacoublay
and the 4ᵉ at Reims in summer 1935. At the
beginning of 1936 115 of both types were on
charge. D510 deliveries began at the end of 1936.
All three types served widely with French fighter
units, including two naval escadrilles. They were
replaced during 1939, thereafter serving with
Escadrilles Régionales de Chasse (reserve units) prior
to the French collapse. The last unit to fly the
Dewoitine was Escadrille I/6 at Dakar, West Africa,
which gave up its six D501s during 1941.

Dornier Do11, Do13 and Do23
Germany

Purpose: Bomber
Makers: Dornier Metallbauten GmbH
In service: From 1932
Photo and Data: Do23G

Engines: See below
Span: 84ft 11.75in
Length: 61ft 8in
Height: 17ft 8.5in
Weight loaded: 20,280lb
Crew: Four
Max speed: 161mph
Service ceiling: 13,775ft
Range: 840 miles
Armament: 7.92mm MG15 machine gun in nose, dorsal and ventral positions. About 2,200lb of bombs

After the Versailles Treaty, which severely restricted the types of aircraft Germany could develop and produce, German aircraft manufacturers built factories in several foreign countries to evade the limitations. At least one of these countries was to live to regret its liberal attitude. Junkers built factories in Russia in 1922 and Sweden, and from a Swiss Dornier factory at Altenrhein there appeared, in 1932, the last of a small batch of so-called freight transport aircraft, the DoF. This first flew on 7 May 1932, and subsequently the decision was made to place the DoF into production in Germany as the Do11, still under the pretence of its civil function although intended as the first Luftwaffe twin-

engined bomber to be designed as such. To aid the cover-up and to enable a nucleus of pilots to be trained, the first aircraft went to the State Railways. About 77 shorter span Do11Ds were built, each with two 650hp Siemens Sh22B engines (Bristol Jupiter type), although they proved relatively unstable in flight. An unusual feature of the aircraft was its retractable main wheels which were manually actuated and lifted into the engine nacelles. Meanwhile, in February 1933, a developed version made its maiden flight as the Do13. This differed from the Do11D in several ways, the most noticeable being the substitution of a fixed undercarriage for the unsuccessful retractable type. The third prototype was the definitive version, with 750hp BMW VI engines, and the Do13 entered production in the 'C' version. The first were delivered in the latter part of 1934, but within a short time several had broken up because of structural failure. Production was begrudgingly stopped and, while the officials moaned at having to wait for more bombers to supplement the Ju52/3ms, the aircraft was redesigned, strengthened and given double-edge flaps and ailerons, and as such received the designation Do13e. Subsequently, when production again got underway, the new aircraft was redesignated Do23F. However, most of the 200 or so aircraft built up to 1935 were Do23Gs, powered by two BMW VIU engines. With their arrival, earlier types were used in secondary roles, and a limited number of Do23s were operated during World War 2 with de-gaussing rings for mine clearance duties.

Fairey IIID
UK

Purpose: Fleet spotter-reconnaissance/General purpose
Makers: Fairey Aviation Co Ltd
In service: 1922-30
Data: Seaplane

Engine: See below
Span: 46ft 1.25in
Length: 37ft 0in
Height: 11ft 4in
Weight loaded: 5,050lb
Max speed: 106-120mph

Crew: Three
Service ceiling: 16,500ft
Range: 550 miles
Armament: One fixed forward-firing Vickers machine gun and one Lewis machine gun in rear cockpit. Light bombs could be carried

The Fairey IIID earned for itself a reputation of quiet reliability, and during its few years of British service was involved only in one real incident, that being to aid the Shanghai authorities in quelling a rebellion in 1927. On this occasion FAA aircraft were used. First

flown in August 1920, it was a direct descendant of the Fairey IIIA, B and C series and a total of 207 was eventually built, mostly for the Fleet Air Arm but a few for the Royal Air Force. In an unusual step, however, reasonable numbers of IIIDs were exported before the British services received the type. Overseas recipients included Australia, Netherlands, Portugal and Sweden. It was indeed the Portuguese Navy IIID named *Santa Cruz* that first brought the type to the attention of the public, when in 1922 it became the first aircraft to cross the South Atlantic. However, this singular feat was not completed by one aircraft named *Santa Cruz* but three, the first two having crashed along the route. In Australia, it appears that the best work carried out by the IIID was in surveying the Great Barrier Reef, which began in 1924 using an aircraft flown from HMAS *Geranium*, subsequently being superseded by Supermarine Seagulls. Various engines were used in the production aircraft, including the 365hp Rolls-Royce Eagle VIII, 450hp Napier Lion IIB and similarly rated Lion V and VA, the latter two engines leading

to the designations IIID Mk II and IIID, Mk III respectively. Capable of operating from land bases or aircraft carriers, and of being catapulted from ships, the IIID first equipped two FAA flights on board HMS *Argus* and HMS *Vindictive* in 1924, the former having been the first flush-deck or 'flat iron' carrier, when completed in 1918 as a conversion of the passenger liner *Conte Rosso* (scrapped in 1947). For carrier operations IIIDs used wheeled undercarriages, initially in conjunction with the arrester hook landing technique. Twin-float undercarriages were standard for use from other types of naval vessels. While ideal for policing duties abroad, it was also an era of 'flag waving' flights, and RAF IIIDs of a special unit flew several long-distance formation flights from March 1926. The first, the Trans-African flight, encompassed cities in Egypt, South Africa, Greece, France and England, a grand total of over 13,900 miles, accomplished to a pre-arranged schedule and claimed at the time to be the first occasion that a long-distance flight under such rigid conditions had taken place.

Fairey IIIF UK

Purpose: Fleet spotter-reconnaissance/Light day bomber/General purpose
Makers: Fairey Aviation Co Ltd
In service: 1928-40
Data: Mk IIIB seaplane

Engine: See below
Span: 45ft 9in
Length: 36ft 4in
Height: 14ft 3in
Weight loaded: 6,300lb
Crew: Three (two for RAF versions)
Max speed: over 120mph
Service ceiling: 20,000ft
Endurance: up to 4hrs
Armament: One fixed forward-firing Vickers machine gun and one Lewis machine gun in rear cockpit. 500lb of bombs could be carried

This beautifully streamlined and popular biplane was used more than any other type by the Fleet Air Arm during the period covered by this book and was also operated in large numbers by the RAF. It is believed that a total of over 620 IIIFs was built, of which all but a small number were ordered for British service, more than any other non-Hawker-built type prior to the rearmament programme of the late 1930s. During their service life several IIIFs were used as trials aircraft for various engine installations (including flight testing a Junkers Jumo from December 1936), testing swept wings and centre floats, and single aircraft were used for target towing and communications work, a departure from the normal duties. A number of IIIFs were converted subsequently into Fairey Gordons. IIIFs served with the FAA as three-seat spotter-reconnaissance aircraft, and over 230 were operated by the RAF, mainly as two-seat general purpose machines, although many were classified officially or unofficially as light bombers. The predominance of Britain's overseas commitments to air control and policing was clearly in the minds of the designers when provision was made for carrying a spare wheel, ration boxes, drinking water and other special equipment. Others were exported, including small numbers to Argentina (with 560hp Siddeley Panther engines), Chile (used by the Navy as land and seaplanes and catapulted from the battleship *Almirante Latorre*), Egypt (ex-RAF IIIF sold in April 1939), Greece (seaplanes), Ireland and New Zealand (seaplanes; see Gloster Grebe). Although designated differently, FAA and RAF versions were generally similar, and the former's versions are covered in the later text. RAF two-seat versions were the Mk IVS of wood and metal construction, the Mk IVCM with wooden stringers added to the metal-constructed fuselage, the Mk IVM of all-metal construction except for the vertical tail, the Mk IVM/A all-metal version, and the Mk IVB with a strengthened fuselage. The prototype IIIF first flew on 19 March 1926 and was followed by a second three-seat prototype, constructed as an all-metal aircraft. 10 pre-production aircraft were then produced, of which one became the prototype for the RAF version and another was used for deck-landing trials. (Since the first deck-landing trials on a moving ship by Sqn Cdr Dunning in a Sopwith Pup in 1917, techniques of stopping the aircraft on the carrier vessel once the aircraft had touched-down went through several stages of development. Unfortunately for Dunning,

the grabbing of straps hanging from the landing aircraft proved unsatisfactory and he was drowned after going over the edge of HMS *Furious*. The original arrester hook and wire method was then adopted for some time, but even this proved accident-prone; so the period in which the IIIF served was mainly that of unassisted landings. Because the IIIF's landing speed was only about 51mph, alighting on a carrier was comparatively easy.) Six other aircraft of the pre-production batch were sent to No 47 Squadron at Khartoum for the 1927 flight from Cairo to Cape Town and back; the remaining two aircraft were sent to India. The first standard production aircraft, designated Mk Is, were powered by the 450hp Napier Lion VA engine and entered service with three FAA flights in 1928. Some of the first Mk Is were, however, sent to the RAF. Next came 32 production Mk IIs for the FAA, powered by Napier Lion XI engines, followed by the Mk III version with metal wings to complete the transition to all-metal structure. These were powered by 570hp Napier Lion XIA engines (as in RAF aircraft) and the final ten, ordered in September 1929, were built as trainers. The last FAA version was the Mk IIIB, which was strengthened for catapulting: 167 were produced, including a few dual-control trainers. IIIFs served on every British aircraft carrier, as well as from capital warships and land stations. They were operated on both cross-axle Vee land undercarriages and floats. Three experimental pilotless radio-controlled aircraft were also produced, known as Fairey Queens.

Fairey Fawn   UK

Purpose: Light bomber
Makers: Fairey Aviation Co Ltd
In service: From 1924
Photo: Mk II

Engine: One 470hp Napier Lion II (Mk I and II)
Span: 49ft 11in
Length: 32ft 1in
Height: 11ft 11in
Weight loaded: 5,834lb
Crew: Two
Max speed: 114mph
Service ceiling: 15,500ft
Range: 650 miles
Armament: One fixed forward-firing Vickers machine gun and one Lewis machine gun in rear cockpit. Up to 460lb of bombs

Official specifications for aircraft produced during the interwar period occasionally restricted the designers to such a degree that inferior products resulted. Perhaps the best remembered example of this was the Supermarine Type 224 fighter of 1933, designed around the Goshawk III engine. An earlier example was the Fawn which, when completed, had a lower performance than the DH9A it was replacing and a lower bomb-carrying capability. Despite all, the Fawn was ordered and served for a short time until the more suitable Hawker Horsley appeared. Developed from the experimental Fairey Type 21 Pintail, which had its rudder situated under the horizontal tail surfaces, the Fawn was the first new day bomber to enter RAF service after World War 1, and became a light companion to the new heavy Vickers Virginia in the inventory. The prototype first flew in March 1923 and retained a short fuselage similar to that of the Pintail. Four more prototypes, with longer fuselages to improve stability and designated Mk II, were put in hand (two ordered with the original Fawn and two after), and the first of these flew in September of the same year. Production of the Fawn II soon commenced, and the first series-built aircraft made its maiden flight in 1924, followed by 49 similar machines. Production continued with 20 Mk IIIs, all except two or three of which were powered by Supercharged Napier Lion V engines.

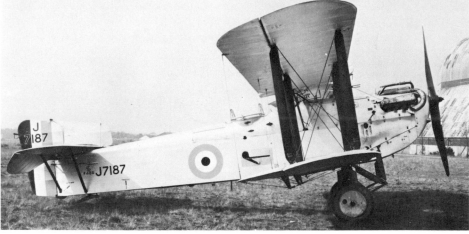

Fairey Flycatcher   UK

Purpose: Fighter
Makers: Fairey Aviation Co Ltd
In service: 1923-35

Engine: One 400hp Armstrong Siddeley Jaguar III or IV engine as standard
Span: 29ft 0in
Length: 23ft 0in
Height: 12ft 0in
Weight loaded: 2,979lb
Crew: One
Max speed: 134mph at 5,000ft
Service ceiling: 20,600ft
Range: 310 miles

Armament: Two fixed forward-firing .303in Vickers machine guns. Four 20lb bombs could be carried

After the end of World War 1, economies imposed by the government reduced naval aviation to a mere skeleton of its former self. The handful of remaining units were expected to perform to the best of their ability the many and varied operational roles, and it was from this poor start that a new beginning had to be made. Overseas operations, like that carried out by mixed British forces against the 'Mad Mullah' in 1919, helped to keep the candle burning until new equipment and new units could be introduced. The first newly designed naval fighter to enter postwar service was the Gloster (Nieuport) Nightjar, followed in the next year by the Flycatcher, which entered service about the same time as the RAF's Grebe (although the Grebe was 20mph faster). The fact that the Flycatcher then remained in service for over a decade is proof enough of its ability as a fighter; yet it also earned the reputation of being a pilot's aircraft, proving easy to fly while retaining a high degree of manoeuvrability. Both Fairey and Parnell had built three prototypes to meet the new naval specification, known as Flycatchers and Plovers respectively. Ten production Plovers were subsequently built and served from 1923-24. The first prototype Flycatcher flew on 28 November 1922, fitted with an Armstrong Siddeley Jaguar II engine. Following satisfactory Service trials, it went in early 1923 for deck trials on board the first flush-deck or 'flat-iron' carrier, HMS *Argus*. The second and third prototypes were completed as a floatplane

and amphibian respectively. Altogether 192 production Flycatchers were built, the first being delivered to a naval flight in 1923, replacing Nightjars. Early production aircraft had arrester hooks, but later aircraft had hydraulic wheel-brakes and could be deck-landed without any further assistance. They were the first FAA (the name Fleet Air Arm adopted in April 1924) aircraft fitted with such brakes. By the latter part of 1924, the FAA had five flights of Flycatchers, increased to eight by 1928. They served on every British aircraft carrier of the time, from shore stations and from gun-turret platforms and were the last aircraft capable of slip flight operations from the below-deck hangars on the carriers *Furious*, *Courageous* and *Glorious*. The Flycatcher was a mixed-construction equal-span biplane, the upper and lower wings being fitted with Fairey Camber Changing Gear. It could be operated on wheels, floats or amphibious gear, and light bomb racks could be fitted to permit use as a dive bomber.

Fairey Fox   UK

Purpose: Light bomber
Makers: Fairey Aviation Co Ltd
In service: 1926-34
Photo and Data: Mk I

Engine: One 480hp Curtiss D12
Span: 38ft 0in
Length: 31ft 2in
Height: 10ft 8in
Weight loaded: over 4,100lb
Crew: Two
Max speed: 156mph
Service ceiling: 17,000ft
Range: 500 miles

Armament: One fixed forward-firing Vickers machine gun and one Lewis machine gun in rear cockpit. Up to 460lb of bombs

In 1925, Air Chief Marshal Sir Hugh Trenchard, accompanied by other officials, watched a demonstration of the new Fairey Fox, with unique consequences. Firstly, sufficient Foxes were ordered immediately to equip one RAF first-line squadron. Secondly, because of seemingly perennial economic restrictions, those 28 aircraft (ordered in three batches and one fitted with experimental towing gear) were the only Foxes that the RAF ever received, although they proved nearly 50% faster than the day bombers then in service. At least they had the effect of stirring the Air Ministry into realising that new and faster fighters would be needed if the RAF had to cope with bombers of such calibre. The beginnings of the Fox can be traced to the 1923 Schneider Trophy contest, when (Sir) Richard Fairey saw the Curtiss D12-engined R-3 Navy Racer in action. Fairey obtained a production licence for the D12, which could be enclosed in a finely streamlined cowling, and in 1924 his company began designing a new bomber round a D12, as a private venture. The result was a breakaway from the usual drag-inducing bombers with radial engines or with frontal radiators. The prototype Fox flew for the first time on 3 January 1925. It was a biplane of wooden construction, fabric-covered, with single-bay wings. The oval fuselage contained a prone bombing position in the

rear cockpit for the bomb aimer, whose defensive Lewis gun was carried on a special high speed mounting for streamlining. The RAF unit which received the Foxes, in the second half of 1926, was No 12 Squadron. It kept them until 1931, by which time some of the aircraft had been re-engined with Rolls-Royce Kestrels and redesignated Mk IAs, and one had been returned to Fairey for use in their steam-cooling experiments. They continued to serve with the Special Duty Flight for another three years. The Peruvian Navy also received six Fox Mk IV seaplanes in the mid-1930s, powered by Kestrel engines, and these joined the inventory of mainly French and American aircraft. In addition, many other Foxes were built, in several versions, by Avions Fairey in Belgium, including Fox IIs, Fox IIIs, Fox VIs, two single-seat Mono-Fox VIIs or Kangourous and Fox VIIs (see separate entry).

Fairey Gordon and Seal   UK

Purpose: (Gordon) Bomber/General purpose
Makers: Fairey Aviation Co Ltd
In service: (Gordon) 1931-38
Photo: Gordon
Data: Gordon I

Engine: See below
Span: 45ft 9in
Length: 36ft 8.5in
Height: 14ft 2.5in
Weight loaded: 5,905lb
Crew: Two
Max speed: 145mph
Service ceiling: 22,000ft
Range: 600 miles

Armament: One fixed forward-firing Vickers machine gun and one Lewis machine gun in rear cockpit. Up to 460lb of bombs

The Gordon was a development of the Fairey IIIF and for a time was known as the IIIF Mk V. Its main attribute compared to the IIIF proper was its considerably higher speed, made possible mainly by a decrease in all-up weight — with slight reduction in bomb-carrying capacity — as well as by the installation of the new and efficient engine. It had unstaggered equal-span two-bay wings of metal construction, fabric covered and fitted with Fairey Camber Changing Gear. The oval-section fuselage was of metal construction, with partial fabric covering, and a cross-axle undercarriage was fitted. Power was provided by a 525hp Armstrong Siddeley Panther IIA radial engine. The forward-firing Vickers gun was mounted externally on the left side of the fuselage, and a prone bombing position was provided in the fuselage. The prototype first flew in 1930 and was a converted IIIF Mk IVM. Initial production aircraft was designated Mk Is, and a total of 163 of this version were built for the RAF (including a few trainers of which three were ordered among the first batch of 20 Gordons). A further nine IIIFs were converted to Gordons while on the production line. The final 24 production aircraft were Gordon IIs, with a more rounded fin and rudder, a modified fuselage and other changes. In addition, about 84 IIIFs were later converted into Gordons. 21 were also exported, one going to China and the rest to Brazil, which operated them as armed reconnaissance seaplanes alongside Vought Corsairs, Curtiss Falcons and Breguet aircraft. Others, from RAF production, were delivered to New Zealand and Egypt. Gordons first entered service with the RAF in April 1931 and were operated in their primary role until late 1938, after which time a few were used for target towing.

The Fairey Seal, known originally as the IIIF Mk VI, was the FAA's equivalent of the Gordon and was operated as a spotter-reconnaissance aircraft. Minor differences from the Gordon included the provision of three seats, a tail wheel, wheel brakes, catapult points, flotation gear, slinging gear and an arrester hook. Its increased weight of about 100lb, partly explained by the increase in bomb load by 40lb, led to a marginally lower maximum speed. Converted from a IIIF Mk IIIB, the prototype made its maiden flight on 11 September 1930. The first production Seal was delivered to the FAA in 1933 and deliveries continued until March 1935. 90 Seals were actually produced (one further Seal ordered but thought not to have been completed). These were operated as landplanes from aircraft carriers and as seaplanes catapulted from warships. By 1938, the Seal had generally been replaced by another biplane in the form of the Blackburn Shark. However, because the RAF was able to operate aircraft of lesser performance for patrol duties overseas in areas where they were less likely to meet with overwhelming opposition, a few Seals were flown from Ceylon by this service during the early war years. Others were sold to Peru (six sometimes stated to be Gordons), Argentina (one seaplane for reconnaissance), Latvia (four seaplanes) and Chile (two).

Fairey Swordfish   UK

Purpose: Torpedo bomber
Makers: Fairey Aviation Co Ltd
In service: 1936-45
Photo and Data: Mk I

Engine: One 690hp Bristol Pegasus IIIM3 radial
Span: 46ft 4in
Length: 35ft 8in
Height: 12ft 4in
Weight loaded: 9,250lb
Crew: Two or three
Max speed: 138mph
Service ceiling: 19,250ft
Range: 546-1,030 miles
Armament: Two .303in machine guns; one

1,610lb torpedo, one 1,500lb mine or equivalent bombs

Affectionately known as the 'Stringbag', the Swordfish was one of the FAA's all-time greats; and despite the fact that it was an antiquated biplane in a hostile world of fast monoplanes, it remained in service throughout World War 2. In its long line of notable war achievements can be counted the decimation of the Italian fleet at Taranto in November 1940 and the crippling of the German battleship *Bismarck*. The prototype Swordfish, known originally as the TSR II, was developed from the earlier TSR I, built as a private venture and first flown in March 1933. The TSR II, modified to counteract the spinning tendencies of the earlier aircraft, made its maiden flight on 17 April 1934, powered by a 690hp Bristol Pegasus IIIM3 engine. In the spring of 1935, the first orders for Swordfish were placed. Of metal construction, fabric covered, the first production Mk Is went into service with No 825 Squadron FAA in July 1936. By 1938, the Swordfish had replaced all other types of torpedo-bomber in FAA service and was alone in this role until 1940, when the Albacore arrived. (It is interesting to note at this point that the Swordfish outlasted the Albacore in service by over a year.) By the outbreak of World War 2, the FAA had 13 Swordfish squadrons, 12 of which were stationed on board the carriers HMS *Ark Royal* (42 aircraft), *Courageous* (24), *Eagle* (18), *Hermes* (9), *Glorious* (36) and *Furious* (18). They served alongside Skuas

and Sea Gladiators, although Martlets subsequently replaced the latter. It was Swordfish from *Ark Royal* that first spotted the Dornier Do18s that Skuas attacked, thus giving the FAA its first victory over a German aircraft. Although the Swordfish was an exceptional aircraft and did a great deal of good work during the war, it was a somewhat perilous mount for the crew, being slow and a relatively easy target for opposing fighters. However, in retrospect, it was the same slow speed that made it a more difficult target for ships' guns than at first would be imagined, because gun control systems was geared to deal with faster attacking aircraft. A total of 993 Mk Is (including prototype) was built, of which 300 were produced by Blackburn Aircraft Ltd. Subsequent versions were produced during World War 2.

Farman F60 Series   France

Purpose: Heavy bomber
Makers: Société des Avions H&M Farman
In service: 1924-1932
Photo: Polish F68s

Engines: See below
Span: 87ft 9.2in
Length: 48ft 5.5in
Height: 16ft 1.7in
Weight loaded: 11,023lb
Crew: Four
Max speed: 99.4mph
Service ceiling: 18,135ft
Range: 342 miles
Armament: Three 7.62mm machine guns. Maximum bomb load 2,293lb (on racks under fuselage and wings)

The Farman Goliath was perhaps the most significant large aircraft of the decade following World War 1. In its airliner versions it was the

mainstay on several important European routes, and a number of developments of the FF60 prototype of 1918 were built in quantity for the French Aéronautique Militaire and several foreign powers. Construction was simple and robust, being built largely of wood with fabric covering. The three-bay equal-span wings had square-cut tips and the single fin and rudder were of distinctive Farman shape. The slab-sided fuselage had open nose and dorsal gunners' cockpits and the pilot was accommodated in a cockpit offset to port below the leading-edge of the upper wing. The main undercarriage struts were contained in streamlined fairings and twin wheels were fitted on either side. The first production bomber was the F60BN2, which was a three-seater despite its designation. It was powered by two 260hp Salmson 9Z engines and the fuselage nose was 'cut down' in British Handley Page Hyderabad fashion to form the forward gunner's cockpit. This version formed the equipment of the 21e Régiment d'Aviation at Nancy and the 22e RA at Chartres. The

F60M of 1923 (310hp Renault 12Fy inline engines) had a redesigned 'blunt' nose. Pilot and co-pilot were seated side-by-side and were protected by a single curved windscreen. This version was used by the French and one aircraft was exported to Japan. A single Goliath with 500hp Farman engines was bought by Italy. The next variant, the F62, had its nose gunner's cockpit located in a 'balcony' with the bomb-aimer's glazed position immediately behind and below. The dorsal gun-ring was on a sliding traverse to permit operation to either side. A number of F62s, powered by 450hp Lorraine-Dietrich engines, were supplied to the Soviet Union where they equipped pioneering Eskadrilas and served to familiarise Soviet aircrew for the first time with large twin-engined aircraft, thus forming the nucleus of the powerful Russian heavy bomber force of the 1930s. 32 F68BN4s with 450hp Jupiter radials were purchased by Poland in 1925 and flew with two 1st Air Regiment squadrons. But the Goliaths, though renowned for their stability in flight, displayed adverse characteristics inherent in their low top speed and were soon relegated to crew familiarisation and parachute training duties. The 380hp Gnome-Rhône Jupiter-powered F65 equipped French Navy Escadrilles 5B2, 6B1 and 6B2, which took part in operations against Rif tribesmen in Morocco during 1925. This version retained the 'blunt' nose of the F60M. It also operated widely on large wooden twin floats with smaller stabilising floats attached directly to the underside of the lower wings. Interestingly, Navy Escadrilles had used a float version of the original Salmson-powered F60 and torpedo-bombing tests had been carried out with F60 Torp seaplanes. Earlier still a civil Farman with floats had been flown by the Navy. The F63 bomber (420hp Jupiters) equipped the 21e RA in 1927.

Farman F160 to F168   France

Purpose: Torpedo bomber/Reconnaissance
Makers: Société des Avions H&M Farman
In service: 1929-37
Photo: F160
Data: F168

Engines: See below
Span: 87ft 7.2in
Length: 48ft 10.6in
Height: 17ft 4.67in
Weight loaded: 15,102lb
Crew: Four
Max speed: 108.1mph
Service ceiling: 14,764ft
Range: 621 miles

Armament: Four 7.62mm machine guns (on twin bow and midships ring mountings)

The success of the Goliath formula induced the Farman company to attempt a modernisation of the design. The F160, F161 and F165 were landplane night bombers. The F160 carried a 3,307lb bomb load and was powered by 500hp Farman engines. The F162, F166, F167 and F168 were naval torpedo bomber/reconnaissance aircraft capable of operating on either wheel or float undercarriages. Of these the F166 and F168 were produced in quantity and featured new carefully contoured fuselages. The uncowled 500hp Gnome-Rhône Jupiter radial

engines had tapering nacelles which extended beyond the trailing edge of the lower wings. The floats were of more modern design and their strut supports were simplified compared with those of the F60 series. The F168 differed from the F166 in having a raised curved decking between the two gunners' cockpits to provide improved visibility for pilot and co-pilot. Some 100 F168s were built and served with a number of Escadrilles of the French Aéronautique Maritime, including 3B1, 3B2 and

4B1, until replaced by LéO 258s built to a similar formula during 1936/37. The Farmans could carry a maximum of 4,409lb of bombs over short ranges or 2,204lb over a 621-mile range. With a standard 1,764lb torpedo the range was 746 miles. For long-range reconnaissance with maximum fuel and no offensive load the range rose to 1,118 miles. After withdrawal from active service, F166s and F168s were attached to French naval air stations at St Raphaël and Hourtin for training duties.

Farman F220 Series

France

Purpose: Heavy night bomber
Makers: Avions Henri et Maurice Farman
In service: 1936-40 (as bombers)
Photo: F221
Data: F222.2

Engines: See below
Span: 118ft 1.25in
Length: 70ft 4.5in
Height: 17ft 0.5in
Weight loaded: 41,226lb
Crew: Five
Max speed: 202mph
Service ceiling: 27,887ft
Range: 745 miles
Armament: Three 7.5mm MAC machine guns, one each in nose, dorsal and ventral positions.
Bomb load (max) 9,259lb

Apart from the fleet of Soviet TB-3s, the Farman F220 series serving in limited numbers with the Armée de l'Air from November 1936 constituted the world's only contemporary four-engined heavy bomber force. The basic design was a high-wing strut-braced monoplane with engines in tandem pairs attached to the tips of lower stub wings. F220 prototype flew on 26 May 1932. With liquid-cooled Hispano-Suiza engines it featured a fixed

undercarriage, enclosed pilot's cabin, open nose and dorsal gunners' positions and a ventral post. F221 differed in having 800hp Gnome-Rhône L4Kbrs radials, enclosed manually-operated nose and dorsal turrets and a retractable ventral position. 10 F221 BN5s equipped Escadre II/15, followed by 11 F222s with retractable undercarriages. 24 F222.2s were built up to 1938, differing in having an entirely redesigned forward fuselage section and dihedral on the outer wing panels. 16 F222.2s had 920hp engines. Only the basic concept of the F223 remained the same, as this version had a new slim fuselage, long finely-tapered wings with strong single struts either side, and a twin fin and rudder tail assembly. Flown originally with radial engines, the eight NC223s completed were re-engined with 1,100hp Hispano-Suiza 12Y50/51 units in 1939-40. By World War 2 some F221s had been modified to F222 standard. The Farmans were engaged on night leaflet raids over Germany during the Phoney War, only making night bombing raids in May/June 1940. Three aircraft were lost on operations. Of three civil F2234 aircraft requisitioned by the French Navy in September 1939, *Jules Verne* made the first Allied raid on Berlin in June 1940. The F2234s were eventually returned to civil use. From June 1940 a number of Farman bombers were converted as transports or liaison aircraft.

Fiat BR Series

Italy

Purpose: Bomber
Makers: Società Anonyma Fiat
In service: 1920-40
Photo and Data: BR3

Engine: See below
Span: 56ft 9.1in
Length: 34ft 7.33in
Height: 9ft 6.5in
Weight loaded: 9,590lb
Crew: Two
Max speed: 142.9mph
Service ceiling: 20,505ft
Normal range: 466miles
Armament: Two 7.7mm machine guns plus bombs

For most of the period between the two world wars, Italian light bombing squadrons relied almost entirely on single-engined biplanes produced by Fiat in the BR series ('B' for Bombardamento and 'R' for Rosatelli, their designer). The original BR was built in 1919. A few were supplied to the Aeronautica Militare and a number were in evidence during ceremonies to celebrate the formation of the independent Regia Aeronautica in 1923. One BR had made the first non-stop Rome-Paris flight (750 miles) on 14 July 1919. Retaining the 700hp Fiat

A-14 engine of the BR, but with a frontal radiator of new design, the BR1 had a divided undercarriage in place of the conventional axle type of its predecessor. Rigid Warren strut wing bracing was introduced and the lower wing, of reduced span, had dihedral. Its unusual bomb-bay had rotating cylinders which permitted the launching of a salvo of three bombs. Armament comprised a single 7.7mm machine gun on a ring mounting operated by the observer. A BR1 was used in torpedo dropping experiments and one of the type established a world record on 23 December 1924, reaching 18,220ft with a 3,307lb payload. The BR2, built in quantity from 1925, represented a considerable improvement with a 1,090hp Fiat A25 engine and undercarriage of new design. Armament comprised one fixed and one flexibly mounted machine gun and a bomb load of up to 1,323lb. The first Squadriglia to equip with the type made a 2,600-mile tour of European capitals in 1925. The BR3 appeared in 1930 and over 100 were built. Most examples had Handley Page slots fitted to the leading edges of the upper wing. The oleo-pneumatic undercarriage was fitted with brakes. The gunner's cockpit had rounded panels at the side with observation windows. BR3s were still serving as trainers in 1940. Aircraft in the BR biplane series were exported to Sweden and Hungary.

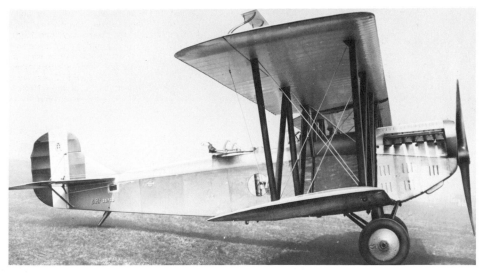

Fiat CR1

Italy

Purpose: Fighter
Makers: Società Anonyma Fiat
In service: 1926-30

Engine: See below
Span: 29ft 4.33in

Length: 20ft 5.67in
Height: 7ft 10.5in
Weight loaded: 2,546lb
Crew: One
Max speed: 167.8mph
Service ceiling: 24,442ft

Normal range: 404 miles
Armament: Two 7.7mm forward-firing machine guns

The CR1 was the first fighter aircraft of Italian design to be adopted by the Regia Aeronautica, and was designed by Celestino Rosatelli in 1923. It was a refined version of his experimental CR and one of two CR1 prototypes built was demonstrated alongside its predecessor at the annual aerial review at Centocelle aerodome (Rome) on 4 November 1924. Series production was initiated and first deliveries took place in 1925. In total 240 CR1s were ordered, with Italian military serials MM1272 to MM1511. Production was shared between Fiat and the OFM and SIAI companies. By 1926 12

squadriglie da caccia were equipped with the type. The CR1 was very distinctive since its lower wing had greater span than the upper wing. The tailplane also had a characteristic shape which later became associated with Fiat biplane designs. W-form rigid wing bracing was introduced. The main legs of the conventional axle-type undercarriage were faired over. Wings were of wood while the fuselage was a trellis construction of metal tubes, covered partly with fabric and partly with plywood. Power was provided by a 300hp Hispano-Suiza liquid-cooled engine with radiator in the upper nose section. Later the Isotta Fraschini 'Asso' engine was adopted. By 1930 the CR1 had been replaced by the CR20 in first-line units. It had proved itself tough and manoeuvrable, but its basic design was seen to be outmoded soon after it had entered service.

Fiat CR20   Italy

Purpose: Fighter
Makers: Società Anonyma Fiat
In service: 1926-1936

Engine: See below
Span: 32ft 1.8in
Length: 21ft 11.75in
Height: 9ft 0.25in
Weight loaded: 3,278lb
Crew: One
Max speed: 171.5mph
Service ceiling: 24,606ft
Normal range: 466 miles
Armament: Two 7.7mm forward-firing machine guns

On 19 June 1926 test pilot Battista Bottalla demonstrated prototype MM60 of the new Rosatelli fighter, the CR20. Although speed was only marginally better than the CR1, the improved manoeuvrability, reliability and structural strength of

the new fighter assured its success. It had a long career, more than 670 machines being built over a seven-year period by Fiat, CMASA and Macchi. Although it retained the Warren wing bracing of the CR1, it reverted to a conventional wing arrangement, with upper wing of greater span. A new powerplant, the 400hp Fiat A20, was installed. The CR20 was Fiat's first all-metal fighter. It established an international reputation for formation aerobatics, flying with the Italian Pattuglie Acrobatiche, and saw action against rebel tribesmen in Libya and in support of the invasion of Ethiopia, the latter towards the end of its career in 1935-6. A high-altitude, fast-climbing version was the CR20AQ. The CR20*bis* of 1929 introduced a more modern undercarriage of split-axle type with brakes and oleo-pneumatic shock-absorbers. The final landplane fighter version was the CR 'Asso', naturally powered by the 450hp Isotta Fraschini engine bearing that name. The CR20 Idro was a twin-float variant which served with the 161 and 162 Squadriglie da Caccia Marittima

from 1930 to 1935. A two-seat advanced trainer, the CR20B, operated in some numbers with Regia Aeronautica flying schools.

Peak of the CR20's career with the Regia Aeronautica was in 1933 when no fewer than 27 landplane fighter Squadriglie were equipped with the

CR20, CR20*bis* or CR 'Asso'. In 1936 the 50° Stormo Assalto at Ciampino Sud and three Squadriglie in East Africa still had the type on strength. CR20s were also exported to Austria, Hungary and Paraguay, the first two countries also receiving a number of CR20B two-seaters.

Fiat CR30   Italy

Purpose: Fighter
Makers: Fiat Aeronautica d' Italia
In service: 1934-1937

Engine: See below
Span: 34ft 5.33in
Length: 25ft 8.25in
Height: 8ft 7.5in
Weight loaded: 4,178lb
Crew: One
Max speed: 217.5mph
Service ceiling: 28,543ft
Normal range: 528 miles
Armament: Two 7.7mm or 12.7mm forward-firing machine guns

The first prototype of the CR30 made its initial flight on 5 March 1932. On 30 July the same year, both CR30 prototypes were entered for the international fighter speed contest, the Dal Molin Trophy, at Zurich, which they won at an average 211mph. On 26 September 1933 a two-seat CR30B carried off the Romanian Bibescu Trophy. The CR30 had been

carefully designed by Celestino Rosatelli to the requirements of Italo Balbo, Italy's Air Minister, for a 'super-fighter'. Of all-metal construction, it showed considerable improvement over the CR20. It had a carefully contoured fuselage and retained the Warren-type wing bracing of its predecessor. It was powered by the reliable 600hp Fiat A30 RA liquid-cooled engine driving a two-bladed metal propeller. A circular 'chin' radiator was housed in a smooth fairing. The sturdy divided undercarriage had wheel spats and the tailwheel was carefully faired to reduce drag. First of 121 CR30s for the Regia Aeronautica were delivered in spring 1934 to the 1° Stormo at Campoformido airfield. In service they justified their designer's confidence, performing the most difficult formation aerobatics while giving few problems in maintenance. Rosatelli, however, soon developed the smaller and more refined CR32 and so production of the CR30 was terminated. A number of single-seaters and two-seat CR30Bs were exported to Austria and Hungary. The CR30B served in the advanced training role with the Regia Aeronautica, a number flying up to the end of World War 2.

Fiat CR32

Italy

Purpose: Fighter
Makers: Fiat/Aeronautica d'Italia
In service: From 1934

Engine: One 600hp Fiat A30 RA
Span: 31ft 2in
Length: 24ft 5.25in
Height: 7ft 9in
Weight loaded: 4,112lb
Crew: One
Max speed: 233mph
Service ceiling: 29,525ft
Range: 466 miles
Armament: Two fixed forward-firing 12.7mm
Breda-SAFAT machine guns

In August 1936 12 Fiat CR32 fighters were sent by sea to Melilla, Morocco, from where they were dispatched to fight with the Nationalist forces under the command of General Francisco Franco, just one month after the Civil War had broken out in Spain and two months after Italy's victory in Abyssinia. In the same month the first German aircraft arrived in the form of He51 fighters and others. During the course of the Civil War Italy supplied about 730 aircraft, including many CR32s, creating the Aviacion de Tercio in Spain, but failed to exploit the situation to the same degree as Germany as a proving ground for new military aircraft. Nevertheless, Italian CR32s and their Spanish Hispano-Suiza HS-132L Chirri

counterparts (about 100 licence-built CR32*quaters*) formed the backbone of the Nationalist fighter force, following the failure of Heinkel He51s to deal with the Russian Polikarpov I-15 fighters of which 550 were supplied to the Republican forces. Perhaps the subsequent appearance of the German Messerschmitt Bf109 in Spain, which was far better than the CR32 in all respects, coincided also with Hitler's final prominence as a leader over Mussolini.

First flown in 1933, the Fiat CR32 was a development of the earlier CR30, which it closely resembled. It was of all-metal structure, fabric covered, and had a shorter wing span than the CR30. With the inevitable weight saving, it was considerably faster than the CR30 and more manoeuvrable, despite being powered by a similar engine. Production started with the standard CR32, later changing to the CR32*bis* version with two extra wing-mounted 7.7mm machine guns and up to 220lb of bombs. More than half of the total production of the CR32 was of these types although neither was the main production version, that distinction going to the CR32*quater,* which followed about 100 CR32*ters*. The CR32*quater* surprisingly had its firepower reduced to that of the original version, a move against the tide of world opinion. Total production of the CR32 amounted to 1,212 aircraft, of which between 300 and 400 remained in Italian service in 1940. CR32s were also exported to other countries, including Austria, China, Hungary, Paraguay and Venezuela.

Fokker CV-A to CV-E

Netherlands

Purpose: Light bomber/Reconnaissance
Makers: NV Nederlandsche Vliegtuigenfabriek (Fokker)
In service: 1924-40
Photo and data: CV-E

Engine: See below

Span: 50ft 2.25in
Length: 30ft 11in
Height: 11ft 10in
Weight loaded: 4,900lb
Crew: Two
Max speed: 158mph
Service ceiling: 23,600ft

Range: 528 miles
Armament: Two machine guns, one forward-firing and one mounted in rear cockpit. Small bomb load carried under wings

During World War 1, Fokker designed the DVII fighter which was one of the most successful combat aircraft ever built. After the war Fokker moved to Holland, and there built an enlarged version of the DVII, known as the CIV. This was a two-seat biplane fitted with a 400hp Liberty engine. From the CIV was then developed the CV, the prototype of which first flew in May 1924. This marked the beginning of one of the most popular series of aircraft to serve during the inter-war period. Of mixed construction, the CV was designed to accept wings of differing areas, a variety of engines, and wheel, float or ski undercarriages, to enable many roles to be performed by the one basic design. The first three models, the CV-A, -B and -C, had parallel-chord wings, with protruding ailerons with wing areas of 403.6sq ft, 439.2sq ft and 496.2sq ft respectively. As well as serving in Holland, -Bs were built for Denmark and -Cs for Bolivia. Most Dutch CV-Cs were fitted with the 450hp Hispano-Suiza engine, although other types were also installed. The designation CV-W covered a small number of floatplanes. However, the main versions were the later CV-D and -E sesquiplanes, on which the wings

were tapered towards the tips and the lower wings had much narrower chord than the upper. Of the two versions, the CV-D (310sq ft of wing area) was more manoeuvrable and was intended for use as a fighter or as a spotter-reconnaissance and army co-operation type; while the CV-E (423sq ft of wing area) was a day bomber and long-range reconnaissance aircraft. Many CV-Ds and -Es equipped the Royal Netherlands air force (LVA), the Naval Air Service (MLD) and the Netherlands East Indies Air Force. The standard CV-D version was fitted with the same engine as the CV-C, but the new engine mounting on the CV-D and -E allowed installation of a greater variety of engines than before, including the Bristol Jupiter, Armstrong Siddeley Jaguar, Napier Lion, Hispano-Suiza 12 and Pratt & Whitney Wasp and Hornet engines. Other CV-D and -Es were exported to Denmark (who also licence-built CV-Es, from 1933, with Bristol Pegasus engines), Finland and Sweden (also licence-built from 1932). Hungary, Switzerland, Norway and Italy also manufactured the type, the Italians designating their aircraft Meridionali Ro1 and Ro1*bis* and fitting them with Jupiter engines. Of the total of about 1,000 CVs built, several hundred were operational in 1939, and some 34 still flew with the LVA when Holland was invaded in May 1940. Indeed, the CV proved so robust and successful that the Fokker company employed the same basic configuration for most of its subsequent military biplanes.

Fokker DXI   Netherlands

Purpose: Fighter
Makers: NV Nederlandsch Vliegtuigenfabrik (Fokker)
In service: From 1924

Engine: See below
Span: 38ft 4in

Length: 22ft 11in
Height: 9ft 2in
Weight loaded: 2,755lb (Hispano-Suiza engine)

Crew: One
Max speed: 140mph (Hispano-Suiza engine)
158mph (Curtiss engine)

Armament: Two fixed forward-firing machine guns

Yet another Fokker aircraft that had its origins in the wartime DVII, the DXI was a sesquiplane of mixed construction, with tapered wings. Special regard was given to its ease of erection and dismantling and interchangeability of parts, and the aircraft featured side mounted radiators which could be retracted into the fuselage to vary cooling. The prototype first flew on 5 May 1923, powered by a 300hp Hispano-Suiza engine fed by a main fuel tank of 250litre and a gravity tank in the upper wing of 45litre. In August of that year it was displayed at the International Air Exhibition in Sweden. The problem now facing Fokker was that the postwar built DVIIs, which had been produced in Holland as the new company's first product, were still considered new and good enough

for Dutch needs and so the DXI was not ordered for home use. Three Curtiss D12-engined DXIs were delivered to the US Army Air Service in 1923, and were designated PW-7s, but although these performed some spectacular feats they remained the only ones ordered for this service. Altogether, 174 other DXIs were produced, of which 49 went to Argentina, Romania, Spain and Switzerland. The remaining aircraft all went to the USSR, later to be joined by Fokker DXIIIs. Indeed, by 1927 the Red air force had nearly 200 Fokker DXI, DXIII, CIV aircraft in service, together with many Junkers, Martinside and other aircraft. Perhaps the greatest contribution made by the DXI was that it confirmed as correct the faith that Fokker placed in the sesquiplane configuration, employed on so many of its subsequent aircraft.

Gloster Gamecock   UK

Purpose: Fighter
Makers: Gloucestershire Aircraft Co
In service: 1926-31
Photo: Gamecock II
Data: Gamecock I

Engine: See below
Span: 29ft 9.5in
Length: 19ft 8in
Height: 9ft 8in
Weight loaded: 2,863lb
Crew: One
Max speed: 155mph at 5,000ft
Service ceiling: 22,000ft
Range: about 365 miles
Armament: Two fixed forward-firing .303in Vickers machine guns

Last wooden biplane fighter to equip the RAF, the Gamecock was developed from the Gloster Grebe of 1923. The first of three prototypes made its maiden flight in February 1925, powered by a Bristol Jupiter

IV radial engine. It retained the short fuselage of the Grebe, but was more rounded in section, and the machine guns were inset in fuselage troughs. Other improvements included a larger fin and a horn-balanced rudder. The third prototype introduced the more powerful (425hp) Jupiter VI engine, and in this form the Gamecock entered production in 1926. A total of 90 Gamecock Is was built for the RAF, with first deliveries to operational squadrons in the spring of 1926. A few months later, the RAF received its new Fairey Fox light bombers, and it must have been agonising for the newly equipped Gamecock squadrons to discover that their aircraft were marginally slower than these Fairey two-seaters. Nonetheless, the Gamecock was popular with pilots, although about one-quarter of the aircraft of this type supplied to the RAF crashed during their service life and the wings had to be fitted with additional Vee struts to correct flutter. To offset some of the other shortcomings of the Gamecock I, the general-purpose Gamecock II of 1928 introduced a top wing centre-section to increase the span, narrower-chord ailerons, revised vertical tail unit and other improvements. The new upper wing gave the pilot a much improved view, although downward vision remained poor; controllability was also better. However, only two more Mk IIs were built in the UK, for export to Finland where, in 1929, Gamecock IIs were manufactured under licence at Valtion Lentokonetehdas, Helsinki. Renamed Kukko, the 15 Finnish-built aircraft were delivered with 420hp Gnome-Rhône-built Jupiter engines, provision for wheel or ski undercarriages and for carrying small bombs. They had the lengthened fuselage and wide-track undercarriage first fitted to a reworked Gamecock I that was flown extensively at the British Royal Aircraft Establishment for a couple of years. Kukkos remained in first-line service in Finland until 1935.

Gloster Gauntlet

UK

Purpose: Fighter
Makers: Gloster Aircraft Co Ltd
In service: 1935-40

Engine: One 640hp Bristol Mercury VIS2 radial
Span: 32ft 9.5in
Length: 26ft 2in
Height: 10ft 4in
Weight loaded: 3,970lb
Crew: One
Max speed: 230mph at 15,500ft
Service ceiling: 33,500ft
Range: 460 miles
Armament: Two .303in fixed Vickers machine guns

The Gauntlet was the last open-cockpit and the penultimate biplane fighter to equip the RAF. In service it was well liked by its pilots, although a number of accidents due to engine failure and air collisions prevented a few squadrons from being at full operational strength for differing periods of time. Another interesting point is that, although many criticisms have been levelled at the signing of the Munich Agreement in September 1938, had the war started in that year the veteran Gauntlet would have served with the Gladiator and Hurricane as one of Britain's main fighters. The prototype Gauntlet, designated SS19B, appeared in 1933. It was a further development of a single re-engined aircraft previously designated SS18/SS19 during 1928-32 and was subsequently powered by a Mercury IVS2 engine. With this power plant, then giving 570hp, the prototype managed 216mph, which represented a fairly dramatic increase of speed over the Bulldog. This was partly due to the care taken in streamlining the new fighter and partly to the great increase in engine power with only 400lb added to the AUW, and it soon passed its acceptance tests. Of metal construction, mostly fabric covered, the Gauntlet had equal-span staggered wings, with dihedral on both upper and lower planes, and Frise ailerons. The fuselage was of oval section, with only the forward part covered in metal. A cross-axle Vee undercarriage was fitted. An initial order for 24 Gauntlet Is was placed (one with Browning machine-gun installation), and the first aircraft entered service with an RAF Squadron, in February 1935, bulk deliveries starting in May. The Mk I was followed by the Mk II version, of which 204 were ordered in 1935: of these 39 subsequently became instructional airframes, 23 went to the Finnish Air Force in 1940 and two to South Africa. Performance was later increased on some Mk IIs by fitting Fairey three-blade metal propellers in place of the two-blade wooden type. By 1937, 14 RAF squadrons operated Gauntlets many of them formed under the expansion programme. In November of the same year, aircraft of No 32 Squadron (equipped with two-way wireless) made the first RAF fighter interception while being directed by ground radar from Bawdsey Manor, homing on an airliner over the Thames. However, by the outbreak of war, only about one-third of the Gauntlets built remained operational, with four home-based Auxiliary squadrons and in the Middle East. They were used as trainers from 1940. A number of Mk IIs were also licence-built in Denmark by Flyvertroppernes Vaerksteder of Copenhagen during 1936-8.

Gloster Gladiator and Sea Gladiator   UK

Purpose: Fighter
Makers: Gloster Aircraft Co Ltd
In service: From 1937
Data: Gladiator Mk I

Engine: One 840hp Bristol Mercury IX radial
Span: 32ft 3in
Length: 27ft 5in
Height: 10ft 4in
Weight loaded: 4,750lb
Crew: One
Max speed: 253mph
Service ceiling: 33,000ft
Normal range: about 410 miles
Armament: Four .303in Browning machine guns, two in fuselage and two under lower wings (early production aircraft armed with two Vickers or two Lewis guns under wings)

Built as a private venture development of the Gauntlet, which it resembled in many ways, the Gladiator was the last and fastest biplane fighter to serve with the RAF and the Sea Gladiator was the last of the type to serve with the FAA. (It was also the last of the four great Gloster biplane fighters that had spanned the interwar period and was a mid-stage development between the Gauntlet and later monoplane types produced by other manufacturers). The prototype first flew in September 1934 and had an open cockpit. After flight trials in competition with other biplane and monoplane types from most of the leading British aircraft manufacturers — including the Bristol 133 monoplane, Hawker PV3, Westland PV4 and Supermarine Type 244 (predecessor of the Spitfire) — it was chosen for production. An initial order for 23 production Gladiator Is was placed in July 1935, each to be powered by the Mercury IX engine and fitted with an enclosed cockpit. One

aircraft from this order went to the Royal Hellenic Air Force. Two months later another 186 were ordered, of which some were cancelled and a few exported to Greece and Iraq, and by the spring of 1940 all production of these and aircraft from subsequent contracts had been completed. The exact number of Gladiators received by the RAF has been quoted at between 310 and 480, but is thought to have amounted to just over 450, of which over half were Mk Is. This version first entered service with the RAF in February 1937. The FAA's Sea Gladiators were first operational at an RN air station in early 1939, and in May of that year Sea Gladiators went to sea on board HMS *Courageous* (first commissioned as an aircraft carrier in 1928). The total number of Sea Gladiators built was 98, of which 38 were Gladiators

modified to Sea Gladiators while under construction. These were powered by Mercury VIIIA engines, as were the RAF Gladiator IIs, which also incorporated certain other refinements and were particularly suitable for warfare in hot climates. Gladiators in Fighter Command had largely been replaced by September 1939 (a total of about 150 remaining in service), and most of the FAA aircraft had been replaced by American Grumman Martlets by late 1940. However, Gladiators served in small numbers in and around Europe and in the Battle of Britain, and will always be remembered for their epic defence of Malta. New and ex-RAF Gladiators were exported before the war to Belgium, China, Egypt, Finland, Greece, Iraq, the Irish Free State, Latvia, Lithuania, Norway, Portugal, South Africa and Sweden.

Gloster Grebe   UK

Purpose: Fighter
Makers: Gloucestershire Aircraft Co
In service: From 1924

Engine: 385hp Armstrong Siddeley Jaguar IV radial
Span: 29ft 4in
Length: 20ft 3in
Height: 9ft 3in
Weight loaded: 2,538lb
Crew: One
Max speed: over 152mph
Service ceiling: over 23,000ft
Range: 400 miles
Armament: Two fixed .303in Vickers machine guns. Small bomb load under wings

After World War 1, it was inevitable that the size of the RAF would have to be reduced and that aircraft of the 1914-18 period would have to continue in service for the next few years. It was not until 1924 that the RAF received its first fighters of postwar design, in the shape of the Gloster Grebe and Armstrong Whitworth Siskin. The Grebe was the first of four Gloster biplane fighters to enter RAF service during the interwar period — a line which ended with the famous Gladiator. Three prototype Grebes were built in 1923 as developments of the Nieuport

Nighthawk basic design which Gloster had refined and produced as the Mars series, culminating for the RAF in the Mars VI fighter. The prototype Grebe differed mainly from the latter in having a high-lift upper wing and medium-lift lower wings of reduced span and chord in place of the equal span RAF 15 wings of the Mars VI. The upper wing was constructed in two sections, therefore doing away with a centre-section, and the gravity fuel tanks were situated in the wings each side of the cabane structure, forming the well-known blisters in the under surface of the wing. Only one row of interplane struts were used each side. The fuselage, tail unit and undercarriage were all similar to those of the Mars VI. Following the prototypes, an initial order for 12 slightly modified production Grebe IIs was placed, followed by orders for 114 further Grebe IIs and IIIs for the RAF. This total included a few two-seat trainers. Grebe IIs first became fully operational with an RAF squadron in 1924, replacing Sopwith Snipes; and one of them became the first British fighter to perform successfully a 240mph terminal velocity dive. On 21 October 1926, two Grebes were launched experimentally from the airship R-33 at heights of around 2,500ft. RAF Grebes were superseded in first-line service by later Siskins in 1928. However, with the exception of the fin and rudder, the basic Grebe shape appeared in

subsequent Gloster designs, the Gamecock, Goldfinch, Gambet and Gnatsnapper. Three Grebes were also operated by the New Zealand Permanent Air Force, later becoming the Royal New Zealand Air Force. In 1931, the strength of this service stood at

nine officers and 48 other ranks, and the aircraft types operated included de Havilland Moth seaplanes, Hawker Tomtits, Fairey IIIFs, Bristol Fighters and Grebes, the last Grebes in operational use.

Grigorovich I-2*bis*

USSR

Purpose: Fighter
Makers: Soviet State Aircraft Factories
In service: 1927-1931

Engine: See below
Span: 35ft 5.2in
Length: 24ft 0.2in
Weight loaded: 3,472lb
Crew: One
Max speed: 146mph
Service ceiling: 17,610ft
Normal range: 373 miles
Armament: Two fixed forward-firing 7.62mm machine guns

Dmitri P Grigorovich, hitherto doyen of Russian flying-boat design, became technical director of GAZ No 1 (State Aircraft Factory No 1) in autumn 1923. He quickly set up a design group and experimental workshop and by the end of January 1924 design of the new I-1 biplane fighter had been completed. A small single-bay biplane with a wooden flat-sided fuselage covered forward with plywood and aft with fabric emerged three months later. Built to the same requirement as Polikarpov's IL-400 low-wing monoplane, the I-1 gave some impressive displays during test flying at Moscow Central Aerodrome in spring 1924. Its performance was not, however, up to specification. It also lacked stability and cooling problems were not resolved by modifications to the twin radiators (attached to the forward undercarriage struts). Great effort was put into a new machine designated I-2. Retaining the basic characteristics of I-1 and powered by the same 400hp M-5 (American Liberty type) engine, the I-2 had a modified engine cowling to improve visibility, a ventral radiator and an oval-section monocoque fuselage. Ailerons were fitted to the lower wing only, which had slightly

greater span than the upper. Single I-type wing bracing struts were fitted either side. A. I. Zhukov test flew the I-2 in autumn 1924. Most of the difficulties with I-1 were eliminated, but to render it suitable for quantity production a number of further changes were made. Zhukov was of slight build and had fitted into the small cockpit. This had to be enlarged for use by the average pilot. The twin 7.62mm machine guns were relocated. Other pilot problems led to redesign of the rudder pedals and raising the cockpit seat to improve visibility. Engine cowling was again modified and the forward fuselage reinforced, a tubular metal framework being introduced which projected forward to form the engine bearers. New profiled bracing wires were introduced and the I-strut attachment points modified. The upper wing centre section fuel tank was also enlarged. With all these changes the production machine was redesignated I-2*bis*. After stress tests between July and September 1926, quantity production was started. When the last aircraft left Zavod No 23 (the 'Red Airman' Factory) in 1929, 43 I-2*bis* fighters had been built there plus 164 at Zavod No 1, bringing the total to 207. The I-2*bis* was structurally strong, but rather complex, and the fighter was rather overweight. Initially poor production standards led to lack of precision in the wing leading edge profile, thus adversely affecting the performance of some aircraft. Additionally, cooling system troubles were never fully overcome. Some machines were built with twin Lamblin radiators between the undercarriage legs but their performance overall suffered accordingly.

Polikarpov's IL-400 rival was a failure, with only 33 aircraft completed. To the I-2*bis* clearly goes the distinction of being the first Soviet-designed single-seat fighter to be produced in quantity and to go into first-line service.

Grumman F2F and F3F USA

Purpose: Fighter
Makers: Grumman Aircraft Engineering Corporation
In service: 1935-41
Photo: F3F-1
Data: F2F-1

Engine: See below
Span: 28ft 6in
Length: 21ft 5in
Height: 9ft 1in
Weight loaded: 3,781lb
Crew: One
Max speed: 237mph
Service ceiling: 27,500ft
Range: 750-985 miles
Armament: Two 0.30in Browning machine guns.
Two 116lb bombs could be carried

Within four months of the first deliveries of the Grumman FF-1 two-seat naval fighter, a new single-seat prototype fighter made its maiden flight, on 18 October 1933, the Grumman XF2F-1. Developed from the earlier aircraft, the XF2F-1 was an unequal-span single-bay biplane of metal construction, with fabric covering only the wings and movable tail surfaces. Power was provided by a 625hp Pratt & Whitney radial engine. It retained the earlier aircraft's undercarriage, which retracted into recesses in the sides of the fuselage, and had a modern type of canopy over the cockpit which was faired into the

rear body. It was a vast improvement over the FF-1 and the older Boeing F4B, and was therefore selected for service. Production F2F-1s for the US Navy were powered by 650hp Pratt & Whitney R-1535-72 14-cylinder radial engines, and deliveries started in 1935. After the production of F2Fs had been completed, the XF3F-1 prototype appeared. This had an extra 3ft 6in wing span and a 1ft 10in longer fuselage, and the first flight was made on 20 March 1935. Production F3F-1s were fitted with 650hp R-1535-84 Twin Wasp Junior engines and served with the Navy from 1936. The line continued with F3F-2s, powered by Wright Cyclone radial engines, and F3F-3s, bringing the total number of Grumman fighters of the series purchased by the US Navy to 216. These equipped all US Navy and Marine fighter squadrons by September 1939, serving at various times on all the American aircraft carriers of the period except for *Langley* (which, incidentally, had participated in an exercise in 1928 in which its aircraft had made a surprise attack on Pearl Harbor). It is also of interest that in December 1936 Grumman delivered a G-22 single-seat aerobatic biplane to the Aviation Manager of the Gulf Refining Company. This was basically a modified F2F fighter fitted with a 1,000hp Wright R-1820-G1 engine driving a three-blade controllable-pitch propeller. This aircraft was reported at the time to have a max speed of 290mph at 12,000ft and a rate of climb of 3,500ft/min.

Grumman FF-1 and SF-1 USA

Purpose: Fighter/Observation
Makers: Grumman Aircraft Engineering Corporation
In service: From 1933
Photo: Canadian built FF-1 *(Grumman Goblin)*

Engine: See below
Span: 34ft 6in
Length: 24ft 6in

Height: 11ft 1in
Weight loaded: about 4,800lb
Crew: Two
Max speed: 216mph
Service ceiling: 22,500ft
Range: 647-920 miles
Armament: Three .30in Browning machine guns, positioned on forward fuselage and in rear cockpit

In the latter part of 1931, the first flight took place of a prototype naval fighter, the XFF-1, which was powered by a 600hp Wright R-1820 Cyclone radial engine. It was unusual in as far as it had an enclosed cockpit for the crew of two, made from telescoping canopy sections, and an undercarriage that retracted into recesses in the fuselage sides. It should be remembered at this point that the two new British naval fighter prototypes that had flown only one year earlier — the Hawker Nimrod and Osprey — were both conventional open-cockpit biplanes with fixed undercarriages. The retractable undercarriage of the XFF-1 was almost an identical copy of the type used on the Dayton-Wright Model RB Racer constructed for the 1920 Gordon Bennett Aviation Cup Race, although this aircraft was a monoplane and the pilot sat inside the completely flush fuselage with little forward view. The XFF-1 was subsequently re-engined with a more powerful 750hp Wright radial engine. An order was placed by the US Navy for production FF-1s, with 750hp Wright R-1820-78 radial engines, and these were delivered from mid-1933. Although the orders for FF-1s and later SF-1s only totalled 60 aircraft in roughly equal quantities, they were large enough to equip one aircraft carrier, the *Lexington*. One of only three American carriers of the time (three more built before 1939), *Lexington* was a converted battlecruiser and could accommodate a maximum of 120 aircraft. It was, however,

the first American aircraft carrier to be destroyed in battle, sunk by the Japanese during the Battle of Coral Sea in 1942, by which time FF-1s had been replaced by Grumman F2Fs (in 1936) and then by Grumman F4F Wildcats. Nevertheless, at the time of going into service, the FF-1s were the US Navy's first operational fighters with retractable undercarriages. Meanwhile, back in 1932, a prototype observation version had been flown. The US Navy ordered production SF-1s, powered by Wright R-1820-84 radial engines, and deliveries started in the spring of 1934. The final production SF-1 was experimentally fitted with a Pratt & Whitney R-1535-80 engine. The end of the line for the FF-1s came when they were finally converted into dual-control trainers and redesignated FF-2s. FF-1 fighters also served in other countries. The Canadian Car and Foundry company built 40 under licence for Turkey. These were soon sent to help the Republican forces in the Spanish Civil War and were the only American designed aircraft to be flown in the war. Considerably lower in performance than the later Nationalist fighters of more conventional biplane configuration, the FF-1s were nevertheless welcome to supplement its near obsolete air force. One FF-1 also went to Japan, where it was studied for possible ideas that could be incorporated into its own designs, one to Nicaragua and 15 to the Royal Canadian Air Force (as Goblin 1s).

Handley Page Harrow UK

Purpose: Heavy bomber
Makers: Handley Page Ltd
In service: 1937-45
Photo: Mk I
Data: Mk II

Engines: Two 925hp Pegasus XX radials
Span: 88ft 5in
Length: 82ft 2in
Height: 19ft 5in
Weight loaded: 23,000lb
Crew: Four or five
Max speed: 200mph
Service ceiling: 22,800ft
Max range: 1,840 miles

Armament: Four .303in Browning machine guns, in nose, dorsal and tail power-operated turrets. Up to 3,000lb of bombs

The Handley Page Company was formed in 1908 but it was not until the closing years of World War 1 that the company established its name as a manufacturer of fine heavy bombers, with the appearance of the O/100, O/400 and V/1500 biplanes. Following later-designed biplane bombers that served with the RAF, such as the Hyderabad, Hinaidi and Heyford, Handley Page produced the Harrow monoplane. As the Heyford had been a great improvement over the RAF's earlier Virginia bomber, so the Harrow proved an equally important milestone in terms of performance, although the maximum bomb load was slightly reduced. Adapted from the earlier HP51 transport aircraft, the HP54 Harrow was one of the first monoplane bombers to equip the RAF when it entered service in the spring of 1937. The first Harrow had made its maiden flight on 10 October 1936, this being one of the 100 production aircraft ordered by the Air Ministry to meet the need for an interim bomber for the RAF's expansion programme. In many ways looking like a Heyford with its lower wing removed and cockpit undercarriage and engine installations revised, the Harrow was a cantilever high-wing monoplane with a fixed divided undercarriage and faired wheels. The metal-structure wing, mostly metal covered, incorporated Handley Page automatic slots and slotted ailerons in the outer section, and hydraulically powered slotted flaps along the inner trailing edges. The fuselage was of all-metal construction, covered with metal sheet

and fabric, and housed the bomb bay below the floor of the centre portion. The bombs were fused and fired electrically by a patented release-gear. The Harrow was not, however, of as modern appearance as the Armstrong Whitworth Whitley of the same year and never achieved the latter's operational record. The initial 39 examples were built as Harrow Mk Is, powered by two 830hp Pegasus X engines, and were followed by Harrow Mk IIs. The Mk I had a maximum speed of 190mph at 10,000ft and a maximum range of 1,880 miles. Some Mk Is were subsequently converted to Mk IIs. Five RAF squadrons operated the type by the end of 1937, but by the beginning of World War 2 all had been re-equipped with Wellingtons. From this point Harrows were restored to their original HP51 purpose, as transports carrying 20 troops (sometimes also called Sparrows). One Harrow I was operated by the Royal Canadian Air Force during the war.

Handley Page Heyford   UK

Purpose: Bomber
Makers: Handley Page Ltd
In service: From 1933
Photo: Mk III
Data: Mk I

Engines: See below
Span: 75ft 0in

Length: 58ft 0in
Height: 17ft 6in
Weight loaded: 16,750lb
Crew: Four
Max speed: 142mph
Service ceiling: 21,000ft
Range: 920 miles
Armament: .303in Lewis machine guns in nose and

dorsal cockpits and in retractable ventral turret. Normal bomb load of 2,800lb. Max bomb load 3,500lb

When the Heyford heavy bomber first entered service with No 99 Squadron on 14 November 1933, the RAF received its last heavy bomber biplane and, at the same time, one of the most unusual looking bombers to enter service. By attaching the fuselage to the underside of the upper wing, the nose and dorsal gunners were given a very clear field of fire; this also made the loading of bombs easy, as they were carried in the centre section of the lower wing. Although some experience was needed to land a Heyford correctly, it proved to be extremely manoeuvrable for its size and was sometimes seen to loop. The prototype first flew in mid-1930, as the HP38, and the first two production versions, the Mk I and Mk IA (of which 38 were built,

one as an intermediate Mk IA/II), were powered by two 575hp Rolls-Royce Kestrel IIIS engines. They were followed by 16 Mk IIs (13 for No 7 Squadron) powered by derated Rolls-Royce Kestrel VIs, and 71 Mk IIIs with 640hp Kestrel VI engines. In the same way as the Heyford had replaced older bombers like the Hinaidi and Vickers Virginia, so in turn it was supplanted by newer types like the Armstrong Whitworth Whitley from March 1937 and, later, the Vickers Wellington, but not by the parent company's Harrow bomber. However, a number of Heyfords were used for training work thereafter. It is of interest to note that in 1936 Flight Refuelling Ltd was formed to continue development of aerial refuelling systems. As well as acquiring Armstrong Whitworth AW23, Boulton Paul Overstrand, Vickers Virginia, Handley Page HP51 and other aircraft for the experiments, a single Heyford III was acquired from the original batch of 20.

Hawker Audax   UK

Purpose: Army co-operation
Makers: Hawker Aircraft Ltd
In service: 1932-42

Engine: One 535hp Rolls-Royce Kestrel IB or 575hp Kestrel X
Span: 37ft 3in
Length: 29ft 7in
Height: 10ft 5in
Weight loaded: 4,460lb
Crew: Two
Max speed: 169mph at 5,000ft
Endurance: $3\frac{1}{2}$hr
Armament: One forward-firing Vickers machine gun and one Lewis machine gun in rear cockpit. 225lb of bombs or other stores

The success of the Armstrong Whitworth Atlas, and the considerable number ordered for the RAF, pointed the way to other manufacturers to explore their own designs of this new type of combat aircraft. Luckily for Hawkers, the extremely fast Hart bomber had already appeared and it was an easy task to modify a Hart I into the prototype Audax. With a

maximum speed 25mph greater than that of the Atlas, the Audax was a winner and was placed in production. Including those sold to South Africa and several transferred to the Straits Settlements Volunteer Air Force, about 652 Audax biplanes were ordered. Others were built for Persia (with Bristol Pegasus and Pratt & Whitney Hornet engines), Iraq (Bristol Pegasus engines) and operated alongside other British aircraft and subsequently Savoia-Marchetti SM79B heavy bombers), Singapore, Canada and Egypt (800hp Armstrong Whitworth Panther X engines — supplied under the Anglo-Egyptian Treaty in which Egypt shared responsibility with Britain for the air defence of Egypt, the Sudan and Canal zone). Audaxes entered RAF service in early 1932 and were deployed at home, where they remained operational until 1938, and in Egypt, the Sudan and India, where they were still flying in 1941-42. Indeed, according to Hawker records, an Audax squadron was used as fighter cover at the Digboi air station in North East Assam in 1942. Interestingly, while the prototype Audax was a converted Hart, so 18 Audaxes were later converted into Hart Specials.

Hawker Demon   UK

Purpose: Fighter
Makers: Hawker Aircraft Ltd and Boulton Paul Aircraft Ltd
In service: 1933-39

Engine: See below
Span: 37ft 3in
Length: 29ft 6in
Height: 10ft 5in
Weight loaded: 4,460lb
Crew: Two
Max speed: 183mph
Service ceiling: 27,500ft
Range: 375 miles
Armament: Usually two fixed forward-firing Vickers machine guns and one Lewis machine gun in rear cockpit

In 1929 the RAF received its first examples of a new two-seat light bomber called the Hawker Hart. With a maximum speed of 184mph, it was very fast for its time and had excellent manoeuvrability; so it was decided that a fighter version should be developed from it. Known originally as Hart fighters, the two prototypes were converted Hart bombers (the first as one of a batch of 15 Harts produced for No 33 Squadron and the second converted to a Demon

abroad), each with a 560hp supercharged Rolls-Royce V (DR) engine, modified rear cockpit, two-way wireless equipment and other changes. In the spring of 1931, six Hart fighters were produced as a batch and were sent for service trials. Eventually, a grand total of 304 Demons (so called from 1932) was built, made up of early Hart fighter prototypes and pre-production aircraft, 77 production aircraft with 525hp Rolls-Royce Kestrel IIS engines (seven produced as instructional airframes and one flown on 22 December 1934 with a Kestrel VI engine of 640hp under Hawker's flight report number 475), 155 with 584hp Kestrel V engines and 64 Demons for the Royal Australian Air Force. The Australian examples were used for additional general duties and so were fitted with bomb racks, a message retrieving hook and other equipment, and were operated alongside Bristol Bulldogs and Westland Wapitis. A large number of RAF Demons were fitted with a Frazer-Nash hydraulically-operated 'lobster-back' shield which protected the rear gunner from the aircraft's slipstream while operating the machine gun, and were called Turret Demons. RAF Demons served at home (also with the RAF Voluntary Reserve) and overseas, finally being replaced from December 1938 by a fighter version of another light bomber, the Bristol Blenheim IF.

Hawker Fury   UK

Purpose: Fighter
Makers: Hawker Aircraft Ltd
In service: 1931-39
Photo and Data: Fury II

Engine: See below
Span: 30ft 0in
Length: 26ft 8.75in
Weight loaded: 3,620lb
Crew: One
Max speed: 223mph at 15,000ft

Service ceiling: 32,000ft
Range: 260-270 miles
Armament: Two fixed forward-firing Vickers machine guns mounted in top of engine cowling

The Hawker Fury II was the last Hawker biplane fighter to be produced for the RAF, although not the RAF's last biplane fighter, that distinction going to the Gloster Gladiator. Not as fast or as attractive as the contemporary Fairey Fantome, which did not achieve operational use, the Fury II was the final

version of the Fury biplane series, which really began in 1928. In that year a new Hawker fighter appeared which subsequently exceeded 200mph in level flight. However, because the Air Ministry changed the specification of its required fighter to include an inline engine instead of radial, the design was developed into the Hawker Hornet of 1929, a single-seat fighter of mixed construction with a Rolls-Royce Kestrel FXIS/FXIIS supercharged water-cooled engine, with which it achieved 206mph at 5,000ft. Following a competition between the Fury, as it was now renamed, and the extremely elegant Fairey Firefly IIM — first flown on 16 January 1930 — an initial production order for Fury Is was placed, the first production Fury I flying on 26 March 1931. Altogether a total of 118 production Fury Is was built for the RAF, with 525hp Rolls-Royce Kestrel IIS engines. The Fury I could achieve 207mph at 13,000ft. In addition, one radial-engined Fury (401), first flown on 5 August 1932, was exported to Norway (Armstrong Siddeley Panther IIIA engine) and 16 to Persia (Pratt & Whitney Hornet engines, the first flown on 29 May 1933). Three inline-engined Furies went to Portugal and six to Yugoslavia (Hispano-Suiza 12 engines; the first flown on 4 April 1931). The initial RAF squadron to receive Fury Is was No 43 in mid-1931, to become the first RAF squadron to be equipped with a fighter capable of over 200mph in level flight. A Fury I won the speed contest for military aircraft over a triangular course at Zurich during an international meeting, at an average speed of 201mph, and in 1934 a flight of Furies went to Canada for the Centennial celebrations at Toronto. Meanwhile, the first flight took place, on 13 April 1932, of a private

venture prototype development of the Fury called the Intermediate Fury, which was basically a civil registered Fury I, initially powered by a Kestrel IIS engine and incorporating some refinements. It was subsequently re-engined with a Kestrel VI with semi-evaporative cooling, with which it first flew on 1 October 1933 and later achieved 230mph. Records show that this aircraft was re-engined in 1934 with a Goshawk III, with which it made its first flight on 17 October, and again with a later Goshawk engine. The initial version of the Intermediate Fury was followed by the experimental High Speed Fury, which first flew on 3 May 1933. This aircraft was known as the High Speed Fury I when powered by a Kestrel engine (achieving 245mph at 1,000ft) and High Speed Fury II when powered by a 695hp Goshawk III engine (achieving 238mph at 16,000ft; first flown on 30 April 1934). In 1934 a Fury I was fitted with a 640hp Rolls-Royce Kestrel VI engine, composite cooling system, modified fuel and oil systems and given streamlined wheel spats, as the Fury II, and first flew on 20 August 1935. Production was started of 23 similar fighters by Hawkers, with increased fuel tankage. Another 89 were ordered from General Aircraft Ltd, six of which were for the South African Air Force. Fury IIs first entered RAF service with No 25 Squadron in 1937; but within two years all RAF Furies had been withdrawn from first-line service, although a number were used subsequently as trainers. Fury IIs were also exported, including 10 to Yugoslavia (Kestrel XVI and Lorraine Petrel engines), six to Persia (Bristol Mercury engines), and three to Spain (690hp Hispano-Suiza 12Xbrs engines, the first flown on 7 April 1936).

Hawker Hart   UK

Purpose: Light bomber
Makers: Hawker Aircraft Ltd
In service: 1930-39

Engine: One 525hp Rolls-Royce Kestrel IB
Span: 37ft 3in
Length: 29ft 4in
Height: 10ft 5in

Weight loaded: 4,635lb
Crew: Two
Max speed: 184mph
Service ceiling: over 21,000ft
Range: 470 miles
Armament: One fixed forward-firing .303in Vickers machine gun and one Lewis machine gun in rear cockpit. Two 250lb bombs standard

During military aviation's short history, there has been a small number of aircraft that, by their advanced design and fine performance, have made other types obsolete just by their presence. One such type was the Hart, which was not only faster than the single-seat fighters then in service, but led to a long line of RAF aircraft that were all developed from it, including the Demon, Audax, Hardy, Hind and Hector. Indeed, Hawker records relate to more than 70 distinct variants developed from the initial design. How good an aeroplane the Hart was can easily be assessed by the fact that some 952 aircraft were built by four manufacturers (Hawkers, Sir W. G. Armstrong Whitworth Ltd, Gloucestershire Aircraft Co and Vickers Aviation Ltd) in several versions, not including the six Hart fighters (see Hawker Demon). These included the standard bomber version (the rear-gunner/bomb aimer using an opening in the fuselage floor for sighting), the dual control Hart Trainer (about 483 built, not including conversions), the Hart C for communications work, and two versions fitted with tropical equipment known as the Hart India (the first flown on 26 August 1931) and Hart Special. Harts were built in the tradition of the fast DH4 and Fairey Fox bombers, and shared the latter's streamlined appearance by the use of a slim engine, closely cowled — a pleasing configuration that the radial-engined Swedish-built Harts did not

have. The prototype Hart first flew at the end of June 1928 at the hands of Flt Lt Bulman and, following its selection against two other aircraft, 15 pre-production examples were built. 12 of these went to No 33 Squadron in late 1929 or January 1930 and one was sent for trials in India. Hart bombers remained in RAF service in India until 1939, and were used in action for the first time on the North-West Frontier in 1932. Many ex-RAF aircraft were acquired by South Africa (used as armed trainers), Egypt and Southern Rhodesia. New production examples were exported to Estonia, Sweden and Yugoslavia; Sweden also built 42 Harts with 580hp Pegasus engines, and used them as standard light bombers, serving alongside Bristol Bulldogs and Fokker CV-D/E army co-operation aircraft. A civil registered Hart was first flown on 15 September 1932 as the Hart II. This aircraft was originally powered by a Kestrel IIS engine, but was subsequently re-engined with a Kestrel VI (first flown on 9 October 1933) and a 660/690hp Kestrel XVI, the latter with which it weighed 4,649lb. It was used mainly for demonstrations at Air Displays and Pageants and for taking air-to-air photographs of other Hawker aircraft. According to Hawker records, it accumulated 627 flying hours from the end of July 1933.

Hawker Hind   UK

Purpose: Light bomber
Makers: Hawker Aircraft Ltd
In service: 1935-39

Engine: See below
Span: 37ft 3in
Length: 29ft 7in
Height: 10ft 7in
Weight loaded: 5,490lb
Crew: Two
Max speed: 188mph
Service ceiling: 26,400ft
Range: 430 miles
Armament: One forward Vickers Mk III or V
machine gun and one Lewis machine gun aft. Two 250lb bombs standard

The dramatic events of 1933 led Britain to look closely at the likely intentions of Germany and its rapidly increasing forces, and in October Winston Churchill gave the first of his famous warnings to Parliament. Proposals to increase the strength of the air forces were put before Parliament in 1934 and 1935, and it was for the expansion programme that aircraft like the Hind were built. Although fast when first produced, events rapidly overtook the Hind and it was totally obsolete by modern standards by the time the Battle and Blenheim replaced it. Not surprisingly, therefore, it became the last biplane bomber to serve with the RAF, and remained in service only a few years. Produced as a replacement for the Hart, from which it was developed (although maximum speeds were very similar), the prototype was a converted Hart and first flew from Brooklands on 12 September 1934. Although initially powered by a Kestrel V engine, the prototype flew six weeks later with a Kestrel VI. The production Hind differed from the Hart in several ways, mainly in having a supercharged Rolls-Royce Kestrel V engine, an improved bomb aiming position and a canted rear cockpit, and was considerably heavier. A total of 528 Hinds was produced. When, in late 1937, the type began to be replaced by monoplanes, many were converted into dual-control trainers, mainly for Volunteer Reserve training schools, and the last

production aircraft were built as trainers. Indeed, nine of the initial production batch of 20 Hinds were so converted in 1938 by General Aircraft, followed by many from every subsequent production batch. The first trainer flew on 5 June 1938. Other ex-RAF aircraft were supplied to overseas countries. Together with new production Hinds, they went to Afghanistan (eight, flown alongside Italian aircraft), Kenya (six), Latvia (three, with Bristol Mercury IX engines, the first flown on 4 May 1938), New Zealand (30), Iran (35 with Bristol Mercury VIII engines), Portugal (four, with Kestrel V and Bristol Mercury engines), South Africa (22), Switzerland (one, with Kestrel V engine and first flown on 23 January 1936), and Yugoslavia (three, with Kestrel XVI engines).

Hawker Horsley

UK

Purpose: Bomber/Torpedo bomber
Makers: H. G. Hawker Engineering Co Ltd
In service: 1927-35
Photo: Mk II bomber
Data: Mk II torpedo bomber

Engine: One 670hp Rolls-Royce Condor IIIA geared engine
Span: 56ft 9in
Length: 38ft 3in
Height: 13ft 7.75in
Weight loaded: 9,655lb
Crew: Two
Max speed: 129mph
Service ceiling: 15,900ft
Armament: One fixed forward-firing Vickers machine gun and one Lewis machine gun in rear cockpit. Up to 1,500lb of bombs or one 2,150lb torpedo

The Horsley went through several stages of development between the years 1926 and 1931 and

was built in two main versions, as a bomber and torpedo bomber. The first prototype flew in 1925 and was followed by a second prototype. They had been built to an Air Ministry specification calling for a Condor III-engined bomber with a maximum speed of not less than 120mph, a range of 1,200 miles and a maximum bomb load of 1,500lb or a torpedo. After competing against the Handley Page HP28 Handcross, the Bristol Berkeley and the Westland Yeovil (first flown in December 1924, March 1925 and summer 1925 respectively), the Horsley was chosen for production. This began with a small number of wooden-constructed Horsley Mk Is, followed by a greater number of Horsley Mk IIs of mixed construction, all from the initial batch of 40 production aircraft. In 1929, the all-metal version of the Mk II appeared and this form of construction was also selected for production Horsleys. Total production, which includes the prototypes, test aircraft and six Horsley IIs built for the Greek Naval Air Service (delivered in 1928 and used for a time alongside Blackburn Velos bombers, until the latter were relegated as naval reconnaissance aircraft), amounted to some 121 aircraft. The bomber version first entered service with the RAF in early 1927, and the first torpedo bombers in the following year. The first aircraft of the final batch of 17 Horsleys for the RAF, which served mainly in the Far East (and were the last in RAF service, remaining operational until 1935), first flew on 28 September 1931 powered by a Condor IIIB engine. The Horsley was well known for its excellent flying qualities and because of these, and its ability to take-off safely under tremendous overload conditions, was selected for several long distance flights. On 20-21 May 1927, a 'long-distance' Horsley, with extra fuel tanks and stronger axle and tyres, flew 3,419 miles from England to the Persian Gulf non-stop in 34 hours, and thus gained for Britain the world long distance record, beating the previous record by about 75 miles. This lasted for much less than a day, because of an American named Lindbergh who flew 3,610 miles from New York to Paris. It was not until February 1933 that

Britain again held the record, on this occasion set up by a Fairey Long-Range Monoplane flying 5,309 miles. Pilot of the Horsley was Flt Lt C. R. Carr. He had intended to fly to India, but technical problems caused a forced landing near Bundar Abbas. A second attempt by the same pilot, but with a different navigator, failed after just an hour of flying due to trouble with the oil system. However, the aircraft was landed safely despite the overload of fuel of nearly 200% of the structural weight, made up of 1,100gal of fuel in three fuselage, two wing centre-section and two top wing tanks. Interestingly, accommodation was provided for a bed as well as other domestic arrangements. A third attempt, again by Carr, ended in Austria, due to (according to contemporary reports) engine overheating on an exceptionally hot day. The Horsley alighted on the River Danube and was badly damaged. During its career the Horsley flight tested several engines, including the 880hp Armstrong Siddeley Leopard IV, 810hp Rolls-Royce H, 450hp Napier Lion and Junkers Jumo.

Hawker Hurricane   UK

Purpose: Fighter
Makers: Hawker Aircraft Ltd
In service: From 1937
Photo and Data: Mk I

Engine: One 1,030hp Rolls-Royce Merlin II or III
Span: 40ft 0in
Length: 31ft 5in
Height: 13ft 1in
Weight loaded: 6,600lb
Crew: One
Max speed: 324mph
Service ceiling: 34,200ft
Range: Internal fuel only, 425 miles

Armament: Eight wing-mounted .303in Browning machine guns

Although the Munich Agreement of 1938 staved off war with Germany for that all-important year, and gave the RAF time to build up over nine squadrons of Spitfires for the coming hostilities, it was nevertheless the Hurricane that equipped the greater number of fighter squadrons during the Battle of Britain, having German bombers as their main targets. Indeed, the highest scoring Allied fighter pilot of the battle was a Czech Hurricane pilot named Sergeant Josef František DFM, who shot down 17 enemy aircraft, and the only Victoria Cross awarded to a pilot of Fighter Command was won on 16

August 1940 by another Hurricane pilot, Flt Lt James Nicolson. The Hurricane was the RAF's first monoplane fighter with an enclosed cockpit and retractable undercarriage, its first fighter capable of over 300mph and its first eight-gun fighter. It was the brainchild of Sydney Camm, who began design in 1934, about the same time as Professor Willi Messerschmitt was working on the Bf109 fighter. An order for one prototype was placed on 21 February 1935 and this flew on 6 November of the same year. attaining a speed of 315mph during trials. In June 1936 an order was placed for 600 production aircraft and the name Hurricane adopted. This was the largest single order for fighters since World War 1, precipitated by events in Germany and, perhaps, Abyssinia. What it does reflect, together with the huge orders placed at the same time for Fairey Battle light bombers, was the RAF's urgent need for modern monoplane combat aircraft. Powered by Merlin II engines, the first Hurricanes entered service with No 111 Squadron RAF in December 1937, and

thus became the penultimate British-designed single-seat fighter to enter service with the RAF during the period covered by this book. Subsequent development of the design brought about several changes before the outbreak of war. These included the fitting of a two-pitch three-blade propeller, the installation of a Rolls-Royce Merlin III engine and metal-covered wings. By the beginning of World War 2, the RAF had 19 Hurricane squadrons, totalling nearly 500 aircraft, but during the Battle of Britain their speed proved slightly inferior to that of the Messerschmitt Bf109E. It was, therefore, the Spitfire that was constantly developed during the war as a fighter, as was the Bf109 in Germany, the Hurricane finding new roles during the conflict at which it proved highly successful, including that of tank-busting and as a sea-going fighter to protect Allied shipping. Other countries that received Hurricanes before the outbreak of war included Belgium, Canada, Poland, Romania, South Africa, Turkey and Yugoslavia.

Hawker Nimrod   UK

Purpose: Fighter
Makers: Hawker Aircraft Ltd
In service: 1932-39
Photo and Data: Mk I

Engine: One 590hp Rolls-Royce Kestrel IIS
Span: 33ft 6in
Length: 27ft 0in
Height: 9ft 9in
Weight loaded: over 3,945lb

Crew: One
Max speed: 192mph at 15,000ft
Service ceiling: 26,000ft
Armament: Two fixed forward-firing Vickers machine guns. Small bombs could be carried

The Nimrod was a third generation postwar carrier-borne fighter and was derived from the Hawker Fury; but, unlike the latter, it never quite achieved 200mph

in level flight status. Compared with the Fury, the Nimrod had a 3ft 6in greater wing span, was strengthened for catapulting and carried hoisting gear and buoyancy bags. Later Mk II aircraft also incorporated deck landing arrester gear and had modified wings and tail unit. Developed via the Hawker Hoopoe, a 185mph naval fighter fitted from 1927 with 400-560hp radial engines. the first prototype HN1 made its maiden flight in 1930, powered by a 480hp Rolls-Royce Kestrel engine. This aircraft was subsequently given a Kestrel IIMS engine, with which it first flew on 20 September 1931. This was followed by the first flight of the initial series production aircraft, accomplished on 14 October 1931. Production totalled 54 Mk Is, most of which served with the FAA on board HMS *Courageous* (a converted light battlecruiser accommodating 48 aircraft), *Furious* (completed in

1917, recommissioned in 1925 and accommodating 33 aircraft), *Eagle* (initially only: the first aircraft carrier with an offset island superstructure and split level aircraft hangar and accommodating 21 aircraft) and *Glorious* (converted from a light battlecruiser and accommodating 48 aircraft), followed in 1933 by 31 Mk IIs, not including the Mk I modified as the Mk II prototype (which first flew on 12 February 1933) but including one further Mk I modified to Mk II standard. Deliveries of Mk IIs started in the spring of 1934. Powered by Rolls-Royce Kestrel V engines, these were the penultimate biplane fighters to serve with the FAA and the last were not finally withdrawn from service until 1939, although several Nimrods had been used as trainers with No 1 Flying Training School between 1935 and 1936. Nimrods were also exported to Denmark (two, with Kestrel IIIS engines), Japan (one) and Portugal (one).

Hawker Osprey UK

Purpose: Fighter/Reconnaissance
Makers: Hawker Aircraft Ltd
In service: 1932-40
Photo: Osprey floatplane
Data: Mk IV landplane

Engine: One 640hp Rolls-Royce Kestrel V
Span: 37ft 0in
Length: 29ft 4in
Height: 10ft 5in
Weight loaded: 4,976lb (seaplane 5,500lb)
Crew: Two
Max speed: 173mph
Service ceiling: 22,000ft
Endurance: 3hr 15min
Armament: One forward-firing Vickers machine gun and one Lewis machine gun in rear cockpit

When the first Ospreys entered service in November 1932 with two FAA Flights, they were operational at a time when Hawker aircraft were being used as fighters, bombers and torpedo bombers with the RAF and as fighters with the FAA. Developed from the Hawker Hart, which had entered service with the RAF in 1930, the Osprey differed in being strengthened for catapulting and in having folding wings for easy storage and special naval equipment. The first prototype (the converted Hart 'high-speed

bomber' prototype) made its maiden flight in 1930 and was followed by two other prototypes proper, the first of which flew on 9 July and 4 September as a landplane and seaplane respectively. Production began with 37 Osprey Mk Is, followed by 14 Mk IIs (later modified as Mk IIIs), 52 Mk IIIs with Fairey Reid propellers and other refinements (including a small number of stainless steel-constructed examples, one of which was exhibited in skeleton form on the Hawker stand at the 1932 Paris Show where, according to Hawker records, it aroused great interest among foreign representatives), and 26 Mk IVs of which several were later modified as trainers and target tugs. The first three versions were all powered by 568hp Rolls-Royce Kestrel IIMS engines, bestowing a maximum speed of about 160mph as landplanes. It is interesting to note that one Osprey was experimentally fitted with a single central float and small wingtip floats, but the twin float layout remained standard on all Osprey seaplanes, especially as this aircraft only achieved 136mph. Ospreys served on board several aircraft carriers and other warships such as the cruisers *York* and *Dorsetshire* (with one Osprey each), first replacing Flycatchers and then IIIFs that had been in service since 1923 and 1928 respectively as fighters and catapult seaplanes. In June 1932 an important step was taken by the FAA when it renumbered

No 404 Flight (Fleet Fighter) as No 420 to become the first fighter-reconnaissance flight, using the Osprey as standard equipment. In 1933, the Swedish air ministry decided to standardise on mainly British aircraft and chose four Ospreys among other new aircraft, each powered by a licence-built Bristol Mercury engine known as Nohab. A number of these eventually served on board the *Gotland,* and Swedish Ospreys remained in service until 1940 as part of the naval co-operation wing alongside Heinkel He5s. In 1934 four Osprey IIIs were taken on charge by No 24 Squadron RAF for communications duties and, according to Hawker records, in the same year the cruiser *Sussex* sailed to Melbourne for the Centenary celebrations, carrying a single Osprey, and aircraft of the type equipped the flagship *Leander*

and cruisers *Neptune, Achilles* and *Orion* of the Second Cruiser Squadron of the Home Fleet. In July 1935 the new cruiser *Ajax* received Ospreys (two), as did other cruisers, and in the following year Ospreys were based at Malta as part of Mediterranean Command. The last FAA Ospreys were withdrawn from first-line service in 1939. Apart from the export aircraft received by Sweden, and noted above, Portugal received two and Spain one, the latter powered by a 690hp Hispano-Suiza 12Xbrs engine and first flying in early 1936. This Osprey presumably played some role during the Spanish Civil War, although whether it was counted among the 57 aircraft supplied by Britain to the Republican Air Force is not clear.

Hawker Woodcock   UK

Purpose: Fighter
Makers: H. G. Hawker Engineering Co Ltd
In service: 1925-28
Photo: Woodcock II

Engine: One 400hp Bristol Jupiter IV radial
Span: 32ft 6in
Length: 26ft 2in
Height: 9ft 11in
Weight loaded: 3,040lb
Crew: One
Max speed: 143mph
Service ceiling: 22,500ft
Endurance: 3hr 30min
Armament: Two fixed .303in Vickers machine guns

The Woodcock was yet another fighter that replaced Sopwith Snipes in RAF service, others being the Gloster Grebe from 1923 and the Armstrong Whitworth Siskin from 1924, and offered little in new design initiative. With the much more exciting 125mph Duiker reconnaissance and fighting parasol-wing monoplane and a re-worked Sopwith Racer, the Woodcock was one of the first products of the Hawker company, which had formed after the Sopwith company had gone into liquidation in 1920

due to losses incurred while producing motorcycles. The latter enterprise was presumably to supplement the postwar development of civil aircraft, which included amongst its numbers the Dove two-seater, Wallaby and six-seat transport, made necessary because of the loss of huge war orders. The first prototype Woodcock appeared in 1923, powered by a 385hp Armstrong Siddeley Jaguar engine, and was followed by a second prototype with a Bristol Jupiter engine, modified wings and vertical tail surfaces. The latter model was designated Mk II and was ordered into production, beginning Hawkers meteoric rise to prominence which lasted throughout the remaining interwar years, and indeed, to the present day. A total of about 67 Mk IIs was ordered, most for the RAF, but only two squadrons received the type. Three aircraft were exported to Denmark, as Dankoks with Jaguar engines, and 12 were licence-built in Denmark from 1927 for the Danish Naval Air Service, these serving for a time as its only fighters alongside Friedrichshafen and Royal Dockyard reconnaissance aircraft and Avro 504K/N trainers. According to Hawker reports, the Dankok had shorter bottom wings, raked struts and a smaller fuselage, all helping to give it a maximum speed of 146mph and good enough general performance to set up a new Scandinavian altitude record.

Heinkel He51 Germany

Purpose: Fighter/Ground attack
Makers: Ernst Heinkel Flugzeugwerke GmbH
In service: 1934-39
Data: He51B-1

Engine: One 750hp BMW VI
Span: 36ft 1.5in
Length: 27ft 6.75in
Height: 10ft 6in
Weight loaded: 4,189lb
Crew: One
Max speed: 205mph
Service ceiling: over 25,350ft
Range: 242-431 miles
Armament: Two fixed forward-firing 7.92mm
MG17 machine guns

It is a misconception to believe that Germany designed and built large numbers of military aircraft of all types from scratch and rebuilt its air force to become one of the most formidable in the world, all in a few short years. It was, in fact, the result of work carried out in secrecy in Germany and more openly abroad, throughout the 1920s, aided to some degree by nations willing to see German companies produce military aircraft in their countries for their own and foreign (non-German) use. Heinkel He51s typify the rearming of Germany during the 1930s. The prototypes were the result of work carried out during the later 1920s; the early aircraft were delivered in secrecy and it was only a short time before they were engaged in combat, during the Spanish Civil War. Progressive development by Heinkel of single-seat biplane fighters had led to the first flight of a new streamlined prototype fighter, the He49, in November 1932. Of mixed construction, it was powered by a BMW VI engine and was followed by

three other prototypes. The last of these was more refined and as such was redesignated He51A. 84 He51As were delivered to the clandestine Luftwaffe, some built by Heinkel and others by Arado, Erla and Fieseler. Together with Arado Ar68s, these were the Luftwaffe's first standard fighters. In 1935 a new version, designated He51B, entered production, with revised undercarriage and a jettisonable 170litre auxiliary fuel tank mounted below the fuselage, which raised the total fuel capacity to 380litre and allowed a range of 431 miles. 70 aircraft were completed, the He51B models fitted out as seaplanes, of which the first handful were converted He51As. The last version built was the He51C ground attack aircraft, many of which served with the Spanish Nationalists, the German Condor Legion in Spain and as He51C-2s with the Luftwaffe. Before this time, six He51Bs had been sent to Spain, in July 1936, together with 20 Junkers Ju52/3m bomber-transports and 85 volunteer airmen and groundcrew, as part of the initial German aid to the Nationalists (where the transports were initially used to fly Moorish troops from Tetouan). Eventually, a total of 135 He51s served with the Spanish and German forces. On the first day of operations with He51s, two aircraft alone destroyed four Republican machines. However, it was only a short time before the Republicans were issued with Russian Polikarpov I-15 fighters, which flew at 224mph, had a service ceiling of over 29,500ft and could climb at a far higher rate. Outmatched as fighters, He51s were switched mainly to ground attack duties until 1939, Fiat CR32s becoming the Nationalists' main fighters. Total He51 production amounted to about 700 aircraft, the Luftwaffe withdrawing the type from fighter squadrons in 1938, although they were subsequently used for other duties including training.

Heinkel He59

Germany

Purpose: Torpedo bomber/Reconnaissance
Makers: Ernst Heinkel Flugzeugwerke GmbH
In service: From 1934
Photo: He59N
Data: He59B-2

Engines: Two 660hp BMW VIs
Span: 77ft 9in
Length: 57ft 1in
Height: 23ft 3.5in
Weight loaded: 20,000lb
Crew: Four
Max speed: 137mph
Service ceiling: 11,475ft
Range: 585-1,090 miles
Armament: Three 7.9mm MG15 machine guns in nose, dorsal and ventral positions. Up to 2,205lb of bombs or a torpedo

By 1939, the He59 was obsolete but remained in service with the Luftwaffe on air/sea rescue duties in small numbers. But, unlike so many aircraft of all nationalities that started life in a combat role and finished as wartime hacks, the He59 had seen combat, albeit in small numbers, during its career. The first prototype He59 to fly, in September 1931, was a landplane. This was, however, the only land version built. In the following year the second

prototype flew as a twin-float seaplane, designated He59B. Following a number of pre-production aircraft built for evaluation trials, the He59B-2 was put in production by Arado, which had been unsuccessful in interesting the Luftwaffe in its Ar66 single-engined biplane trainer and had most of its 15,000sq m of factory space going spare. Next came the He59B-3, produced for long-range maritime reconnaissance duties. A total of about 140 He59s was produced. Ten He59B-2s were sent to Spain during the Civil War in that country, serving with the Condor Legion. These were used mainly as night bombers to disrupt Republican coastal areas and prevent supplies reaching their destinations, although some were fitted with a 20mm cannon as attack aircraft. By 1938, the He59 was becoming long in the tooth and potentially more than a little vulnerable to the modern fighters coming off the production lines in most European countries. The Heinkel He115 and Dornier Do18 had already proved themselves suitable production material and it was decided therefore to convert the He59s to perform other non-combat roles. The resulting conversions gave rise to versions for armament and navigational training, air/sea rescue and photographic reconnaissance duties. It is worth recalling that on 3 September 1939, the day the Luftwaffe lost the most aircraft during the Polish campaign, an He59 was among the 22 German aircraft destroyed.

Henschel Hs123

Germany

Purpose: Ground attack
Makers: Henschel Flugzeugwerke AG
In service: 1936-44

Engine: See below
Span: 34ft 5.25in
Length: 27ft 4in
Height: 10ft 6in
Weight loaded: 4,884lb
Crew: One
Max speed: 214mph at 4,000ft
Service ceiling: 29,500ft

Range: over 530 miles
Armament: Two fixed 7.9mm MG17 machine guns. One 550lb bomb, or four 110lb or smaller bombs, or two 20mm cannon

Henschel started as an aircraft manufacturing company in 1933. Its first two products were high-wing monoplanes for fighting, training and armed-reconnaissance roles, but they did not enter service. However, in May 1935 came the maiden flight of the first Hs123 dive bomber prototype. This was a metal-constructed biplane, powered by a 650hp BMW 132 radial engine driving initially a three-blade propeller. It had single-bay sesquiplane wings, with ruggedly faired undercarriage legs and wheels as independent units under the lower wings. The fuselage was an oval monocoque structure. All-in-all, it was a strong and well built aircraft with a more than reasonable turn of speed. Two more prototypes were built, and these proved much better than their rival, the Fieseler Fi98, which had the speed and look of an outdated aircraft. However, all was not to be plain sailing for the Henschels. In the course of the trials, two of the prototypes broke up in the air, as a result of which the wings were strengthened. The Hs123 was then put into production as a stop-gap dive bomber, to serve until the Junkers Ju87 Stuka was ready for service. Production Hs123A-1s joined the first designated unit in October 1935. Just over a

year later a small number arrived in Spain and soon proved outstanding as ground attack aircraft. Others subsequently arrived from Germany. The arrival into service of the Ju87 in 1937 should have ended the biplane's career and undoubtedly would have if it had not been for its newly found success in the ground attack role. Although dive bomber squadrons re-equipped with Ju87s, Henschels remained operational in their own right, and during World War 2 fought in the Polish campaign, in Belgium, the Netherlands, France and then the Russian Front, continuing in service with the Luftwaffe until 1944 when, so outmatched by the new Russian fighters, they were virtually annihilated. Of course, the type had previously suffered casualties, Hs123s being counted among the losses suffered by the Luftwaffe during the worst two days of the Polish and Belgium campaigns.

IMAM Ro37   Italy

Purpose: Reconnaissance/Attack
Makers: SA Industrie Meccaniche e Aeronautiche Meridionali
In service: 1935-43
Data: Ro 37*bis*

Engine: See below
Span: 36ft 4.2in
Length: 28ft 1in
Height: 10ft 3.75in
Weight loaded: 5,346lb
Crew: Two
Max speed: 198.8mph
Service ceiling: 23,622ft
Normal range: 932 miles
Armament: Two or three 7.7mm machine guns plus anti-personnel bombs

Built to replace the Ro1 (Fokker CV built under licence), the Ro37 prototype (serial MM220) flew for the first time on 6 November 1933 piloted by test

pilot Nicolo Lana. An unequal-span biplane braced either side by pairs of parallel struts, the Ro37 had a fuselage and tail unit of steel tube construction with dural sheet covering forward and fabric covering aft of the observer's cockpit. The metal wings were staggered and had dihedral. Ailerons were fitted on the upper wing only. Wings were covered partly with plywood and partly with fabric. The divided undercarriage and tailwheel had spat-type fairings. The pilot and observer/gunner (the latter an Army Officer or NCO in service aircraft) were close together in tandem. The observer had a partially enclosed position with glazed side fuselage panels, and operated a 7.7mm machine gun and an OMI camera. While the first prototype had a 600hp Fiat A30 inline engine, the second prototype had a 650hp Piaggio PIX radial in a long-chord cowling. Both versions went into quantity production, the Ro37/A30 in July 1935 and the radial-engined Ro37*bis* two months later. Grand total built between the IMAM, Caproni-Taliedo and AVIS factories up to

May 1939 was 637. Five Squadriglie operated in Abyssinia during the Italian invasion in 1935-6. They were engaged on machine gunning and anti-personnel bombing attacks, and subsequently on colonial policing duties. The Ro37*bis* operated successfully with the Italian Aviazione Legionaria in Spain from September 1936, carrying out photographic reconnaissance, artillery observation and ground attack duties with few losses. The 128 Squadriglia developed the 'Las Cadinas' attack technique, the aircraft approaching the target in Indian file, dropping their bombs and strafing the enemy in quick succession. When Italy entered World War 2, 296 of both versions were still in first-line service. They operated in East and North Africa and then in the campaign against Greece. Subsequently they were relegated to anti-guerilla duties in the Balkans. Apart from the flexibly mounted machine gun, the Ro37 had one or two 7.7mm fixed synchronised weapons and carried either two 79lb bombs or a special launcher for 72 4.4lb anti-personnel bombs. Although robust and reasonably manoeuvrable, the Ro37 had the misfortune to be obsolescent soon after going into Squadriglia service. Nevertheless, examples were exported to Afghanistan, Austria, Ecuador, Hungary and Uruguay.

IVL A-22   Finland

Purpose: Reconnaissance
Makers: Finnish Aviation Force Aircraft Factory
In service: 1922-36

Engine: See below
Span: 52ft 0in
Length: 36ft 5in
Height: 9ft 7.75in
Weight loaded: 4,683lb
Crew: Two
Max speed: 98.17mph
Service ceiling: 13,124ft
Range: 200 miles
Armament: One 7.62mm machine gun on a ring mounting over the rear cockpit

The A-22 was a low-wing twin-float seaplane manufactured in quantity by the Ilmailuvoimien Lentokonetehdas, the state-owned Finnish air arm factory established in 1920, two years after Finland obtained its independence from Russia. A policy decision was made early on to concentrate on seaplanes (that could be fitted with skis for winter operations) for national defence in view of the thousands of Finnish lakes and the country's long seaboard with the Baltic. The search for a suitable machine led to the decision to build the German Hansa-Brandenberg W33 under licence as the IVL A-22, especially as Hansa-Brandenberg seaplanes had achieved great success with German forces during World War 1. The principal Finnish version was powered by a 300hp Fiat A12*bis* engine with a frontal radiator, although some earlier machines had a radiator of different design located under the fuselage. The A-22 was distinguished by its wide chord wings and multiplicity of struts connecting the twin floats with the underside of the fuselage and wing. The distinctive horizontal tailplane was mounted on top of the rear fuselage with a balanced rudder extending behind and below the sternpost. Production continued from 1922 to 1925, a total of 122 of the type being delivered. A robust and dependable aircraft, which represented an advanced design when it first went into service, the A-22 soldiered on well past any normal span of years into the mid-1930s, by which time it was totally obsolete.

Junkers Ju52/3m Germany

Purpose: Bomber/Transport
Makers: Junkers Flugzeug und Motorenwerke AG
In service: 1934-45
Data: Ju52/3mg3e

Engines: Three 725hp BMW 132A-3 radials
Span: 95ft 11in
Length: 62ft 0in
Height: 14ft 10in
Weight loaded: 24,200lb
Crew: Two or three (plus up to 18 troops in transport version)
Max speed: 165mph
Service ceiling: 19,000ft
Range: 800 miles
Armament: Two 7.9mm MG15 machine guns, one in dorsal position and one in semi-retractable ventral position. Up to 1,100lb of bombs

In 1930, there appeared a passenger or freight carrying monoplane powered by a single 800hp Junkers L88 engine. The type entered production as the Ju52, with a 750hp Junkers Jumo 4 engine, later becoming known as the Ju52/1m. However, in April 1931, the first flight took place of a modified, three-engined version designated Ju52/3m and production of the type was started for Deutsche Luft Hansa and for foreign civil airlines (particularly in South America and including three operated by British Airways as mail freighters). With the creation of the German Luftwaffe auxiliary bomber force in 1933, Ju52/3m 'Iron Annies' were converted as temporary bombers, considered only as a stop-gap until Do11s arrived. Hold-ups in production of the

latter aircraft meant that the force had to rely on the earlier type for longer than expected. In 1935, the Ju52/3mg3e improved bomber version entered production, powered by three BMW 132A-3 engines and with dorsal and ventral 'dustbin' gun positions. In August of the following year, the first 20 Ju52/3m bomber-transports arrived in Spain, together with Heinkel He51b fighter biplanes and volunteer air and groundcrew. Their first task was to transport 10,000 Moorish troops from Morocco to help the Nationalist uprising. Soon the aircraft began bombing raids, and by November had been joined by Ju52/3mg4e bombers serving also with the German Condor Legion. But in the following year these were handed over to the Spanish Nationalist forces, after the arrival of more modern types. From 1937, Ju52/3ms in Luftwaffe service were withdrawn as bombers and began a further career as general-purpose transports. At the outbreak of war the Luftwaffe had over 550 Ju52/3ms in service, including a number of Ju52/3mg5es with interchangeable land, float or ski undercarriages, and Ju52/3mg6es with land or float undercarriages. Military Ju52/3ms were also exported to Austria, Portugal and Switzerland. During World War 2 the Ju52/3m proved highly successful as a transport and in other non-combat roles, although it was an easy target for fighters. This was well demonstrated on 10 May 1940 when Germany invaded the Netherlands and Belgium. On that day the Luftwaffe lost 157 Ju52/3ms, more than half the total aircraft lost, some 37 of which were brought down in one aerial combat by a formation of Dutch Fokker DXXIs. Production totalled 4,800 aircraft by 1944.

Junkers W33, W34 and K43 Germany

Purpose: General purpose
Makers: Junkers Flugzeugwerke AG
In service: 1926-39
Photo: K43
Data: W34

Engine: see below
Span: 58ft 2.75in
Length: 33ft 8in
Height: 12ft 0.5in
Weight loaded: 5,950lb
Crew: Two

Max speed: 137mph
Service ceiling: 22,300ft
Armament: One machine gun on flexible mounting in cockpit (two machine guns in two dorsal gun positions in K43)

In 1919 there appeared the first-ever all-metal transport aircraft, the Junkers F13. Powered by a 310hp Junkers L-5 engine, it had a maximum speed of 126mph and carried a crew of two and four passengers. From it were derived, in 1926, the W33 and W34 two-seat general-purpose aircraft, and these entered production in both civil and military versions. (199 and 1,790 produced respectively, including K43s.) Fitted with a variety of engines — although the standard powerplants were the 320hp Junkers L-5 and the 650hp BMW 132 or 575hp Hornet (licence-built Pratt & Whitney) respectively — they were operated with land, float and ski undercarriages and served in Germany, Canada, Colombia, Finland, Greece, Japan and Sweden (where W34s were built by the Swedish Junkers company with Mercury engines). They were used mainly for coastal patrol, transport, communications,

instrument training and ambulance work, although, with the rebirth of the Luftwaffe in 1933, W34s were used for a few years as a stop-gap light bomber. From the W34 was developed the K43. Powered subsequently by the 575hp Hornet radial engine, K43s were built in Sweden and exported to Colombia, Portugal and Finland where they were fitted with floats normally or skis for winter flying. Between 12-13 April 1928, a W33 named *Bremen* made the first east-west crossing of the North Atlantic, crewed by Hauptmann Köhl, Baron von Hünefeld and Cmdt Fitzmaurice, flying from Dublin, Ireland, to Greenly Island, Labrador.

Kawasaki Type 92

Japan

Purpose: Fighter
Makers: Kawasaki Jukogyo KK (Kawasaki Industries Ltd)
In service: 1932-36

Engine: See below
Span: 31ft 4in
Length: 23ft 1.6in
Height: 10ft 2in
Weight loaded: 3,748lb
Crew: One
Max speed: 198.8mph at sea level
Service ceiling: 31,168ft
Normal range: 528 miles
Armament: Two synchronised 7.7mm machine guns

Derived from the experimental KDA-5 designed by Dr-Ing Richard Vogt, the Type 92 fighter made use of the most up-to-date constructional techniques available in the early 1930s. Basic structure was all-metal, the equal-span wings had contoured I-struts and the undercarriage was of split-axle type. The KDA-5 had a 600hp BMW VI liquid cooled engine. The same engine, uprated to 750hp, powered the Type 92 Model 1, which had the pilot's headrest completely faired into the upper rear fuselage decking, a fin and rudder assembly of improved configuration and a modified 'chin'-type radiator. Five KDA-5 prototypes were tested during 1930-1 and 180 Type 92 Model 1s were built by Kawasaki in the two following years. The Type 92 Model 2, incorporating structural strengthening and further

revision to the tailplane, was produced from 1933 to 1934. 200 Model 2s were delivered to the Imperial Japanese Army.

The Type 92 proved to be an outstanding interceptor with excellent manoeuvrability and a good rate of climb, reaching 9,849ft in four minutes. It was rated greatly superior to the Nakajima Type 91 parasol monoplane. However, it saw little action, as it did not reach the Army's Air Regiments until after the conclusion of the Shanghai Incident in May 1932. Some Type 92 Model 1s served briefly in Manchuria before the fighting there terminated in 1933, but both Model 1 and Model 2 had been phased out of front-line service by the time large-scale war between Japan and China broke out in July 1937. A number of Type 92s were utilised as advanced trainers, several still flying in that role at the time of Pearl Harbor in December 1941.

Kawasaki Ki-3 Japan

Purpose: Light bomber
Makers: Kawasaki Jukogyo KK (Kawasaki Heavy Industries Ltd)
In service: 1934-39

Engine: See below
Span: 42ft 8in
Length: 32ft 8in
Height: 9ft 10in
Weight loaded: 6,837lb
Max speed: 161.6mph
Service ceiling: 22,966ft
Armament: Two 7.7mm machine guns. Up to 1,103lb of bombs

The Ki-3 was the last Japanese Army biplane bomber. It had unequal-span, staggered wings and was developed from the KDA-6 private venture reconnaissance prototype (which was later purchased by the Asahi Shinbun newspaper group, fitted with a glazed crew canopy and used for liaison and propaganda flights as the A-6). The Ki-3 prototype, like the KDA-6, was designed by German engineer Richard Vogt, who later returned to Europe to become Chief Designer for Blohm und Voss. KDA-6 had been powered first by a 500hp BMW VI engine and later by a 660hp BMW VIII. The first Ki-3 flew in March 1933 and featured a rather unusual annular cowling with a nose radiator for its engine. During development a more conventional, but distinctly rakish, chin radiator became standard. Series aircraft bore the designation Army Type 93 Light Bomber and 203 were built by Kawasaki plus a further 40 by Tatchikawa, between January 1934 and 1937. Despite the fact that it was not particularly successful in service, never overcoming difficulties with its liquid-cooled powerplant and having what was generally regarded as poor performance, the Type 93 received considerable foreign publicity and was subject to a considerable, though unsuccessful, foreign sales campaign by Kawasaki, largely directed at the South American market. In appearance the type was quite impressive, with its rugged lines, large wide-track divided undercarriage with wheel spats and carefully contoured I-form wing struts. Of metal structure with fabric covering, the Ki-3 was armed with one fixed synchronised cowling machine gun and a second weapon on a ring mounting over the observer's cockpit. Bombs were carried on six underwing racks. It first went into service in Korea with the 6th Mixed Air Regiment and in autumn 1936 equipped the newly formed 9th, 10th and 16th Air Regiments. It participated in the China Incident from the outset in 1937, but during the summer of 1938 replacement by monoplanes was initiated. The Ki-3 ended its career in the support and supply-dropping roles.

Kawasaki Ki-10   Japan

Purpose: Fighter
Makers: Kawasaki Jukogyu KK (Kawasaki Heavy Industries Ltd)
In service: 1936-40
Data: Ki-10-I (Type 95 Model 1)

Engine: See below
Span: 31ft 4in
Length: 23ft 7.5in
Height: 9ft 10.1in
Weight loaded: 3,638lb
Crew: One
Max speed: 248.5mph at 9,843ft
Service ceiling: 32,808ft
Normal range: 621 miles
Armament: Two 7.7mm machine-guns

The Ki-10 fighter biplane was developed by designer Takeo Doi to a Japanese Army September 1934 requirement. Four prototypes underwent intensive testing, proving considerably more manoeuvrable and only slightly slower than the rival Nakajima Ki-11 low-wing monoplane. The Army, which laid emphasis on dogfight superiority, selected the Kawasaki biplane for production as the Army Type 95 Model 1 Fighter. In its definitive form the Ki-10-I was powered by a 850hp Kawasaki Ha-9-IIa inline engine driving a three-blade metal propeller. It was an unequal-span biplane with N-form bracing struts. Ailerons were fitted to the upper wing only. The fixed undercarriage was provided with wheel fairings.

Construction was all-metal with alloy sheet and fabric covering. Three hundred of the initial production version were built, followed by 280 Model 2 machines (or Ki-10-II). These differed in having wings of greater span and fuselage of increased length (1ft 6.5in and 1ft 2.25in respectively). Production of the second version lasted until December 1938. Meanwhile two more streamlined experimental versions had been tested, Ki-10-I KAI and Ki-10-II KAI. The latter had an enclosed cockpit and cantilever spatted main undercarriage units. A top speed of 276.5mph was achieved. Series Ki-10s were flying with six squadrons in China soon after hostilities broke out with that country in July 1937. Due to weak air opposition they were involved in few dogfights and were mainly employed in providing close support for Japanese troops. Later, Soviet equipment reached the Chinese and in one large scale air engagement with Polikarpov 1-15*bis* biplanes over Koitoh, on 10 April 1938, 12 Type 95s of the 2nd Air Battalion claimed destruction of 24 enemy aircraft. This was one of a series of engagements in which Japanese fighters achieved supremacy over the Chinese. By the summer of 1939, however, the Type 95 was obsolescent and proved relatively ineffective in the border fighting at Nomonhan with the Soviet air force, largely equipped with Polikarpov I-16 monoplanes. Soon afterwards the Ki-10 was completely replaced in the front line by the Nakajima Ki-27 and relegated to advanced training duties.

Kawasaki Type 88   Japan

Purpose: Reconnaissance/Light bomber
Makers: Kawasaki Dockyard Co Ltd
In service: 1928-39

Engine: One 450hp Kawasaki-built BMW VI
Span: 49ft 2in
Length: 40ft 3.5in
Height: 11ft 1.25in
Weight loaded: 6,270lb (reconnaissance); 6,835lb
Crew: Two
Max speed: 137mph (reconnaissance)
Service ceiling: 20,300ft

Armament: Two or three 7.7mm machine guns, forward-firing and rear mounted. Normal load of 550lb of bombs under wings

Designed as a two-seat reconnaissance biplane, the first of three prototype Kawasaki Type 88s (designated KDA-2s) appeared in 1927. During flight tests, the prototypes proved so outstanding that the type was ordered into immediate production as the sleek Type 88-I. This version carried three machine guns for its protection and equipment included a camera and wireless apparatus. When the Army subsequently made known its need for a new light bomber, Kawasaki produced a derivative of the Type 88 as the Type 88-II of 1929, armed with just two machine guns but carrying a very reasonable warload under its wings. This version also entered production and service, although in lesser numbers than its reconnaissance counterpart. Some Type 88-IIs were later used in the non-combat role. Type 88-Is served alongside Mitsubishi Type 92

reconnaissance monoplanes during the early 1930s, while the Type 88-IIs paired with the older Mitsubishi 2MB1s or Type 87s. Total production of both variants of the Type 88 was 1,117, completed by Kawasaki and by the Tachikawa Army Air Arsenal. Type 88s of the Japanese Army were involved in fighting the Chinese around Shanghai in 1937, and undertook missions in Manchuria, a region which had suffered periods of attack and occupation by Japanese forces since 1931.

Keystone Bombers

USA

Purpose: Bomber
Makers: Keystone Aircraft Corporation
In service: 1927-36
Photo: B-3A
Data: B-3A

Engines: See below
Span: 74ft 8in
Length: 48ft 10in
Height: 15ft 9in
Weight loaded: 12,952lb
Crew: Four
Max speed: 114mph
Service ceiling: 12,700ft
Normal range: 860 miles
Armament: Three 0.30in Browning machine guns. 2,200lb of bombs

For nearly a decade the American public was impressed to see lumbering twin-engined Keystone

bomber biplanes hitting the headlines in all manner of ways. In late 1927 brand-new LB-5s of the 2nd Bombardment Group from Langley Field demolished with bombs a long highway bridge over the Pee Dee River in North Carolina. Keystones also took part in the National Air Races — like the LB-7s of the 20th Squadron which showed they could turn at pylons at 45° angles. And when the air mail was in difficulty it was aircraft like the Keystone B-4A which stepped into the breach. All this publicity was good for the US Army Air Corps, but it concealed the fact that when the first production Keystones were delivered in August 1927, their speed and general performance were little better than that of the old NBS-1 biplanes they replaced. By 1936, when the design was hopelessly obsolete, it still formed part of the equipment of several bombardment squadrons. Even as the series was still in production and thrilling Americans with mass formation flights the warning

had gone out. After the Pacific War Games in 1930, in which Keystones of two Bombardment Groups participated, it was officially recommended that they be replaced by lighter and faster machines. However, production of the B-4A and the B-6A did not terminate until 1932 (during 1931-2 over 100 were built). Construction was of steel tube, with fabric covering except for the forward part of the wing which was faced with plywood. All versions were equal-span two-bay biplanes with fixed wide-track undercarriages. Nose and midships gunners' cockpits had 0.30in Browning machine guns on ring mountings. Pilot and co-pilot were seated side-by-side in open cockpits protected by a single windscreen. The original XLB-5 'Pirate' was a twin-engined version of the single-engined LB-1. It was followed by 10 LB-5s and a single XLB-3, with twin auxiliary fins and rudders in addition to the large main fin and rudder of the XLB-5. The twenty-five

LB-5As differed in having twin fins and rudders. All versions thus far were powered by Liberty engines. The last LB-5 was completed as the XLB-6, in which the wing taper was eliminated and the wing span was increased. It was powered by the new 525hp Wright R-1 750-I Cyclone radial engine and was followed by 18 525hp Pratt & Whitney R-1690-3 Hornet-powered LB-7s and 17 Cyclone-powered LB-6s. After a number of 'one-off' modifications came 36 B-3As, with lengthened fuselages, and the definitive tailplane — a single fin with rounded and balanced rudder, five Y1B-4s with Hornet engines, 27 B-5As, six Y1B-6s with Cyclones, 39 Cyclone-powered B-6As and 25 Hornet-powered B-4As, most with three-bladed propellers. Altogether, 207 aircraft in this series were built, 120 serving in the continental United States and the rest in American overseas possessions in Hawaii, the Philippines and the Panama Canal Zone.

Latécoère 290 France

Purpose: Torpedo bomber
Makers: Société Industrielle d'Aviation Latécoère
In service: 1933-39

Engine: One 650hp Hispano 12Nbr
Span: 63ft 2in
Length: 44ft 9in
Height: 10ft 11.5in
Weight loaded: 10,249lb
Crew: Three
Max speed: 124.3mph at sea level
Service ceiling: 15,575ft
Range: 435 miles
Armament: One fixed forward-firing 7.62mm Vickers machine gun and twin Lewis 7.62mm machine guns on a dorsal ring mounting. One torpedo or 661lb of bombs

The Latécoère company had, by 1930, become famous for producing a long series of mail and passenger carrying aircraft to operate the pioneering Aéropostale routes across the Mediterranean, to West Africa and across the South Atlantic to Brazil, Uruguay and Argentina. The Laté 28, of which about 70 were built, had a number of specialised variants including the Laté 28.3 and the record-breaking Laté 28.5. It was from these machines that a prototype for naval aviation was developed under the

designation Laté 290. A high-wing strut-braced cabin monoplane with an interchangeable wheel or twin float undercarriage, the Laté 29.01 prototype (the first of two prototypes) flew for the first time in early 1931. Official testing as a seaplane began at St Raphaël on 21 October, concluding successfully with an order for 20 series machines placed on 9 December 1931. An additional order placed on 5 October 1933 brought the total production aircraft ordered to 40. Intended for coastal patrol duties, the Laté 290s were all delivered with wheel undercarriages, being converted to seaplanes at St Laurent de la Salanque. Apart from the fixed machine gun operated by the pilot, the gunner operated a twin-dorsal mounting housed under a glazed cupola. The third crew member was the radio operator/navigator whose cabin was in the fuselage amidships. Experimental variants included the Gnome-Rhône radial-engined Laté 29.3 and Laté 29.4, the latter with modified wings and rear fuselage. Initial series Laté 290s were delivered to Aéronavale Escadrille 4T1 at Berre in 1933. The newly formed Escadrille 1T1 at Cherbourg received Laté 290s in 1935. Relegated to training duties at the end of 1938, several Laté 290s were subsequently issued to the newly-formed Escadrille 1S2 at the beginning of World War 2. These flew coastal patrols until evacuated from Cherbourg in face of the German Blitzkrieg in June 1940.

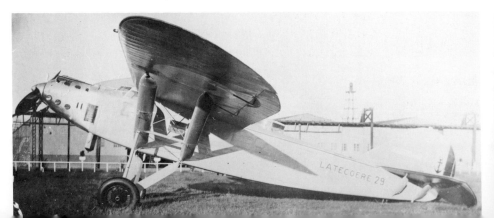

Latécoère 298

France

Purpose: Torpedo bomber/Reconnaissance
Makers: Société Industrielle d'Aviation Latécoère
In service: 1939-46
Data: Latécoère 298D

Engine: See below
Span: 50ft 10.25in
Length: 41ft 2.5in
Height: 17ft 1.25in
Weight loaded: 10,582lb
Crew: Four
Max speed: 180.2mph at 6,562ft
Service ceiling: 21,325ft
Range: 497 miles (with torpedo)
Armament: Two fixed 7.5mm Darne machine guns plus another on a flexible mounting. One 1,447lb torpedo or 1,100lb of bombs

Intended as a multi-role twin-float seaplane, the Latécoère 298.01 prototype made its maiden flight on 8 May 1936. Its slim oval fuselage had stressed skin covering and its underside was concave so that when a torpedo was carried it was partially enclosed. As with the series-built aircraft, its 880hp Hispano-Suiza 12Ycrs 12-cylinder water-cooled engine drove a Ratier constant-speed propeller. The four crew men

were housed under a raised glazed canopy. 130 Laté 298s of all versions were built, 20 of them for the French Vichy regime. The Laté 298A was the initial production model with an entirely new crew canopy; the Laté 298B had folding outer wing sections and tailplane tips for stowage aboard seaplane carriers; the Laté 298D had a fourth crew member; the one-off Laté 298E had a large ventral gondola; and the Laté 298F was the Vichy-built series version. Among the missions intended for the Laté 298 was long-range oversea reconnaissance (with extra tanks), coastal daylight reconnaissance, night reconnaissance, torpedo bombing and shallow dive-bombing attacks on enemy vessels and coastal targets. What actually happened when the Germans launched their Blitzkrieg on France in May/June 1940 was that French Naval Latécoère 298s of Escadrilles T1, T2 and T3 based first at Boulogne and then at Cherbourg were launched in desperate overland attacks on the advancing German armoured columns, making shallow dive bombing attacks on bridges over the Somme on 23 May 1940. Mediterranean-based units saw action against Italian naval vessels during the brief Italo-French conflict in June of that year. A few Laté 298s remained in service with Escadrille 3S for postwar policing duties until the end of January 1946.

Letov S-16

Czechoslovakia

Purpose: General purpose
Makers: Letov Vojenská továrna na letadla
In service: 1928-37

Engine: See below
Span: 50ft 2.5in
Length: 33ft 5.75in
Height: 11ft 2in
Weight loaded: 5,026lb

Crew: Two
Max speed: 146mph
Service ceiling: 22,966ft
Range: 621 miles
Armament: Three 7.62mm machine guns plus normally 661lb of bombs (see below)

The S-16 first appeared in 1926 when the prototype was displayed at the Paris Salon Aéronautique. Impressed with the new design by Alois Smolik, Latvia and Turkey soon placed production orders. All series aircraft had a redesigned fin and rudder which eliminated the angular lines of the prototype's tailplane. The S-16 was of all-metal construction with fabric covering overall. It had a deep square-cut fuselage, narrow-chord single-bay wide-span wings and a conventional axle-type undercarriage. 22 S-16Ls exported to Latvia in 1927 had 450hp Hispano-Suiza engines. One Latvian machine, flown by Letov test pilot Alois Jezek, achieved a world record by attaining 143.4mph over a 62.14-mile (100km) closed circuit while carrying a 1,000kg (2,204lb) payload. 16 S-16Ts went to Turkey in 1929. Like the prototype, they were powered by Lorraine Dietrich engines. Meanwhile, the Czech

Army Air Force had already placed an initial order to equip its light bomber-reconnaissance units. Total production for Czechoslovakia was 115 aircraft, most of which were powered by Lorraine-Dietrich engines. One Czech S-16 was flown by Lt-Col Skála, with Taufer his mechanic, to Tokyo in 1927 via Moscow, Siberia and Manchuria. Yugoslavia bought the S-16J, a 600hp Hispano-Suiza-powered twin-float version. A number of variants of the S-16 were also built, most varying only in the power plant utilised. The highest powered version was the S-516, which had an 800hp Isotta-Fraschini 'Asso' water-cooled engine installed. The S-16 remained in first-line service for a decade from 1928. It proved robust and was popular with both air and ground crews, as well as with the Czech public to whom it became a familiar sight during routine flights and at air displays. It typified the rugged, commonsense reliability of the Czech engineering and aviation industries between the two world wars. Armament comprised a fixed forward-firing Vickers 7.62mm machine gun plus twin Lewis guns on a ring mounting operated by the observer. Over short ranges bomb load could be increased from the normal 661lb to 1,320lb.

Letov S-328 and S-528

Czechoslovakia

Purpose: General purpose
Makers: Letóv Vojenska tovarna ná letadla
In service: 1934-44
Photo: S-328 prototype
Data: S-328

Engine: See below
Span: 44ft 11.75in
Length: 33ft 11.75in
Height: 10ft 11in
Weight loaded: 5,820lb
Crew: Two
Max speed: 174mph at 5,905ft
Service ceiling: 23,622ft
Range: 435 miles
Armament: Two fixed forward-firing 7.92mm Zbrojovka (upper wing) machine guns plus twin weapons of the same type on Skoda mounting (observer). Normally 772lb of bombs

Three S-328s achieved fame flying with Slovak insurgents against the occupying Germans in

August-October 1944, operating out of Tri Duby airfield. The 463 S-328s built between 1934 and 1940 had placed the type second only to the Avia B-534 fighter in terms of numbers during the lifetime of the interwar Czechoslovak Republic. In these circumstances it is remarkable that the prototype S-328F, which flew on 19 June 1933, was designed to a Finnish requirement! The Czech Government came to the aid of the firm when the Finns cancelled the order, by ordering 61 machines in 1934. These initial aircraft went to the 6th Air Regiment at Prague, flying in the reconnaissance/light bomber role. With subsequent deliveries, the S-328 became the unspectacular Czech workhorse for five years. One vice was, however, never wholly overcome: its tendency to get into an uncontrollable spin. The S-328 itself was an open-cockpit single-bay biplane, with slim, tapered-tip, staggered wings and had a robust wide-track divided undercarriage. The circular-section all-metal fuselage structure was fabric covered, except for light alloy panelling

forward. Standard equipment included R/T and a camera, either hand-operated or automatic. The S-328 had a Walter-built Bristol Pegasus II radial engine with a Townend ring, but six S-528s built for the Czech Frontier Guard (MVP) had 800hp Gnome-Rhône Mistral Major radials in long-chord cowlings. Four twin-float S-328V target tugs and 13 S-328N

night fighters (with two additional fixed machine guns) were also built. A number of captured S-328s were pressed into Luftwaffe service for training and target-towing. The puppet Slovak regime acquired others and 62 examples were handed over to Bulgaria, which operated some on Black Sea coastal patrols.

Lioré et Olivier 20   France

Purpose: Heavy bomber
Makers: Société anonyme des Etablissements Lioré et Olivier
In service: 1927-36

Engines: See below
Span: 73ft 0in
Length: 45ft 2in
Height: 16ft 6.75in
Weight loaded: 12,037lb
Crew: Four
Max speed: 123mph at sea level
Service ceiling: 18,865ft
Range: 621 miles
Armament: Twin 7.62mm machine guns in nose and dorsal cockpits and a single 7.62mm machine gun in a ventral turret. Bomb load 1,102lb

Developed via the LéO 12 and LéO 122, the Lioré et Olivier 20 Bn3 constituted the French night bomber

force from 1927 to 1936, when it was replaced by the Bloch MB200. It had equal-span three-bay wings with square-cut tips. A large single fin was fitted with a balanced rudder. The main undercarriage units had large 'trouser'-type fairings. Power was provided by twin uncowled 420hp Gnome-Rhône Jupiter 9Ady radial engines. The LéO 20 emerged first in a series of tests in the 1926 French Air Ministry heavy bomber competition, the prototype establishing a world distance record with a payload of 4,409lb (2,000kg) on 16 September, covering some 1,130 miles in 9hr 30min flying time. The first series of 50 aircraft was ordered at the end of 1926 and the 311th machine was delivered to the Armée de l'Air in December 1932. These were allocated initially to the 12 night bomber escadrilles of the 21e and 22e Regiments d'Aviation at Nancy and Chartres respectively. Six aircraft of the 22e RA began a long-distance formation flight on 11 June 1931 which eventually took in Milan, Zagreb,

Belgrade and Bucharest, making the return flight in one day on 22 June, covering a distance of some 870 miles with refuelling stops at Zagreb and Milan. Six escadrilles of the 12ᵉ RA at Reims were next to receive the LéO 20 Bn3 (three-seat night bomber), while the strategic reconnaissance escadrille attached to the 34ᵉ RA at Le Bourget was re-equipped with the LéO 20 RN4, a night reconnaissance version fitted with radio-goniometer and additional fuel tanks. In fact the night bomber version was normally flown as a four or even five-seater with the pilot and co-pilot seated in open side-by-side cockpits in front of the wings, the bomb aimer in a glazed 'balcony' position in the extreme nose and the gunner in an open cockpit immediately behind. The dorsal gunner had an open cockpit, but the ventral gunner was accommodated in a retractable 'dustbin'. Nine LéO 20s were also exported, seven to Romania and two to Brazil. At the outbreak of World War 2, 79 LéO 20s were still in flying condition, serving as crew trainers and as target-tugs.

Lioré et Olivier 25 Series

France

Purpose: Bomber-reconnaissance
Makers: Societé anonyme des Établissements Lioré-et-Olivier
In service: From 1932
Data: LéO H-257*bis*

Engines: See below
Span: 83ft 7.8in
Length: 57ft 6.75in
Height: 22ft 3.7in
Weight loaded: 20,679lb
Crew: Four
Max speed: 155.3mph
Service ceiling: 26,247ft
Range: 1,243 miles
Armament: Four 7.62mm Lewis machine guns (later 7.5mm Darne) on flexible mountings under nose cupola, in open dorsal cockpit and in retractable ventral 'dustbin'. One 1,477lb torpedo or up to 1,323lb of bombs

The original LéO 25 Bn4 was intended as a successor to the LéO 20. It had more powerful Hispano-Suiza liquid-cooled engines driving four-bladed propellers but showed only slight improvement in performance. The prototype, registered S-362, flew in May 1928. Modified with frontal radiators for its 575hp Mbr engines (in place of radiators carried above the engines) and with a rudder of revised outline, it became the LéO 252.01, which was converted to a seaplane with twin floats and tested by the French Navy at St Raphaël in 1931. The LéO 25 No 2 was a landplane bomber bought by Romania and three LéO 253 landplanes, differing only in detail, were sold to Brazil. Two LéO H-254 seaplanes flew in 1932. Each had open pilot's and gunners' cockpits and were intended for coastal bombing, maritime reconnaissance and torpedo-dropping duties. The single H-255 had new engines and was tested on wheel and float undercarriages, the latter with simplified strut-bracing. Flying the H-255 on 26 January 1936 pilot Bourdin reached an altitude of 31,273ft with a 1,102lb payload, establishing a new world seaplane record. The LéO H-256 was developed in parallel, having increased wing area, and the LéO H-257 was tested on the Seine in March 1933. The latter aircraft featured an enclosed pilot's cabin designed by LéO engineer Verrisse. The French Aéronavale ordered 60 LéO H-257*bis* aircraft powered by 870hp Gnome-Rhône 14Kfrs radial engines and with the bow gunner's position housed in a glazed cupola. Unfortunately, problems with the engines led to delays and the LéO 258 was ordered to fill the gap. The latter had the lower-powered Hispano-Suiza engines of the H-256 fitted, but otherwise closely resembled the LéO H-257*bis*, although with poorer performance, particularly at altitude. Twenty-six LéO 258s were delivered from June 1935, initially equipping Escadrilles 3B1 and 3B2 at Berre. A year later the LéO H-257*bis* machines started to arrive, equipping Escadrilles B1, B2, B3, E7, 3S4. Others of the same type, with land undercarriages, went to equip Armée de l'Air Groupe GB II/25 in North Africa. The LéO seaplanes carried out Mediterranean neutrality patrols during the Spanish Civil War and a number were still in service during the first year of World War 2. They operated over the Mediterranean, the Channel and the French Atlantic coast. Flung into action against the German Blitzkrieg in May/June 1940, they suffered heavy losses. The last flight was by a LéO H-257*bis* stationed in French North Africa towards the end of 1944.

Loire 46   France

Purpose: Fighter
Makers: Ateliers et Chantiers de la Loire
In service: 1936-39

Engine: One 850hp Gnome-Rhône 14Kfs radial
Span: 38ft 8.5in
Length: 25ft 5.5in
Height: 13ft 6.5in
Weight loaded: 4,630lb
Crew: One
Max speed: 228.67mph at 19,685ft
Service ceiling: 38,550ft
Range: 466 miles
Armament: Four fixed forward-firing 7.5mm MAC 1934 machine guns in the wings

Developed from the inline-engined Loire 43 and the radial-engined Loire 45, the Loire 46 prototype was clearly inspired by the success of the Polish PZL gull-winged fighters. The fuselage was of round section and the fixed, divided undercarriage had wheel spats. The horizontal tailplane was strut-braced to the tail fin. The gull wing, considerably modified from that of the Loire 45, gave generally good visibility, although

there were some inevitable blindspots. R/T was fitted. The prototype first flew on 1 September 1934. After some development problems and structural strengthening, 60 series machines were ordered for the Armée de l'Air. The first of them were delivered in the summer of 1936, 22 reaching operational units by the end of the year and the balance of the order being delivered by July 1937. As an undercover operation five Loire 46s from the Armée de l'Air were ferried to Spain in September 1936 and placed at the disposal of the Republican forces in the Civil War. Two machines were shot down and two others lost through failure of the 14K engine. Pilots found the type rather heavy, but nevertheless manoeuvrable. It climbed well, but was hypersensitive to the controls. Its main problem, however, was undoubtedly the unreliability of the Gnome-Rhône engine. After serving in France until 1939 with four fighter escadrilles of the 6 Escadre (comprising Groupes GC I/6 and II/6), stationed at Chartres and Reims respectively, surviving Loire 46s were passed to the École de Tir (Air Gunnery School) at Cazaux near Bordeaux, where they flew until the French collapse in June 1940.

Loire-Gourdou-Leseurre 32C1   France

Purpose: Fighter
Makers: Sociefe anonyme des Ateliers et Chantiers de la Loire/Société anonyme des Établissements Gourdou-Leseurre
In service: 1927-34

Engine: See below
Span: 40ft 0.25in
Length: 24ft 9.25in
Height: 9ft 8.25in
Weight loaded: 3,034lb
Crew: One
Max speed: 147.3mph at 9,843ft
Service ceiling: 31,824ft
Range: 410 miles

Armament: Two fixed forward-firing 7.62mm Vickers machine guns

Designed to compete in a French Air Ministry (1924) competition for single-seat fighters powered by engines in the 400hp range, the LGL-32 was selected with the Wibault 7 for series production in preference to a number of biplane designs. Both types chosen were parasol-wing monoplanes. The rounded fuselage was built up of dural tubing, with metal sheet covering at the front and fabric covering at the rear. The wing was of mixed construction without any sweepback and had square-cut tips. It was supported by a pair of parallel struts either side. The large fin and rudder assembly had a curved leading edge. Originally the undercarriage was of a simple narrow-track axle type but later aircraft had improved divided main legs. Powerplant was an uncowled Gnome-Rhône Jupiter 9Ac radial engine of 420hp. Prototype tests indicated an excellent rate of climb and manoeuvrability and the first series of 16 machines was ordered in September 1925. Production finally totalled some 460 machines, most built by the Loire company. Over 380 aircraft were delivered to the French Aéronautique Militaire, 15 went to the French Navy and 63 were exported, including 50 for Romania, 12 for Turkey and a single example for Japan. The LGL-32C1s went into French service in late 1927. They equipped four Escadrilles of the 3e Regiment d'Aviation de Chasse at Chateauroux, the 6e Escadrille of the 32^e RA at Dijon, three Escadrilles of the 35^e RA at Lyons, four Escadrilles of the 38^e RA at Thionville, the 1^e and

2 GALD (Light Defensive Aviation Groups) at Sidi-Ahmed in Tunisia; the Cercle de Chasse (Voluntary Reserve Fighter Unit) at Le Bourget and Escadrilles 3C1 and 3C2 of the French Navy. The French fighters made numerous publicity formation flights over the home country until they were relegated to training duties in 1934. About a dozen of them were sold to the Spanish Republican Government in 1936 and a further 12 or 13 went to the Basques in the north of Spain. These were apparently newly-built and had modern divided undercarriages with Messier shock-absorbers. Armed with bombs they were instrumental in sinking the Nationalist battleship *Esparta* in 1937. The unique LGL-633 was a strengthened dive bomber development with rounded wingtips. It too found its way to the fighting in the Basque Provinces and later in Catalonia.

Martin B-10 and B-12   USA

Purpose: Bomber
Makers: Glenn L. Martin Company
In service: From 1934
Photo and Data: B-10B

Engines: Two 700hp Wright R-1820-33 Cyclone radials
Span: 70ft 6in
Length: 44ft 8.75in
Height: 15ft 5in
Weight loaded: 14,995-16,450lb
Crew: Four
Max speed: 213mph
Service ceiling: 24,300ft
Range: 590-1,240 miles
Armament: Three .30in Browning machine guns in nose, dorsal and ventral positions. Over 2,200lb of bombs

The Martin B-10 was a mid-way development between the old and extremely slow MB-2 bomber and the wartime B-26 Marauder, although it was much closer to the latter in terms of configuration. Its

place in the annals of the US forces was secured when it became the first American all-metal bomber to go into quantity production, the first to be fitted with a gun turret (a feature found on a British bomber as far back as 1934) and the first standard cantilever low wing monoplane bomber of the USAAC. Its rival for production contracts had been the Boeing B-9, itself a revolutionary aircraft that had, in turn, effectively stopped the Army ordering more than eight Douglas YB-7 bombers, which were officially the first monoplane bombers built for the USAAC and appeared to offer great advantages over the Keystone biplanes of the 1920s. Compared with the Boeing B-9, the Martin bomber was considerably faster — in fact also faster than the Army's Boeing P-12 or Curtiss P-6 Hawk single-seat fighters then in service. The design allowed the crew to be accommodated in open cockpits initially — situated at the nose of the fuselage, just forward of the wing leading-edge (pilot, and with compartment inside the fuselage for the wireless operator), and in the rear fuselage — but these were later changed to fully enclosed cockpits. The bomb aimer had control over the doors of the internal weapons bay, although this could be controlled by the pilot in an emergency situation, while auxiliary flight controls were mounted in the rear cockpit together with movable dorsal and ventral guns. The prototype first flew in early 1932, powered by 600hp Wright Cyclone radial engines. It was subsequently fitted with 675hp Cyclones and taken on charge by the Army as the XB-10. An order for evaluation and full production aircraft was placed in 1933, the first being delivered in the follcwing year. Aircraft from this batch comprised 700hp Wright-engined YB-10s, 700hp Pratt & Whitney Hornet-engined YB-12s and Hornet-engined B-12As, totalling 46 bombers. A number of these were subsequently fitted with huge twin floats for coastal defence duties. Production of the type for the US Army Air Corps ended in 1936 after more than 100 B-10Bs had been built, and these served in the USA and at other US bases. Interestingly, the bomber was even more successful as an export type. Production for export totalled nearly 190 aircraft, the majority of which went to the Netherlands East Indies Army Air Service but significant small numbers also went to China, Siam (joining Avro 504s, Curtiss Hawks and Vought Corsairs) and Turkey.

Martin MB-1, MB-2/NBS-1 USA

Purpose: Bomber/Torpedo bomber
Makers: Glenn L. Martin Company
In service: 1920-28
Photo: MB-2
Data: NBS-1

Engines: Two 420hp Liberty 12A engines
Span: 74ft 2in
Length: 42ft 8in
Height: 14ft 8in
Weight loaded: about 12,100lb
Crew: Four

Max speed: 99mph
Range: 560 miles
Armament: Five .30in machine guns, two in open nose, two in open dorsal and one in ventral position. 2,000lb of bombs, carried internally or externally

The MB-1 and -2 biplane bombers were basically similar, and were among the first combat aircraft of home design to be operated by the US forces post-war. Neither version was ever used in combat and the MB-2 is only really remembered as the first US aircraft to sink a capital warship by bombing. The

ship was the ex-German *Ostfriesland* and was used as a stationary target by the famous Brigadier-General William Mitchell on 21 July 1921 to prove that the aeroplane was the offensive weapon of the future and should be given a greater share of the dwindling military expenditure. This point was further enforced by other bombers and flying-boats on the same occasion, which sunk a submarine, a cruiser and a destroyer. Despite these demonstrations, and others carried out in 1923 against surplus American warships, bombers were still given low priority compared with traditional naval vessels. As for Mitchell, he was later court martialled and died before his beliefs proved correct in the air offensives of World War 2.

The MB-1 made its first flight on 15 August 1918 as the American answer to the British Handley Page O/400, but US officials proved reluctant to put money into an untried home-designed bomber. Only a handful were built for the US Army Air Service as bombers, reconnaissance and transport aircraft, in each case powered by two 400hp Liberty engines; and it may have been significant that the first of these production aircraft to fly was one of the reconnaissance variants. Two others were built as

MTB-1 torpedo bombers for the USMC and four more MB-1s became government mailplanes. Interestingly, the original MB-1 was sometimes referred to as the WF Night Bomber or 'Seven Ton' bomber, while one MB-1 became a prototype commercial type (sometimes named the WF Commercial, MB-1 Commercial or T-1). No American bombers were built during 1919 and it was not until 1920 that renewed interest was shown in an improved development of the MB-1 known as the MB-2. This had larger equal-span wings than the earlier model, a divided undercarriage with a single wheel under each nacelle (instead of the four-wheel undercarriage of the MB-1), modified twin tail unit, and 420hp Liberty engines. A total of 130 MB-2s was eventually produced by Martin, Curtiss, Lowe-Willard-Fowler and Aeromarine, more than half as short-range night bombers or NBS-1s. These remained in service until the late 1920s. In fact, Martin bombers, followed by Keystone bombers, were the mainstay of the US Army Air Service/Corps during most of the interwar period, before giving way to more modern monoplane designs of which the Army had an abundance of prototypes in the early 1930s (see Martin B-10).

Martin T3M/T4M and Great Lakes TG   USA

Purpose: Torpedo bomber
Makers: Glenn L. Martin Company
In service: 1926-37
Photo: T4M-1
Data: T3M-2

Engine: See below
Span: 56ft 7in
Length: 41ft 4in
Height: 15ft 11in
Weight loaded: 9,500lb
Crew: Three
Max speed: 109mph
Service ceiling: about 8,000ft
Range: 366-755 miles
Armament: One .30in machine gun in rear cockpit. One 18in torpedo or bombs

During 1926, Martin built 24 T3M-1s for the US Navy as combined bombers, torpedo-bombers and long-range scouting aircraft. They were a development of the SC-1 and SC-2 types, designed by Curtiss and delivered during 1925. The main differences between the types were the rearrangement of the crew accommodation — the pilot and navigator/bomber sat together in a large cockpit forward of the wings and the rear gunner had a separate cockpit which was slightly restricted by being too near the wing trailing-edge — use of an all-welded metal structure fuselage instead of the welded and riveted fuselage of the SC, a new split-type undercarriage sprung by rubber chord and a 575hp Wright T3B engine. The rear gunner actually had an upper gun on a rotatable ring mounting and a ventral gun. T3M-1s were followed into production

by 100 T3M-2s, ordered in March 1927 and powered by 730hp Packard 3A-2500 engines. The configuration of this version differed mainly in having equal-span wings (still of mahogany ply and spruce, fabric covered), a new undercarriage with oleo-pneumatic suspension and tandem cockpits for the crew. Deliveries began later that year and the type served initially on board the new second-generation aircraft carrier USS *Lexington* as well as the first US carrier *Langley*. Reports of the time suggest that the T3M-2 was capable of 121mph, but this is believed to apply to the prototype which differed from production aircraft in several minor ways. One month after the T3M-2s had been ordered, the prototype of the T4M-1 appeared, with a 525hp Pratt & Whitney Hornet radial engine, 3ft 7in shorter span wings (of metal construction, fabric covered), and a balanced

rudder. Just over 100 T4M-1s were built, first going to the carriers *Lexington* and the new acquisition the USS *Saratoga*. Most T4M-1s were operated as landplanes but, like the earlier versions, could be fitted with twin duralumin long single-step floats. Again the crew sat in tandem, with the front cockpit occupied by the bomber, while the rear gunner had a modified cockpit with a small windscreen. Despite the smaller engine, the T4M-1 had a maximum speed of 116mph. T4M-1s were followed by 40 generally similar but improved TG-1s and TG-2s built by the Great Lakes Aircraft Corporation. These last two models were powered by 550hp Pratt & Whitney R-1690-28 Hornet and 575hp Wright R-1820-86 Cyclone engines respectively, and were the last of the type to be produced.

Messerschmitt Bf109 Germany

Purpose: Fighter/Fighter-bomber
Makers: Bayerische Flugzeugwerke AG/Messerschmitt AG
In service: From 1937
Photo: Swiss Bf109E
Data: Bf109E-1

Engine: One 1,100hp Daimler-Benz
Span: 32ft 4.5in
Length: 28ft 4.25in
Height: 8ft 2.25in
Weight loaded: 5,520lb
Crew: One
Max speed: 342mph at 13,125ft
Service ceiling: 34,500ft
Range: 410 miles
Armament: Four 7.9mm MG17 machine guns in early production aircraft. One 550lb or four 110lb bombs as fighter-bomber

A thoroughbred aircraft in the same class as its rival, the Spitfire, the Bf109 was the main German fighter of the late 1930s. Although it is usually designated with the Bf prefix, it is interesting to note that even among Luftwaffe officials it was often designated

Me109. Its development started in 1933, when the RLM placed a contract with the Bayerische Flugzeugwerke AG (BFW) for the development of a new fighter. The first prototype Bf109V1 flew in September 1935, powered by a 695hp Rolls-Royce Kestrel V engine and embodying many features of the Bf108 two-seat low-wing cabin monoplane with retractable undercarriage, built for the 1934 Challenge de Tourisme Internationale. Following flight trials, a further 10 pre-production aircraft were ordered. The intended power plant for the Bf109V1 had been the 610hp Junkers Jumo 210A, but this was not available at that time. The subsequent prototypes were, however, powered by Jumo engines. During February and March 1937, three of them were evaluated in Spain. Others won a number of victories in the military aircraft competitions at Zurich; and on 11 November, a Bf109, with a boosted DB601 engine of 1,650hp set up a new landplane speed record of 379.4mph. Earlier, in the spring of 1937, a number of Bf109B-1s, with 635hp Jumo 2100 engines, had entered Luftwaffe service. Although only a smaller number of this version was built some became operational in Spain. They were joined in 1937 by an initial batch of Bf109B-2s, serving

with the Condor Legion. In turn, Bf109B-2s were followed to Spain in 1938 by Bf109Cs, so that there was a total of over 50 Bf109B-1s, B-2s and C-1s serving in Spain by July 1938. It was also in 1938 that the Bayerische Flugzeugwerke AG was transformed into Messerschmitt AG. Experience gained in Spain led to further changes, particularly in armament; and after the 910hp DB600-engined Bf109D series of aircraft had been in production for a short time, they were superseded by the Bf109E, which entered Luftwaffe service in February 1939. By the outbreak of World War 2, the Luftwaffe had nearly 1,060 Bf109s on strength. Bf109s were also acquired before the war by other countries, including Spain, Hungary and Switzerland.

Mitsubishi B1M Japan

Purpose: Carrier-borne torpedo bomber
Makers: Mitsubishi Nainenki Kaisha (Mitsubishi Internal Combustion Engine Co Ltd)
In service: 1924-38
Photo: 2MT5

Engine: See below
Span: 48ft 5in
Length: 32ft 1in
Height: 11ft 6.6in
Weight loaded: 5,948lb
Crew: Two/Three
Max speed: 130mph
Service ceiling: 14,764ft
Armament: Three 7.7mm machine guns. One torpedo or two 529lb bombs

The Mitsubishi company employed British designer Herbert Smith to design a series of aircraft to meet Japanese Navy and Army requirements. Most successful of these was the 2MT1, the prototype of which was completed in January 1923. A three-bay two-seat biplane, it was placed in quantity production for the Japanese Navy under the designation Type 13 carrier-borne attack aircraft. Later versions were the 2MT2 and 2MT3. Considerable redesign resulted in the Type 13-2(B1M2) or 2MT4 and 2MT5. Final variant was the Type 13-3 (B1M3) three-seater with the firm's designation 3MT2, 88 of which were produced by Mitsubishi in 1930. 197 B1M1s and 117 B1M2s were built respectively. The Hiro Navy arsenal completed an additional 40 B1M3s. The B1M was of wooden construction with fabric covering. It was powered by a 450hp Napier Lion engine in its early B1M1 version, while the B1M2 and B1M3 versions had 450hp Hispano-Suiza engines.

The conflict known as the Shanghai Incident, which broke out in January 1932, resulted in the Japanese aircraft carriers *Kaga* and *Hosho* being despatched to Chinese waters. The 1st Air Wing aircraft deployed included 32 Type 13 attack aircraft from *Kaga* and nine from *Hosho*. From the beginning of February daily attacks were made on Chinese military installations in and around Shanghai, but chief activity was co-operation with ground forces. On 5 February two Type 13s, escorted by three Type 3 carrier fighters, were engaged in air combat with Chinese Corsair biplanes. On 22 February three Type 13s with fighter escort, on a mission from *Kaga*, were attacked by the American volunteer pilot Robert Short flying a Boeing P-12. The escort commander Lt Ikuta in a Type 3 fighter shot down Short, but one of the Type 13s had already been downed by the American with the loss of Lt Susumi Kotani, the formation commander. When the 1932 Type 92 (B3Y1) attack bomber proved a disastrous failure, a number of B1M3s were retained in service, although hopelessly obsolescent, and remained into the mid-1930s.

Mitsubishi B2M1-2   Japan

Purpose: Carrier-borne torpedo bomber
Makers: Mitsubishi Nainenki Kaisha (Mitsubishi Internal Combustion Engine Co Ltd)
In service: 1932-36
Data: B2M1

Engine: See below
Span: 49ft 11in
Length: 33ft 8in
Height: 12ft 2in
Weight loaded: 7,940lb
Crew: Three
Max speed: 131.75mph
Service ceiling: 14,305ft
Armament: Two 7.62mm machine guns. One torpedo or 1,764lb of bombs

When the Japanese Navy issued a requirement for a new torpedo bomber in February 1928, Mitsubishi was determined to win the production contract. The company management decided that Japanese design talent was not yet able to guarantee success and consequently approached several British companies for designs. They ultimately chose the aircraft of G. E. Petty, chief designer of the Blackburn firm. The first 3MR4 prototype was built in Britain. Three subsequent prototypes were built at Mitsubishi's factory under Petty's personal supervision. Development was difficult and prolonged and the type was not adopted until March 1932 under the designation B2M1 or Navy Type 89-1. Powered by a 650hp Hispano-Suiza liquid-cooled inline engine, the B2M1 showed considerable innovation, being constructed largely of metal. An equal-span two-bay biplane, it had square wing tips, but rounded tail surfaces. Its divided undercarriage was of wide track and extremely robust, showing much improvement over that of the B1M. In 1934 the B2M2 appeared, a much modified development which featured an entirely new angular fin and rudder assembly. Production of both versions totalled 200 aircraft in addition to prototypes. Series production lasted from 1931 to 1935 and some machines saw service during the Shanghai Incident, flying medium-level bombing missions as well as supporting ground troops with lower-level raids near the front line.

Mitsubishi 1MF   Japan

Purpose: Carrier-borne fighter
Makers: Mitsubishi Nainenki Kaisha (Mitsubishi Internal Combustion Engine Co Ltd)
In service: 1923-29
Data: 1MF3B

Engine: See below
Span: 29ft 0in
Length: 22ft 6.9in
Height: 9ft 10in
Weight loaded: 2,502lb
Crew: One

Max speed: 139.8mph
Service ceiling: 20,013ft
Armament: Two fixed forward-firing 7.7mm machine guns

Designed by Herbert Smith, formerly of the British Sopwith Company, this small and nimble single-seat single-bay biplane was accepted for service by the Imperial Navy in 1921 as the Type 10 Carrier Fighter (the figure 10 standing for the tenth year of the reign of the Emperor Taisho). In February 1923 it was a Type 10-2 which made the first successful take-off

by a Japanese-built aircraft from Japan's first aircraft carrier, the *Hosho*. Production terminated in 1928 with the 138th machine. The type 10-1 had a frontal radiator for its 300hp Hispano-Suiza V8 engine, while the Type 10-2 had twin Lamblin radiators fixed side-by-side between the undercarriage legs. The Type 10-2 bore the company designation 1MF3, the designation 1MF2 having been applied to a variant with modified ailerons on the upper wing. The 1MF4 had revised equipment and the pilot's cockpit set further forward along the fuselage, while the 1MF5 had a redesigned tail assembly of better aerodynamic contours. It was on the Type 10 Carrier Fighter that many of the fighter unit leaders in the Japanese Navy that fought during World War 2 learned their craft.

Mitsubishi 2MR

Japan

Purpose: Carrier-borne reconnaissance
Makers: Mitsubishi Nainenki Kaisha (Mitsubishi Internal Combustion Engine Co Ltd)
In service: 1923-30

Engine: See below
Span: 39ft 6in
Length: 26ft 1in
Height: 9ft 6in
Weight loaded: 2,910lb
Crew: Two
Max speed: 126.7mph
Armament: Two 7.7mm machine guns. Up to 198lb of bombs

Another successful design by Herbert Smith, formerly of Sopwith but working under contract to the Mitsubishi company, the prototype 2MR1 was completed on 12 January 1921. It was intended to operate as a reconnaissance aircraft from the first Japanese aircraft carrier *Hosho*, commissioned on 27 December 1922. Going into service in 1923 as the Type 10 Carrier Reconnaissance Aircraft, 159 of the type were eventually built up to 1930. A two-bay equal-span biplane, it was powered by a 300hp Hispano-Suiza water-cooled engine. The original 2MR1 had a frontal radiator but many variants were completed, differing either in shape of the fin and rudder or in the type of radiator. A powerful armament included twin cowling 7.7mm machine guns and twin guns of the same calibre on a ring mounting over the observer's cockpit. Three 66lb bombs could be carried. Its robust design kept many of the type flying through the 1930s, either civilianised or as Navy trainers.

Mitsubishi Ki-2   Japan

Purpose: Light bomber
Makers: Mitsubishi Jukogyo (Mitsubishi Heavy Industries Ltd)
In service: 1934-41
Data: Ki-2-II

Engines: See below
Span: 65ft 5.8in
Length: 41ft 8in
Height: 15ft 2.5in
Weight loaded: 10,362lb
Crew: Four
Max speed: 175.8mph
Service ceiling: 22,966ft
Normal range: 560 miles
Armament: Two 7.7mm machine guns plus 1,102lb of bombs

The Ki-2 was a most successful design, although built in relatively small numbers by Japanese standards of the '30s. It was developed from the Junkers K-37, an example of which had been imported from Germany in 1931 and donated by collections from Japanese citizens to the Imperial Army. In fact it bore the distinction of being named 'Aikoku 1', first of many such patriotic gifts, sparked off by the Army's involvement in Manchuria against the Chinese. The Ki-2 prototype flew for the first time in the spring of 1933. A cantilever low-wing monoplane powered by twin 570hp Nakajima Kotobuki radial engines with Townend rings, it was distinguishable by its corrugated alloy decking and twin fins and rudders. The fixed divided undercarriage had wheel fairings which in practice were often discarded. Nose and dorsal gunners' cockpits had built-up glazed sections and the open pilot's cockpit had a faired headrest. Maximum speed was 139.8mph. The Ki-2-I received the Army designation Type 93 Twin Engined Light Bomber and saw action in China from the early part of the Sino-Japanese 'Incident' in July 1937. It was joined by the Ki-2-II or Type 93 Model 2, which had two 750hp Ha-8 radials with long-chord cowlings, an enclosed manually operated nose gun turret, a glazed canopy over the pilot's cockpit and main undercarriage legs which retracted into the engine nacelles. Maximum speed was improved by 36mph. Normal bomb load for both versions was 661lb, which could be increased to 1,102lb over short ranges. 113 Model 1s and 61 Model 2s were built. A number survived in the training role until 1941. A civilianised version of the Ki-2-II named 'Otori' (Phoenix), registered J-BAAE, made international news when it left Tatchikawa military airfield on 5 December 1936, flying to Bangkok via Taipei (Taiwan), a distance of 3,063 miles covered in a flying time of 21hr 36min.

Nakajima Type 91   Japan

Purpose: Fighter
Makers: Nakajima Hikoki KK (Nakajima Aircraft Co Ltd)
In service: 1932-36

Engine: See below
Span: 36ft 1in
Length: 22ft 11.5in
Height: 9ft 2.9in
Weight loaded: 3,307lb
Crew: One
Max speed: 186.4mph
Service ceiling: 29,528ft
Normal range: 311 miles

Armament: Two fixed forward-firing 7.7mm machine guns

Three major Japanese aircraft manufacturers — Kawasaki, Mitsubishi and Nakajima — submitted prototypes to meet a Japanese Army requirement of 1927 for a new single-seat fighter. All were parasol-wing monoplanes designed in Japan by engineering teams either wholly or partly led by European engineers. During tests in June 1928 the Mitsubishi prototype, the Hayabusa (Falcon), broke up in a dive. As a result Army examiners insisted on putting the two surviving aircraft through extensive ground loading tests. Both proved insufficiently stressed and all three contenders were eliminated from the competition. Nakajima's prototype, bearing company designation NC, had a slim monocoque fuselage, an uncowled Jupiter radial engine and elaborate strut bracing connecting the wings to the fuselage and to the wide-track axle-type undercarriage. Nakajima persevered with the design and six consecutive development prototypes were built. The last was extensively tested by the Army and was found to be rugged and manoeuvrable, with an excellent rate of climb, reaching 9,800ft in four minutes. It was accepted for production as the Army Type 91 Fighter. It incorporated a new wing with rounded tips, an advanced elliptical cantilever horizontal tailplane and a fin and rudder assembly with rounded contours. Wing bracing was simplified, with a pair of parallel struts either side. The divided undercarriage was of new design. The engine was a 450hp

Nakajima-built Bristol Jupiter enclosed in a Townend ring. The two-bladed propeller had a pointed spinner. Production of the Type 91 lasted into 1934 and terminated with the 450th machine (including prototypes). Twenty-two were Model 2s with modified engine cowls. Type 91s, intended primarily to operate as air superiority fighters, were introduced into the Army fighter squadrons from 1932, replacing Nieuport-Delage 29C1 biplanes, built under licence with the designation Ko-4 by Nakajima. They were first deployed in action with the four squadrons of the 11th Air Battalion operating with the Army Kanto Command in conflict with the Chinese in Manchuria, which terminated in complete occupation of the province by the Japanese in 1933. By then the Type 91 was the principal Army fighter and formed standard equipment for the newly-formed Air Wings (Hiko Rentai).

Nakajima A2N   Japan

Purpose: Carrier-borne fighter
Makers: Nakajima Hikoki KK (Nakajima Aircraft Co Ltd)
In service: 1931-38
Photo: A2N1

Engine: See below
Span: 30ft 8.9in
Length: 20ft 3.4in
Height: 9ft 11in
Weight loaded: 3,417lb
Crew: One
Max speed: 182.2mph
Service ceiling: 29,528ft
Normal range: 311 miles
Armament: Two fixed forward-firing 7.7mm Vickers machine guns

The A2N series of carrier fighters were developed from the Navy Type 3 Carrier Fighter, the Nakajima-built version of the British Gloster Gambet. The prototype, company designation NY, first flew in 1930. A small unequal span single-bay biplane, it had stylishly tapered wings with elliptical tips and considerable stagger. Ailerons were fitted on upper and lower wings, which were braced either side by a pair of N-struts. Tail surfaces were angular in form, the horizontal tailplane being braced either side by a single strut. The wheels of the divided undercarriage were provided with 'spat' type fairings, which appear to have been discarded after the initial series of production machines. Power was provided by a 500hp Nakajima Kotobuki radial, developed from the Bristol Jupiter VI, with a Townend cowling ring. The NY was accepted for service at the end of 1930 as the Navy Type 90 Carrier Fighter. The A2N1 and

A2N2 versions had dihedral on the lower wings only, whereas the A2N3 had dihedral on both wings. Standard armament was two 7.7mm Vickers machine guns, but on the A2N1 these were installed in blast troughs on the lower side of the forward fuselage, while in the later versions they were fixed just beneath the upper fuselage decking in front of the pilot. Production lasted until 1935 and totalled 106. Subsequently, 66 of a two-seat advanced trainer version, the A3N1, appeared. It seems likely that most, if not all, of the latter were conversions of the A2N. They differed solely in having a second open cockpit (with dual controls) immediately behind that of the pilot. Immediately after the outbreak of war between Japan and China on 7 July 1937 (having flown in the 1932 'Incident'), Nakajima A2Ns flew in operations over the Shanghai area, having been embarked from an aircraft carrier, which formed part of the Second Carrier Division of the Imperial Fleet. The little fighter, already popular with its pilots, confirmed its serviceability and agile flight characteristics. Many pilots were reluctant to give it up when required to convert to its successor, the A4N1 (Type 95).

Nakajima A4N1   Japan

Purpose: Carrier-borne fighter
Makers: Nakajima Hikoki KK (Nakajima Aircraft Co Ltd)
In service: 1935-40

Engine: See below
Span: 32ft 9.7in
Length: 21ft 9.4in
Height: 10ft 0.8in
Weight loaded: 3,880lb
Crew: One
Max speed: 218.8mph
Service ceiling: 25,394ft
Normal range: 526 miles
Armament: Two fixed forward-firing 7.7mm machine guns

The A4N1 was essentially a stop-gap fighter. In 1932 a number of the more farsighted Japanese

Navy air officers noted the advanced techniques which were going into monoplane designs abroad, realising also the immediate need for more fighters for the Navy's carrier force and for a replacement for the ageing A2N Type 90. A 7-shi competition for a new fighter had produced two prototypes, both monoplanes — Mitsubishi's 1MF10 was a cantilever low-wing type and Nakajima had submitted a development of the parasol-wing Army Type 91 Fighter. Both demonstrated poor flight characteristics and disappointing performance. In this situation the Navy, influenced partly by their fighter pilots' predilection for the reliable, manoeuvrable biplane, authorised the Nakajima company to develop the A2N design to give improved performance. The resulting A4N1 was accepted for series production by the Navy as the Type 95 Carrier Fighter. 221 were built between 1935 and 1938. With the outbreak of the Sino-

Japanese War, originally known in Japan as the 'China Incident', the Japanese Navy moved carriers to the coast off Shanghai and also established air bases on the mainland. The A4N1, the main Navy fighter in the first year of conflict, was used widely against Chinese aircraft and troops. In addition to its twin 7.7mm synchronised machine gun armament, there was provision for carrying two 66lb bombs on underwing racks for close-support duties. The evidence indicates that a jettisonable streamlined fuel tank could be fitted to the underside of the port wing close to the junction with the fuselage, no doubt to improve the normal rather limited range. Only six of the new Mitsubishi A5M monoplanes had been delivered when war broke out on 7 July 1937. By the end of 1938, however, the A4N1 was on the

way out, two-thirds of the Navy's fighter units being equipped with the Mitsubishi fighter. Like the final production version of the A2N, the A4N1 had dihedral on both wings. A single strut joined the upper and lower ailerons either side. The tailskid was replaced by a tailwheel and the main undercarriage was of axle type, simpler and stronger than that on the A2N. There was no provision for wheel spats. The pilot was provided with a headrest with streamlined fairing. The more powerful 730hp Hikari radial engine required a longer chord cowling than the A2N's 500hp Kotobuki engine. The A4N1 was undoubtedly exceptionally manoeuvrable, but although faster, showed relatively few advances in design compared with its predecessor, introduced into service five years earlier.

Naval Aircraft Factory P Series   USA

Purpose: Patrol flying boat
Makers: Naval Aircraft Factory and others
In service: 1925-37
Photo: Douglas PD-1
Data: PN-12

Engines: Two 525hp Wright R-1750D Cyclone radials
Span: 72ft 11in
Length: 49ft 2in
Height: 16ft 4in
Weight loaded: 14,122lb
Crew: Five
Max speed: 114mph
Service ceiling: 10,900ft
Range: over 1,300 miles

The Naval Aircraft Factory carried out a great deal of experimental work on the development of flying-boats for the US Naval Air Service during the 1920s. In an attempt to improve upon the Felixstowe type F-5L flying-boats of World War 1 vintage then in service, the Factory developed the PN-7. This had a traditional wooden hull but new biplane wings, the lower of which had some dihedral and small floats attached to the outer sections. The twin 575hp Wright Tornado engines, driving two-blade propellers, were enclosed in cigar-shaped fairings and installed between the wings. Only two examples were built, but these began a line of NAF-built PN

flying-boats that ended with the PN-12 after only a very small number had been built as prototypes for testing developments that could be incorporated into mass-produced types. Major changes in design came with the PN-8 and PN-11, which featured a metal hull and a redesigned hull without the usual three-quarter length sponsons respectively. Interestingly, the PN-12 — numerically the last of the series — had a duralumin riveted all-metal two-step Vee section hull similar in shape to that of the F-5L (with six main fuel tanks), and it was with this version that it was decided the aircraft should go into production. As it was not the function of the NAF to produce aircraft in quantity against the established trade, the PN flying boat design was offered to several manufacturers for its ultimate development and production. The Glenn L Martin Company produced 55 as PM-1s and PM-2s, powered by Wright Cyclone radial engines of 525hp and 575hp respectively; the Keystone Aircraft Corporation produced 18 as PK-1s; and the Douglas Aircraft Company produced 25 as PD-1s. Those produced by Douglas were reported to be modifications of the PN-10 and PN-12, weighing 14,880lb and with a maximum speed of 120.8mph, and were delivered to the Navy from 1929. Keystone PK-1s were produced alongside OL-9 amphibians, while the Martin PM-2 had a guaranteed speed of 123mph and range of 1,450 miles (but in fact achieved a lesser speed although still impressive as they weighed

considerably more than the PN-12). One further variant should be mentioned. In 1929 the Hall-Aluminium Aircraft Company produced the PH-1 flying-boat based on the PN-11. The company went on to produce nine production examples with fully-enclosed cockpits and powered by 625hp Wright R-1820E engines (with maximum speeds of 135mph and 129mph respectively as patrol and attack aircraft) and a few PH-2s before the war for the US Coast Guard with 875hp Wright SGR-1820-F51 engines (giving a maximum speed of 150mph). A four-engined derivative of the PH-1 designated Hall XP2H-1 and powered by Curtiss Conqueror engines, remained a prototype only.

Nieuport-Delage 29C1 France

Purpose: Fighter
Makers: Société Anonyme Nieuport-Delage
In service: 1920-31

Engine: See below
Span: 31ft 10in
Length: 21ft 3.5in
Height: 8ft 4.8in
Weight loaded: 2,628lb
Crew: One
Max speed: 140.6mph
Service ceiling: 27,887ft
Range: 360 miles
Armament: Two Vickers 7.62mm (.303in) forward-firing machine guns

Stemming from a September 1918 official requirement, the Nieuport 29 prototype single-bay biplane did not reach the altitude laid down for new French single-seat fighters and so a second prototype with a wider two-bay wing and Lamblin radiators was completed. This did reach the 29,931ft required on 14 June 1919 and was ordered into production as the Ni-D 29C1. It equipped Escadrilles 101, 102 and 103 of the French Aéronautique Militaire in 1920. Over 250 were built for France by Nieuport and seven other contractors. At the peak of their use they equipped 25 Escadrilles. The Ni-D 29V racing variant retained the streamlined monocoque fuselage of the fighter. It won the 1919 Coupe Deutsch competition with an average 165.5mph. Of other Ni-D29Vs built, one, flown by Sadi-Lecointe, won the 1920 Gordon Bennett Cup. The racers had the 300hp Hispano-Suiza 8Fb engine of the fighter boosted to 320hp. The Ni-D29 also formed the main fighter elements of the Belgian and Italian air arms as well as the Imperial Japanese Army air force. Belgium imported 21 in 1922 and built 87 under licence, while the corresponding figures for Italy were six and 175. The Japanese were the greatest users of the type. After importing a single machine, Nakajima built 608 Ni-D29C1s under licence, designated Ko-4s. Japanese Army Ko-4s remained in front line service for a decade from 1923. In September 1931 one squadron from the 6th Army Air Wing was sent to Shenyang to support Japanese ground troops during the Manchuria Incident. Other Ni-D29s followed and served in Manchuria until 1933. With little air opposition they were employed in troop support and ground attack. Spain also operated 30 Ni-D29s (10 built under licence) and Sweden nine. The Ni-D29C1 in French service hit the headlines on 27 May 1927 when Charles Lindbergh, fresh from his Transatlantic triumph, flew one of the type over Paris, engaging in a mock dogfight over Le Bourget airfield. His opponent was Sadi-Lecointe, who had been given official recognition the year before for his achievement in commanding a unit of modified Ni-D29 bombers which had operated successfully against Rif tribesmen in Morocco, each carrying 132lb of bombs. In 1931 surviving Ni-D29s were relegated to a training role, in which they served for a further two years.

Nieuport-Delage 52C1   France

Purpose: Fighter
Makers: Société Anonyme Nieuport-Delage/
Hispano Aviaçion
In service: 1928-38

Engine: See below
Span: 39ft 4.8in
Length: 25ft 0.75in
Height: 9ft 10.1in
Weight loaded: 3,968lb
Crew: One
Max speed: 155.3mph
Service ceiling: 19,685ft
Range: 310 miles
Armament: Two fixed forward-firing 7.62mm
Vickers machine guns

The Ni-D29 biplane had proved its value during
Spain's Moroccan campaign and for a replacement it
was natural to look to the same French firm. The
Ni-D41 sesquiplane was evaluated and
Hispano-Aviaçion obtained the licence to build its
successor the Ni-D52. 34 French machines were
imported and the first Spanish-built aircraft was
tested by Gomez Spencer at Gefate airfield in 1930.
The Ni-D52 was a sesquiplane of all-metal
construction, except for the main wing and movable
control surfaces which were fabric covered. A plane
type fairing over the axle of the undercarriage gave
the Ni-D52 (at some angle of flight) the appearance
of a triplane and it was so nicknamed by several
Spanish pilots! Power was provided by a 580hp

Hispano-Suiza 12Hb inline engine. The Spaniards
were not happy about the twin undercarriage
radiators favoured by the manufacturer and so a
single large radiator under the nose was standard. In
fact, this change seems to have improved general
performance. A Spanish-designed Amadio Diaz twin-
bladed propeller was fitted to the aircraft built at
Hispano's Guadalajara factory, where 91 Ni-D52s
were completed between 1929 and 1936. They
formed the backbone of the Spanish air arm for
seven years and proved manoeuvrable and robust,
but with inadequate speed. By July 1936 only three
home-based fighter groups were still equipped with
the type — the 11th at Getafe, 12th at Granada and
13th at Prat de Llobregt. Each group had two
squadrons with nine machines per squadron. With
the outbreak of the civil war only about a dozen
Ni-D52s fell into Nationalist hands, all the rest flying
with the Republican forces. In the initial stages of the
fighting little use was made of the Ni-D52s, although
two were among four aircraft destroyed by two
Nationalist Heinkel He51s during the Germans' first
day of operations in the civil war on 18 August
1936. By the time they did go into action on a large
scale they were pitted against the far superior Fiat
CR32. After a few months they were relegated either
to coastal patrol duties or for training new young
fliers for the Republic. The Guadalajara workshops
built about 20 more Ni-D52s from available spare
parts. By 1938, however, the type was regarded as
having no further value and all remaining machines
were scrapped.

Nieuport-Delage 62C1

France

Purpose: Fighter
Makers: Société Anonyme Nieuport-Delage
In service: 1926-39
Photo: Ni-D629C1
Data: Ni-D622C1

Engine: See below
Span: 39ft 4.5in
Length: 25.75ft
Height: 9ft 10in
Weight loaded: 4,144lb
Crew: One
Max speed: 168mph
Service ceiling: 26,903ft
Range: 311 miles
Armament: Two fixed forward-firing 7.62mm
machine guns

Although it appeared in 1927, the same year as the Ni-D52, the Nieuport-Delage 62C1 retained the wooden monocoque fuselage of the 1926 Ni-D42 (25 of which served with the French Aéronautique Militaire), while the Ni-D52 was constructed largely of metal. The Nieuport-Delage 62C1 was built in large numbers during the interwar years, 315 examples of the basic version alone appearing between 1928 and 1931. Of these 50 went to the Aéronautique Navale and the balance to military aviation. It differed from earlier Nieuport-Delage designs in having wings of greater chord, but with smaller ailerons, increased vertical tail surface area and was powered by the 500hp Hispano-Suiza 12Hb with twin radiators attached to the forward undercarriage legs. Three specialised trainers were built as Ni-D621s, and three Ni-D62s were

converted to twin-float seaplanes to train French Schneider Trophy contestants. While the original series machines had compared favourably with foreign aircraft when they were first introduced, the basic concept was already outdated when the Ni-D622 development was ordered into production in 1931. The H-S 12Mb engine was supercharged for altitude performance, full-span ailerons were fitted and a metal propeller replaced the two-blade wooden airscrew of the Ni-D62. 322 were built, 62 for the Navy. By 1933 they formed the main strength of French fighter Escadrilles, but their shortcomings became evident to the French people when Ni-D622s were ordered to escort General Balbo's famous Savoia S55 flying boats on the first stage of their formation flight to the United States. Over Strasbourg the tiny French fighters found it impossible to keep pace with the large twin-hulled Italian aircraft. Twelve of the Ni-D626 version were exported to Peru in 1933 and France ordered 50 Ni-D629s, which had 500hp 12Mdsh engines with new Szydlowski-Planiol superchargers, Lamblin radiators and modern Messier-design undercarriages with oleo-pneumatic shock-absorbers. However, when they were finally delivered in 1935 they were obsolete. A number of experimental versions were tested, including two aircraft specifically for record-breaking and two monoplane variants. At their peak in 1932 the Ni-D62 series fighters equipped two-thirds of the French Escadrilles de Chasse, but from 1935 onwards they were systematically replaced by Dewoitine D500 low-wing monoplanes. By September 1938 about 140 of all versions remained for second-line duties. A number of reserve regional units still had Ni-D622s and 629s on strength at the outbreak of World War 2.

Northrop A-17

USA

Purpose: Light attack bomber
Makers: Northrop Corporation
In service: 1935-40
Data: A-17A

Engine: See below
Span: 47ft 8.5in

Length: 31ft 8.5in
Height: 12ft 0in
Weight loaded: 7,545lb
Crew: Two
Max speed: 220mph
Service ceiling: 19,400ft
Range: over 730 miles

Armament: Four fixed .30in Browning machine guns and one in rear cockpit. Up to 600lb of bombs

In the early 1930s, two Northrop commercial aircraft were in service — the freight carrying Gamma and the eight-passenger Delta cantilever, low-wing monoplanes. Of all-metal construction, each was powered by a single 575hp Cyclone engine and had a cantilever trousered undercarriage. In 1933 Northrop built a prototype attack bomber variant of the civil aircraft, designating it Model 2C. In the following year this was acquired by the US Army Air Corps for evaluation as the YA-13, and 1934 also saw the appearance of the improved Model 2E. This retained the general lines of the Gamma monoplane, although an enclosed cockpit canopy covered the crew of two in the area that had been reserved for freight in the former type; and it was powered by the more powerful 750hp Wright radial engine. One Model 2E was bought by the British Air Ministry for evaluation; and at the close of 1934, the US Army ordered 110 production aircraft, designated A-17s. These were built with 750hp Pratt & Whitney Wasp Junior radial engines, and also differed from the YA-13 in having only the undercarriage legs and rear

portion of the wheels enclosed, in much smaller fairings, two separate cockpit hoods for the crew, internal instead of external bomb racks, perforated flaps and a three-blade propeller. The A-17 was followed in production by 131 improved A-17As, with 825hp Pratt & Whitney R-1535-13 Wasp Junior radial engines and retractable undercarriages, improving the maximum speed by 15mph. Export aircraft, produced by Northrop and Douglas Aircraft as 8A-1s (A-17s), 8A-2s (with Cyclone engines and fixed undercarriages) and 8A-3s (usually with Cyclone engines and retractable undercarriages) before the beginning of World War 2, included 30 8A-3s for Argentina (840hp Cyclone engines), approximately 150 8A-1s for China, 18 8A-3s for the Netherlands (1,050hp Pratt & Whitney engines) and 10 8A-3s for Peru (1,000hp engines). Sweden also licence-built more than 100 8-A1s as B5s (875hp Bristol Pegasus engines at Svenska's Linköping factory). During World War 2, Great Britain and France received ex-USAAC A-17As, the former being given the name Nomad. The Nomads were not up to the expectations of the RAF and all but one were transferred to the South African Air Force. From the basic A-17 was subsequently developed the naval BT-1 dive bomber.

Polikarpov I-3   USSR

Purpose: Fighter
Makers: Soviet State Aircraft Factories
In service: 1929-34

Engine: See below
Span: 36ft 5in
Length: 26ft 6.1in
Weight loaded: 4,070lb
Crew: One
Max speed: 186.5mph
Service ceiling: 23,620ft
Normal range: 363 miles
Armament: Two fixed forward-firing 7.62mm PV-1 machine guns

Polikarpov's I-3 fighter was a workmanlike aircraft

which owed a great deal to the two-seat fighter 2I-N1 or DI-1. This was a single-bay unequal-span biplane powered by a 450hp Napier Lion engine. It had a monocoque fuselage with a covering of shaped layers of glued plywood. The wings had plywood covering over the leading edge with the remaining area covered by fabric. The two-seater was of clean construction and great attention had been paid to detail in the design. Poor workmanship, however, led to wing fabric coming adrift from its supposed fixing points in the course of high-altitude tests. The fault remained undetected and during a later high-speed run the fabric began to balloon and tore away causing a fatal crash on 31 March 1926. The disaster shook the entire design collective and it was not until six months later that work started on the

2I-N1's derivative, the single-seat I-3. After some deliberation it was decided that a good top speed was the most important consideration and with that in mind the inline water-cooled M-17 engine was selected as a power plant. The engine drove a two-bladed airscrew with pointed spinner. A mockup of the I-3 was accepted for construction in May 1927 and two prototypes were completed in the spring and summer respectively of 1928. Clark Y profile was selected for the wings, which were two-spar structures with plywood ribs. Ailerons comprised a dural framework, fabric covered. Similarly, the tailplane was a dural tube structure again with fabric covering. The fuselage was built up along four longerons and had 13 frames. A conventional axle-type undercarriage with rubber shock-absorbers could be fitted either with wheels or floats. The engine radiator was located between the rear undercarriage struts. Armament was two 7.62mm Vickers machine guns. After tests, which indicated good speed and reasonable manoeuvrability, the I-3

was accepted for series production. It entered service in 1929 and proved popular with Soviet fighter pilots. The Vickers guns of the prototypes were replaced by 7.62mm PV-1 machine guns synchronised to fire through the propeller disc. The I-3 was characterised by its sleek, slim fuselage, wings which were rakishly staggered with ailerons on the upper wing only, and beautifully curved tail surfaces. The wingtips were also rounded and the lower wing was considerably smaller in area than the upper, with much reduced span and chord. Soviet records refer to 399 I-3s being completed. They served in first-line units over a five-year period. Polikarpov developed a two-seat version of the I-3, thus completing the circle started by the I1-N1. Designated D-2 (or DI-2) it had increased dimensions compared with the I-3 and a redesigned tailplane. The rudder was of greater area and horizontal tail surfaces had 10° dihedral. The gunner had a twin-gun mounting. Tests were successful and a small batch was produced.

Polikarpov I-5 USSR

Purpose: Fighter
Makers: Soviet State Aircraft Factories
In service: 1930-36

Engine: See below
Span: 33ft 5.5in
Length: 22ft 3in

Weight loaded: 2,987lb
Crew: One
Max speed: 173mph
Service ceiling: 23,950ft
Normal range: 329 miles
Armament: Two fixed forward-firing 7.62mm machine guns. 88lb of bombs (see below)

The I-5 project was listed in the Soviet 'Five-Year Plan for Experimental Aircraft' published in 1927. Andrei Tupolev was to design this new mixed construction single-seat fighter biplane. He was, however, fully occupied with large all-metal aircraft and no progress was made until a special design bureau was allocated the urgent task of producing the new fighter. Polikarpov and Grigorovich were both members and submitted designs for consideration. Polikarpov, drawing on recent experience with the experimental all-wood I-6 biplane, was successful. A mockup was approved in March 1930. The urgent need led to rapid completion of the VT-11 first prototype, which was flown for the first time by test-pilot B. L. Bucholz on 29 April, just 40 days later! Powered by a Gnome-Rhône Jupiter VII radial engine with individually helmeted cylinder heads, the VT-11 was intended for high-altitude operation. The second prototype, named *Klim Voroshilov* after the Soviet who had taken considerable interest in the project, had a Jupiter VI engine and was intended for the low and medium-level role. The final prototype had an M-15 radial engine with a NACA ring cowling. It flew on 1 July 1930. Later, wheel spats were fitted. The M-15 engine was not accepted for production and the M-22 of 480hp (based on the Jupiter VI) was selected in its place. During August and September 1930 seven pre-production I-5s were built for service testing. They performed well and the I-5 was

accepted for production. The new fighter was to be built at Zavod No 21, a new factory still not wholly completed. Nevertheless, a special engineering group, led by I. M. Kostkin, helped initiate mass production and finally 803 I-5s were built. The production I-5 was a stubby workmanlike unequal-span biplane. The rounded section fuselage was built up on a metal tubular framework and the pilot's cockpit had a faired headrest. The fabric covered wooden wings were braced with N-struts, while the undercarriage was of conventional axle type. An attractive fighter, with good flying qualities, it was closely comparable with its foreign contemporaries and remained in large-scale service until 1936. Several I-5s were used, along with other types, in Zveno parasite fighter experiments. In these two or three I-5s, attached to the upper wing or fuselage surfaces of a TB-3 'mother ship', were air launched. The LSh ground attack variant of the aircraft had four machine guns. Standard armament of the fighter was two synchronised 7.62mm PV-1 machine guns, although 10 aircraft from a late production batch had four PV-1 guns. There was also provision for 88lb of light bombs on underwing racks. Two examples of a two-seat dual-control trainer version of the I-5 were also tested. I-5 advanced trainers were still in use when Germany attacked the Soviet Union in June 1941, when two units of the Black Sea Fleet air force used I-5s operationally in the ground attack role.

Polikarpov I-15 and I-15*bis* USSR

Purpose: Fighter
Makers: Soviet State Aircraft Factories
In service: 1935-39
Data: I-15 series

Engine: See below
Span: 31ft 11.9in
Length: 20ft 7.25in
Height: 7ft 3.3in
Weight loaded: 3,027lb
Crew: One

Max speed: 228mph
Service ceiling: 32,152ft
Normal range: 311 miles
Armament: Four fixed forward-firing 7.62mm machine guns

One of the most important aircraft participating in the Spanish Civil War, the I-15 unequal-span biplane was designed in 1933 by Nikolai Polikarpov under the bureau designation TsKB-3. The fuselage was of steel tube, fabric covered. The upper two-spar wing

was gulled into the top of the fuselage ahead of the pilot's cockpit. Wings were braced either side by single profiled I-struts. The fixed undercarriage comprised single cantilever struts and wheel spats were provided. The first flight of the prototype, powered by an imported 630hp Wright Cyclone SGR-1820F-3 radial, was made at the hands of pilot Valery Chkalov in October 1933. However the only engine available for the first production machines (delivered from early 1934) was the 480hp M-22. The next version, which went into production the following year, was powered by a 715hp M-25 in a NACA cowling. It drove a two-bladed metal propeller in place of the original wooden type. Armament was four synchronised PV-1 7.62mm machine guns. Four 55lb bombs could also be carried on underwing racks. A specially lightened I-15, piloted by Vladimir Kokkinaki, set up an altitude record of 47,818ft on 29 November 1935. With the outbreak of the civil war in Spain, I-15s were sent to aid the Republican forces, the first 13 reaching Cartagena on 13 October 1936. At least 234, named 'Chato' by the Spaniards, went into service with the Republicans. A number of the other 53 I-15s sent and partially assembled at the time of the Republican collapse were completed and used during the 1940s by the Franco regime. Experience in Spain showed that the I-15 was highly aerobatic, provided an exceptionally stable gun platform and was controllable in spins. These qualities, combined with its ability to out-turn any potential opponent, made it a true pilot's aircraft. It proved superior in respect of manoeuvrability and rate of climb to the redoubtable Fiat CR32, although slower in the dive and with virtually equal top speed. A number of Spanish aces made their 'kills' on the Chato, including Miguel Zambudio, Manuel Aguirre and Garcia Lacalle. The I-15bis (or I-152) development of the I-15 was intended to provide improved pilot visibility. Mass produced from 1937, it had a redesigned upper wing of increased span with a conventional centre section supported by a pair of N-form cabane struts. As with the I-15, wheel spats were provided but often discarded under operational conditions. The 750hp M-25V engine had a long chord cowling, its two-bladed metal propeller supporting a large spinner. The heavier engine, structural alterations and additional equipment resulted in a loaded weight some 1,058lb higher than that of the I-15, with a consequent reduction of 13mph in maximum speed. I-15bis fighters sent to Spain arrived too late to be used in operations, but the type flew against the Japanese over the Khalkin Gol and Nomonhan in 1939 and was also supplied to the Chinese Nationalist air arm. Used in some numbers against the Finns during the Winter War, it had largely been relegated to ground attack regiments when the Germans launched Operation 'Barbarossa' against the Soviet Union. Armament was four 7.62mm PV-1 machine guns. Later I-15bis machines and Spanish I-15s still in service during 1938 were armed with the more rapid firing 7.62mm ShKAS guns. Six RS-82 rockets could be carried underwing plus a maximum bomb load of 331lb. A total of 674 I-15s was produced and 2,408 I-15bis.

Polikarpov I-16　　　　　　　　　　　　　　USSR

Purpose: Fighter
Makers: Soviet State Aircraft Factories
In service: 1935-44
Data: I-16 Type 24

Engine: See below
Span: 29ft 6in
Length: 20ft 1in

Height: 7ft 11in
Weight loaded: 4,215lb
Crew: One
Max speed: 311-326mph
Service ceiling: 31,070ft
Range: 249-373 miles
Armament: Four fixed forward-firing 7.62mm ShKAS machine guns; or two 7.62mm ShKAS plus

two 20mm ShVAK cannon; or two 7.62mm ShKAS and one 12.7mm UBS machine gun. Either six RS-82 rockets or two 220lb bombs

One of the few aircraft designs to merit the description 'epoch-making', Nikolai N. Polikarpov's I-16 was the first cantilever low-wing monoplane single-seat fighter with a retractable undercarriage to go into service anywhere in the world — the true forerunner of the machines which contested the skies during World War 2. The stubby fuselage, the radial engine, the manually-operated inward-retracting main wheels, the curved tapered wing trailing-edge and horizontal tailplane leading-edge profiled into the fuselage so that they almost met, all helped to make the I-16 very distinctive. The wooden monocoque fuselage had a plywood skin while the leading edge and centre section of the metal wing had aluminium alloy skinning, remaining surfaces being fabric covered. The ailerons doubled as landing flaps. Valery Chkalov flew the TsKB-12 prototype on 31 December 1933. About 30 Type 1s were built, five of them drawing public attention for the first time during the May Day fly-past in 1935. The prototype and Type 1 aircraft had Soviet 480hp M-22 engines, while the TsKB-12bis second prototype had the imported 710hp Wright Cyclone SR-1820-F3 radial. The Types 4 and 5 had the 700hp M-25 radial the latter having a new cowling and an enclosed cockpit with a one-piece windscreen-capony which slid forward, and was the first to be truly mass-produced. Top speed was 282.1mph and loaded weight 3,219lb, impressive figures for 1935! All I-16s up to that time had just two wing-mounted 7.62mm machine guns. The I-16 proved lighter and more manoeuvrable than its contemporaries, but needed careful handling. To meet a pressing need a two-seat advanced training version of the Type 5 was built as the UTI-4. After a limited number of four-gun 750hp M-25A-powered Type 6s, the Type 10 was produced, eventually being built in greater numbers than any other version. It had a new short windscreen and open cockpit and incorporated considerable structural strengthening. It was armed with four 7.62mm ShKAS machine guns, two in the wings and two in the cowling of its 750hp M-25V engine. The I-16P of 1938 had two 20mm ShVAK cannon as armament and the Type 17,

intended for ground attack, had a supplementary 12.7mm UBS machine gun under the forward fuselage and carried 441lb of bombs on underwing racks. The tailskid used on previous I-16s was replaced by a tailwheel. From 1939 standard I-16s had six underwing launchers for RS-82 rockets. In the same year the I-16 Type 18 went into production with the supercharged 920hp M-62 radial and four 7.62mm ShKAS guns. Final large-scale production version was the Type 24 with the M-62 or 1,100hp M-63 engine. The wing was redesigned and external auxiliary fuel tanks could be fitted. Production finished in mid-1940, but was reinstated in the 1941 emergency. The total number of single-seaters built was 7,005, plus over 1,600 UTI-4 two-seat trainers.

The I-16's combat career began in October 1936 when a few Type 5s were despatched to the Republican Government in the Spanish Civil War. From then on 'Mosca' (Fly), as the I-16 was named by the Republicans, played a considerable role in the conflict. After additional Type 5 and some Type 6 aircraft had been sent in during 1937, large numbers of Type 10s were delivered in the following year, known as 'Super Moscas' due to their improved performance. Final deliveries totalled 278, and 10 of 100 machines being built in Spain under licence had been completed by the Republicans before the close of the war. Subsequently, the Nationalist Government completed 30 of the remainder. Meanwhile Chinese I-16s (piloted by Chinese and Russians) had fought against the invading Japanese from 1937. Then, in 1939, during Russo-Japanese border fighting at Nomonhan, I-16s again achieved prominence, particularly after the introduction of the cannon-armed Type 17 and the operational debut of the RS-82 rockets. By World War 2, however, the nimble speedy world-beater of 1935 was well and truly obsolescent. Strenuous efforts had increased speed, but at the expense of weight and manoeuvrability. After participation (usually mounted on skis) in the Winter War of 1939-1940 with Finland, the I-16 met its greatest challenge with the German attack on the Soviet Union in June 1941. Despite enormous initial losses (many on the ground), the I-16 gave a reasonable account of itself. About two-thirds of the Soviet fighter force at that time flew I-16s and they remained in service until the end of 1943, usually outclassed but scoring victories and winning medals for a number of their more experienced pilots. I-16s also participated in two interesting operational techniques during the first year of the war. Prewar 'Zveno' parasite fighter experiments led to the creation of a special unit based in the Crimea which operated four-engined TB-3 mother-ships each with two I-16s underwing, each adapted to carry two 551lb bombs apiece. Air-launched, the I-16s made dive bombing attacks on important targets in Romania. They subsequently had sufficient fuel to make their way back to base. The second tactic, which won considerable fame for the I-16 during the darkest days of the war, was the so-called 'taran' attack in which I-16s were deliberately rammed into German aircraft, many of which were destroyed, while the Soviet pilots frequently saved themselves by parachute.

Polikarpov I-153 USSR

Purpose: Fighter
Makers: Soviet State Aircraft Factories
In service: 1939-44

Engine: See below
Span: 32ft 9.7in
Length: 20ft 3.1in
Height: 9ft 2.2in
Weight loaded: 4,098-4,652lb
Crew: One
Max speed: 275.25mph
Service ceiling: 36,090ft
Normal range: 432 miles
Armament: Four fixed forward-firing 7.62mm machine guns

Misreading the signs and misled by the relative success of the Fiat CR32 and Polikarpov I-15 in the Spanish Civil War, the Soviet Command requested Nikolai Polikarpov and his assistant Aleksei Shcherbakov in October 1937 to design the I-153 in the belief that biplane fighters would still have a role to play in any future major war. The new fighter was accepted for production in autumn 1938 after successful testing. Three thousand, four hundred and thirty-seven I-153s had been completed when production ceased at Zavod No 156 at the end of 1940. The other aircraft factory involved, Zavod No 1, had turned over to MiG monoplanes four months earlier. The I-153 (or I-15ter) had the Clark YH wing profile of the I-15bis but reverted to the gulled upper wing of the earlier I-15. The wooden wings were fabric covered and were braced with I-type struts either side. The fuselage was built up of light alloy tubing with dural skinning forward and fabric covering aft. The open pilot's cockpit had a faired headrest. The main undercarriage legs retracted in a rather complex manner to lie smoothly in the fuselage. Powered by a 775hp M-25V radial, which allowed a top speed of 258mph, the new fighter had good flying qualities and excellent manoeuvrability, but was disappointing when sent to the Far East against Japanese Ki-27 monoplanes at Nomonhan in 1939. Nevertheless, full-scale production continued, the later aircraft fitted with the 1,000hp M-62 radial. Subsequently the four fuselage-mounted synchronised ShKAS 7.62mm machine guns were replaced by 12.7mm UBS weapons. Two auxiliary tanks, each with a capacity of 22gal of fuel, were provided. A small number of I-153Ps had two synchronised 20mm ShVAK cannon in place of the machine gun armament. Underwing launchers for six or eight RS-82 rockets became standard and up to 331lb of bombs could be carried. Some 80 I-153s were supplied to the Chinese Nationalists in early 1940, while that same year many new Soviet fighter regiments equipped with the type. During the German invasion of Russia many I-153s were lost on the ground or in the air but a number of more experienced Soviet pilots did well on the type, utilising its manoeuvrability and tight turning circle. The last front-line and target defence (PVO) fighter units relinquished their I-153s during the first six months of 1942. By the summer of 1943 the I-153 was used mainly by ground-attack regiments and in this role achieved considerable success. Finland used 22 I-153s, obtained from a variety of sources, for tactical reconnaissance until 1944. Experimental I-153GK and I-153TGK variants had pressurised cabins for high-altitude operations. Merkulov DM-4 auxiliary ramjets were mounted under the wings of an I-153 in late 1940 and tests proved an increase of 32mph in top speed at 6,600ft. The solitary I-190 had a 1,100hp M-88V radial and reached 304mph at 19,700ft.

Polikarpov R-5　　　　　　　　　USSR

Purpose: Reconnaissance/Light bomber
Makers: Soviet State Aircraft Factories
In service: 1930-44

Engine: See below
Span: 50ft 10.24in
Length: 34ft 10.5in
Height: 11ft 9.7in
Weight loaded: 7,158lb
Crew: Two
Max speed: 141.5mph
Service ceiling: 21,000ft
Range: 684 miles
Armament: Two 7.62mm machine guns. 551lb of
bombs

The R-5 was a classic two-seat biplane which
showed its qualities soon after entering service in
1930 by winning an international contest for light
reconnaissance bomber aircraft staged at Teheran.
The design dated from a 1928 prototype. A classic
biplane, constructed largely of wood with fabric
covering, it had unequal span wings braced with N-
struts. Pilot and observer-gunner were seated close
together in tandem, the pilot beneath a 'cut out' in
the upper wing trailing edge. The BMW VIb engine of
the prototype was replaced in series machines by the
Soviet-built 680hp M-17B. Its radiator was located
under the fuselage just in front of the undercarriage.
The wheels of the conventional axle-type

undercarriage were interchangeable with skis for
winter operations. 7,000 R-5s were completed in
many versions by 1937. Apart from the U-2 (later
Po-2) it was the most numerous Soviet military
aircraft of the 1930s. Armament was one fixed
7.62mm PV-1 synchronised machine gun and one
7.62mm DA-1 on a ring mounting operated by the
observer. The 551lb of bombs were carried on
underwing racks. Variants included the R-5Sh for
ground attack (five fixed and two flexible machine
guns plus 1,102lb bombs); R-5T single-seat torpedo
bomber (50 built); the twin-float R-5a (or MR-5); and
the SSS with a 715hp M-17F engine, spatted
undercarriage and ShKAS machine gun armament.
Civil versions were the P-5 of 1931 and P-5a of
1933, the latter with a four-passenger cabin and
enclosed position for pilot. Considerable numbers
were used in the Arctic with skis. Soviet R-5s fought
in the Spanish Civil War, where 31 R-5s flew with
the Republicans under the nickname 'Rasante'
(razor), in the Far East against the Japanese (1938-
39) and in the Winter War against Finland (1939-
40). During World War 2 the Russians employed
several hundred R-5s as night 'nuisance' bombers,
regiments being raised to fly alongside Po-2s in the
defence of Moscow in autumn 1941 and later taking
part in the battle for Stalingrad. Also used were
ambulance variants with two underwing panniers for
two patients. Many other R-5s were used for
training.

Polikarpov R-Z　　　　　　　　　USSR

Purpose: Reconnaissance/Attack bomber
Makers: Soviet State Aircraft Factories
In service: 1937-42

Engine: See below
Span: 50ft 10.25in
Length: 31ft 9.9in
Weight loaded: 7,716lb
Crew: Two
Max speed: 180.2mph

Service ceiling: 26,247ft
Normal range: 621 miles
Armament: Two 7.62mm machine guns plus 880lb
of bombs

The R-Z, used as a ground support, reconnaissance
and light bombing aircraft, was the ultimate
development of the Soviet Polikarpov R-5 series.
1,000 were built from 1936 onwards. Powered by
an AM-34R engine, which delivered 820hp at low

altitude, it was a robust and reliable aircraft and could carry an effective bomb load of eight 110lb bombs on underwing racks. Armed with a single synchronised forward-firing 7.62mm PV-1 machine gun and a single 7.62mm ShKAS KM-35 gun fitted to a heavy ring mounting and used by the observer, the R-Z gave a reasonable account of itself. The main external differences from the R-5 included a completely redesigned fin and rudder, the ventral radiator relocated between the undercarriage legs, elimination of the upper wing trailing edge 'cut-out' over the pilot's cockpit, introduction of additional fuel tankage and the provision of a glazed canopy over the cockpits. The undercarriage was stronger than that of the R-5 but the spat-type fairings fitted to the wheels of the prototype R-Z were eliminated on series aircraft. While the R-Z saw action in Far East border incidents, which culminated in the Russo-Japanese air battles over Nomonhan in summer 1939, and was still in service during the first year of the German invasion of the Soviet Union, its claim to fame undoubtedly rests with its contribution to the Republican cause during the Spanish Civil War. R-Z biplanes arrived in Spain in February 1937, serving with Group 20. They were soon named 'Natazah' by the Republicans. They participated in the bombing of

Italian columns at Guadalajara and then Toledo and Jarama. Missions were remarkably trouble-free, the first losses not occurring until the battle of Huesca. But at Brunete four machines were destroyed during a single attack. During 1937 Groups 30 and 31 were formed with four squadrons each. R-Z squadrons usually met at an agreed rendezvous and then flew in formation to their objective at an average 10,000ft, if possible with an escort of I-15 Chato fighters, which followed up the bombing with machine gun attacks. Bombing approach was in echelon, with a gentle dive to about 2,500ft, increasing speed to render AA fire inaccurate. When confronted by enemy fighters R-Zs quickly got into tight formation and went into a shallow dive, stepped up to ensure defensive crossfire from their quick-firing ShKAS weapons. In this way R-Z groups suffered more from anti-aircraft fire than from enemy fighters. After bombing, the aircraft returned to base singly and at low altitude. R-Zs survived remarkably well; Group 30, in particular, remaining in the Southern Zone at full strength until March 1939. Of 62 aircraft which arrived in Spain, 36 were captured intact by the Nationalists, although nearly all had been damaged by machine gun and AA fire.

Potez 25 France

Purpose: Reconnaissance/Army co-operation
Makers: Établissements Henry Potez
In service: 1926-45
Photo and Data: Potez 25 TOE

Engine: See below
Span: 46ft 4.75in
Length: 29ft 10.25in
Height: 12ft 0.5in
Weight loaded: 4,934lb
Crew: Two
Max speed: 129.25mph at sea level
Service ceiling: 19,119ft
Range: 391 miles
Armament: One fixed 7.62mm or 7.5mm machine gun plus twin guns of same calibre on flexible TO7 mounting. Up to 441lb of bombs

One of the classic military aircraft of the period between the two world wars, the Potez 25 prototype flew for the first time in early 1925. A compact unequal-span biplane with pilot and observer seated close together in open tandem cockpits, 1,948 examples of the TOE (Colonial) version were produced for France, while a further 322 were exported. The French TOEs 'kept the peace' for many years throughout that country's colonial empire, a formation of 33 TOEs making a 'show-the-flag' tour of French Africa between November 1933 and January 1934 led by General Vuillemin. The exploit was popularly known as the *Croisière Noire* (Black Cruise) and achieved considerable and much-needed worldwide fame for French military aviation. The TOE was powered by a 450hp Lorraine 12Eb water-cooled engine with frontal radiator. Many other

versions of the Potez 25 were produced for a variety of roles with a large choice of engines, radial and water-cooled. A number of Hispano-Suiza, Salmson and Farman-powered Potez 25s also had redesigned rudders of increased surface area. A considerable number of Potez 25A2s served in metropolitan Observation Escadrilles. The type was exported to no fewer than 17 countries. In addition 150 were built under licence in Poland, over 200 in Yugoslavia and a batch of 27 in Portugal. A small number of Potez 25s, including nine Gnome-Rhône Jupiter-engined ex-Latvian aircraft, saw limited service on the Republican side during the Spanish Civil War. Potez 25s remaining in France had been relegated to training and liaison duties by the outbreak of World War 2, but the type continued in front-line service in overseas territories, being caught up in subsequent conflicts in North Africa, Syria and French Indo-China. It was in the latter territory that the last of the type to remain in flying condition were reported in 1945. Total production of the Potez 25 in France alone exceeded 4,000 aircraft.

Potez 54 Series

France

Purpose: Reconnaissance-bomber/Transport
Makers: Établissements Henry Potez
In service: 1935-45
Photo and Data: Potez 540

Engines: See below
Span: 72ft 6in
Length: 53ft 1.8in
Height: 12ft 9in
Weight loaded: 13,025lb
Crew: Five
Max speed: 192.6mph at 13,124ft
Service ceiling: 19,685ft
Range: 528 miles
Armament: Three 7.5mm Darne machine guns, one each in nose, dorsal and ventral positions. Bomb load 1,987lb

Designed as an 'aerial cruiser', without any defensive blindspots, the prototype Potez 54.01 flew for the first time on 14 November 1933. It was a strut-braced high-wing monoplane, with enclosed cabin and nose turret, open dorsal gunner's cockpit and retractable ventral position. Series aircraft had a large single fin and rudder in place of the original twin assembly, plus an enclosed dorsal turret. The main undercarriage units retracted into the nacelles of the twin 690hp Hispano-Suiza Xirs/jrs engines. 192 were delivered to the Armée de l'Air together with 67 Potez 542s (with 720hp Lorraine engines). Most served with reconnaissance groupes. Immediately before World War 2 some aircraft were re-engined with high-altitude Hispano-Suiza 12-Y engines, disarmed and used by Air HQ for covert photographic missions over northern Italy and the

Siegfried Line. Withdrawn from front-line service during World War 2, French machines were converted for military transport and liaison duties. The solitary Gnome-Rhône radial-engined Potez 541 bomber, and 10 similarly powered Potez 543s, were exported to Romania. Early in the Spanish Civil War six Potez 540s were sold to the Republican Government. 13 more Potez machines were delivered surreptitiously, seven of them Type 542s. The Spanish machines were expended in a number of daylight single bombing sorties, most being shot down within the first 18 months of conflict. Because

of the heavy losses caused as a result of the reckless use of the Spanish Potez 54s, the type was rather unfairly nicknamed 'Flying Coffin' or 'Widow Maker'. As World War 2 progressed, more and more Potez 54s were converted for the transport role, principal external modification being the fairing over the nose section. A number flew with Vichy Groupe de Transport GTII/15 during the fighting in Syria in 1941. Later they served with the same Groupe in greater numbers in Algeria, subsequently operating with the Free French.

PZL P-7

Poland

Purpose: Fighter
Makers: Panstwowe Zaklady Lotnicze
In service: 1932-39
Photo: P-7a

Engine: See below
Span: 33ft 9.5in
Length: 23ft 6in
Height: 9ft 0.25in
Weight loaded: 2,976lb
Crew: One
Max speed: 197mph
Service ceiling: 32,808ft
Range: 435 miles
Armament: Two fixed forward-firing 7.7mm Vickers machine guns

The predilection for gull or parasol-wing monoplanes by the Polish Air Force in the 1930s is self-evident, for not only did that service come to rely on its PZL fighters for the greater part of the decade but acquired more RWD-8 trainers than any other Polish-built aircraft, not to mention Lublin RXIIIs and others, all serving up to the 1939 onslaught. It can be argued that the line really began with the PWS10

fighter, which was quickly replaced by the P-7. Developed from the 190mph P-1 fighter of 1929, the P-7 prototype first flew in October 1930, powered by a Bristol Jupiter VII radial engine. Retaining the gull-type wings (known as the Pulawski wing after its designer), divided undercarriage and tail unit of the P-1, with the wings tapering towards the tips in chord and thickness — the P-7 prototype had a neat all-metal oval-section fuselage, an open cockpit, and an elaborate close-fitting engine cowling. This last feature was superseded on subsequent aircraft by a smooth cowling ring. While flight trials were still underway in 1931, the first few fighters were ordered from PZL, embodying alterations to various parts of the structure including a redesigned rear fuselage and a Skoda-built Bristol Jupiter VIIF radial engine of 485hp. The Polish Air Force began to receive the production P-7a fighters in the latter part of 1932, and deliveries eventually totalled some 150 aircraft. By the close of the following year, the Polish Air Force could claim to be the first in the world to have only all-metal monoplanes in front-line fighter service. These durable and highly manoeuvrable fighters remained operational throughout the remaining 1930s. Accordingly, they failed to keep

pace with the performances gained by later fighters with enclosed cockpits, retractable undercarriages and more powerful engines, and, more importantly, did not move with the trend away from two light machine guns for attack and defence, to four, six or eight guns or cannon. Even in 1939, over two-thirds of all P-7as built were still flying — 27 as fighters — although sadly outdated by later types; the rest were used for training. So when Germany invaded Poland on 1 September 1939, the handful of P-7 fighters fought with P-11s against Luftwaffe types, which included some 200 Bf109s. Within four weeks Warsaw had surrendered and the country was divided by Germany and Russia. Most of the P-7a fighters had been destroyed but a few, plus a number of trainers, escaped to Hungary and Romania and subsequently served in secondary roles with other friendly air forces.

PZL P-11   Poland

Purpose: Fighter
Makers: Panstwowe Zaklady Lotnicze
In service: 1934-39
Photo: P-11b
Data: P-11c

Engine: See below
Span: 35ft 2.5in
Length: 24ft 9.5in
Height: 9ft 4in
Weight loaded: 3,593lb
Crew: One
Max speed: 242mph at 18,000ft
Service ceiling: 36,075ft
Range: 503 miles
Armament: Four 7.7mm machine guns, two in fuselage and two in wings. Two 27lb bombs could be carried

When the P-11 first appeared, it was one of the finest fighters in the world and attracted great interest from foreign air forces. Compared with the Bristol Bulldog then in RAF service, it was some 67mph faster and had the excellent flying qualities of the earlier P-7. However, even the best aircraft become outdated and by 1939, when the heady race by other nations to build the best fighter in Europe had produced the Spitfire and Bf109, the most numerous fighter in Polish service was still the P-11, by which time the design was over eight years old. Despite the odds, P-11s and the few P-7s fought on until two-thirds of their number had been lost, although Polish aircraft of all kinds, plus ground forces, destroyed 203 Luftwaffe aircraft. But it is noticeable from the records that the superiority of German aircraft soon showed, despite the Polish campaign lasting four weeks, as 116 of the German aircraft destroyed were successfully engaged in the first week of fighting, the numbers sharply tailing off as Polish air power became overwhelmed.

Developed from the P-7, the P-11 was another single-seat monoplane with a high, braced gull wing. The first prototype made its maiden flight in August 1931 while powered by a Gnome-Rhône-built Jupiter IX engine. The main aims with the new fighter were to improve the structure, pilot's view and performance over the P-7, the latter by allowing much more powerful engines to be fitted. Following trials with this and other prototypes, an order for 30 production two-gun P-11as was placed. Power was to be provided by licence-built 500hp Mercury IV-S2 engines. These entered service in 1934. The next

version ordered was the P-11b for Romania, 50 of which were built with 595hp IAR-built Gnome-Rhône K9 Mistral engines. Then, in the latter part of 1934, the P-11c entered production for the home air force. It differed from earlier versions in having the engine lowered and the pilot's seat raised to improve further the forward view (in a manner also favoured by the French Loire 46 fighter), the addition of two guns in the wings and other refinements. A total of 175 aircraft of this type was completed up to 1937, the original Skoda-built Mercury V-S2 engines being replaced by Polish-built Mercury VI-S2s of 645hp on later production machines. P-11s equipped every

PAF fighter squadron except three right up to the German invasion. In addition, about 80 P-11s were licence-built in Romania as P-11fs, a crossbred version of the P-11b and 'c'. When, in September 1939, Poland was invaded, the air force had nearly 680 first-line aircraft, which included 27 P-7s and 12 squadrons of P-11s, totalling 129 fighters. Interestingly, Stanislaw Skalski, the highest-scoring Polish pilot to serve with the RAF during World War 2, flew a P-11 during the invasion, shooting down five German aircraft before escaping to England.

Savoia-Marchetti SM81 Pipistrello (Bat)   Italy

Purpose: Bomber/Transport
Makers: Societa Italiana Aeroplani Idrovolanti Savoia-Marchetti
In service: From 1935

Engines: Three 700hp Piaggio PX RC35 radials, although other types could be fitted including the Alfa 125 and 126, Piaggio PIX and Gnome-Rhône K-14, all in the 580-1,000hp range
Span: 78ft 9in
Length: 58ft 6in
Height: 14ft 7.25in
Weight loaded: 20,500-22,000lb
Crew: Six
Max speed: 211mph
Service ceiling: 22,975ft
Max range: 1,242 miles
Armament: Five or six 12.7mm machine guns in dorsal, ventral and side gun positions. 3,307-4,400lb of bombs

Entering service with the Regia Aeronautica in 1935, the SM81 was developed with the SM73 18-passenger airliner of the early 1930s, which also had tapered cantilever low-wings and a fixed and faired divided undercarriage. During the Abyssinian campaign, which started in October 1935, SM81s

were operated alongside Caproni Ca133s and performed bombing raids, bomb and machine gun attacks and harassed ground forces, in addition to supplying ammunition and other supplies to Italian ground forces. In all these roles it proved highly successful. Interestingly, reports made at the time mention the use of gas to break the morale of the Abyssinian forces, often only comprising of horsemen armed with rifles. The gas is said to have been sprayed from aircraft and to have caused heavy casualties among the bewildered enemy. With the outbreak of the civil war in Spain in the following year, Italy sent SM81s to aid the Spanish Nationalists, and these were operational by August. Later, SM81s also equipped the Aviazione Legionarie, being used as bombers, transports and reconnaissance aircraft. Although having a higher designation number, the SM81 was in service some time before the SM79, which subsequently joined it in Spain and later replaced it in service. About 100 SM81s of 534 built were on strength as bombers when Italy entered World War 2, most of them deployed by the East African Command, later becoming paratroop and general-purpose transports. A small number of twin-engined SM81Bs were also built and used for experimental work, although some are believed to have been exported to Romania.

Sopwith Snipe
UK

Purpose: Fighter
Makers: Sopwith Aviation Company and others
In service: 1918-26
Data: 7F 1 Snipe

Engine: One 230hp Bentley BR2 rotary
Span: 30ft 0in
Length: 19ft 10in
Height: 9ft 6in
Weight loaded: 2,020lb
Crew: One
Max speed: 121mph
Service ceiling: 20,000ft
Endurance: 3hr
Armament: Two forward-firing Vickers machine guns. Four 25lb bombs could be carried

The Sopwith Snipe was a development of the Camel, and was indeed designed as a replacement for it. It was one of several excellent new conventional and radical fighters that were vying for production contracts in the first months of 1918, most of which were not considered despite the policy of pressing ahead with a continual stream of new combat planes in case the war dragged on into and beyond 1919. It was evolved to make use of the new Bentley BR2 rotary engine for which great things were expected. The prototype Snipe first flew with a BR1 engine of only 150hp, but even with this it was clear that the fighter was a winner, although some modifications were made to the airframe of the second prototype which had the BR2 installed. Further modifications to the design resulted in a third prototype (of six) and this aircraft set the seal on production. Orders for 4,000 Snipes were placed with 14 manufacturers in 1918, but only about 100 had been delivered to the RAF in France by the Armistice, equipping just three squadrons from the summer of 1918. Nevertheless, it was sufficient to prove the Snipe the best all-round fighter of the war, with few of the Camel's handling difficulties. Indeed, it is thought likely that the first four-point hesitation roll was performed in 1918 by a Snipe. A long-range version of the fighter was also built as the 7F 1a Snipe. Perhaps the best remembered exploit of a Snipe was when Major W. G. Barker won the Victoria Cross for his dramatic singleton fight against 15 Fokker DVIIs only a couple of weeks before the Armistice. The war over, production of the fighter continued, bringing the total to 497. As the first standard postwar RAF fighter, it remained in service at home and in the Middle East until replaced by Gloster Grebes, Hawker Woodcocks and Armstrong Whitworth Siskins. A small number were also converted into two-seat trainers. As mentioned under the DH9A entry, a squadron of Snipes were among the aircraft operated on the first air control operation. The fighter was also flown after the war by the Canadian Air Force. The Sopwith Company went into liquidation in 1920 having incurred financial losses producing motorcycles.

SPAD 61
France

Purpose: Fighter
Makers: Société Anonyme Blériot-Aéronautique
In service: 1925-30
Photo: S61-4
Data: S61-2

Engine: See below

Span: 31ft 3.2in
Length: 22ft 2.9in
Height: 9ft 2.25in
Weight loaded: 3,375lb
Crew: One
Max speed: 147.25mph
Service ceiling: 29,500ft

Range: 375 miles
Armament: Two fixed forward-firing 7.62mm machine guns

Designed in parallel with the 300hp S81, ordered by the French Air Force, the prototype S61-1 fighter appeared later and flew for the first time on 6 November 1923. A biplane with straight staggered wings and single I-type bracing struts, the S61 had a monocoque fuselage and a tailplane of a shape associated with its designer André Herbemont. In the following year the S61-2 appeared with wooden wings, a frontal radiator for its 450hp Lorraine 12We engine and conventional strut-bracing between the fuselage and wing in place of the faired structure of the prototype which had obstructed the pilot's vision. Successful testing led to a Polish order for 250 aircraft, followed by one for 100 machines from Romania. Subsequently, the Polish Francopol and PZL factories built a further 30 S61-2s. No French orders came, but the type became well-known in France when the S61-6b F-ESAU was piloted by Pelletier d'Oisy to victory in the 1924-5 cross-country air race, the Coupe Michelin. Leon Challe flew the S61-6d F-AIIU to victory in the 1926/7

event and the same pilot came second in the 1928/9 contest despite the fact that his S61-9 F-AJCR had a Lorraine radial engine of only 230hp.

The S61-2 equipped Polish fighter squadrons from 1925, going first to the 11th Fighter Regiment, then to the 4th, 3rd and 2nd respectively. All 250 imported machines had been delivered by December 1928 and all Polish fighter units had a few of the type on strength. Others were held in reserve storage. S61-2 series aircraft proved sensitive to the controls but were difficult to pull out of a spin, while having a tendency to go into a flat spin. Futhermore, the type was criticised for having an insufficiently strong structure when several Polish aircraft lost their wings in flight. Nevertheless, Captain Pilot Stachón, CO of the 11th Fighter Regiment, secured Poland's first ever world air record while flying an S61-2, reaching 6,000m (19,685ft) in 14min 38sec on 5 April 1926. He congratulated designer André Herbemont on the S61-2 thus: 'Your masterpiece will remain a beautiful jewel and a most delightful diversion for my comrades and myself.' By 1930 S61-2s had been withdrawn from first-line service but some 80 were used thereafter as advanced trainers.

Supermarine Southampton UK

Purpose: Reconnaissance/Bomber
Makers: Supermarine Aviation Works (Vickers) Ltd
In service: 1925-37
Photo and Data: Southampton II

Engines: Two 500hp Napier Lion V
Span: 75ft 0in
Length: 51ft 1 in
Height: 22ft 4in
Weight loaded: 15,190lb
Crew: Five
Max speed: 108mph
Range: over 900 miles

Armament: Three Lewis machine guns, one in bow and two in dorsal positions. 1,100lb of bombs or two 18in torpedoes

The Supermarine Aviation Works was founded in 1912 and, until the Type 224 and Spitfire proper appeared in the 1930s, was devoted almost exclusively in designing and building flying-boats. The obvious exceptions to this were the S5/S6/S6B Schneider Trophy racing seaplanes of 1927 to 1931, which were never intended as production aircraft but had direct effect on the later fighters mentioned above and the Sparrow light plane. Before World

War 1, the company built a number of flying-boats for Germany, but the war soon put a stop to the delivery and the company thereafter concentrated on building Admiralty flying-boats and a number of experimental types. Following the end of hostilities, the company again concentrated on its own designs, producing the Seagull for the Fleet Air Arm. Among the flying-boats appearing at this time were the Sea Lion Schneider Trophy racers, the Naval Training F-B, the Scarab bomber and the Swan. The latter was a passenger-carrying amphibious flying-boat with accommodation for 12 passengers, and was claimed at the time as being the first of its type in the world. Internal accommodation included an elaborately decorated saloon and buffet area, while the crew sat in open cockpits. From the Swan, of which two were ordered by the Air Ministry, was evolved the Southampton, which became the first postwar flying-boat to enter RAF service. Like those of the Swan, the Southampton's engines were suspended between the biplane wings on struts, and the rounded-section hull swept sharply upward at the rear, where a triple tail-assembly was fitted. A significant change from the Swan was in the crew accommodation, where open cockpits were provided in front of the wings for the gunner/bombardier and two pilots, all in tandem. Behind the wings were staggered cockpits for two rear gunners. The prototype Southampton had a wooden hull — a feature also of the initial production aircraft. It was

recorded at the time that design and construction of the first Southampton were completed in under seven months and that the aircraft was delivered to the RAF at Felixstowe the day after its first flight. It is thought that this refers to the prototype Southampton, although it cannot be substantiated. Production Southampton Is entered service with a coastal reconnaissance Flight of the RAF in September 1925. Most of the 78 Southamptons built were, however, Mk IIs with lightened duralumin hulls. Metal wings were also developed. RAF Southamptons flew many spectacular long-distance missions, the most famous being that flown by four aircraft of the Far East Flight during 1927 and 1928. Setting off from England, they flew to Singapore, then around the Australian continent, returning to Singapore where they were then based. The cruise, totalling about 27,000 miles, was performed to a schedule and without serious trouble of any kind. Also built were the Southampton III of 1928, with two Bristol Jupiter VIII engines, the Mk IV with two Rolls-Royce Kestrel III engines, and the triple Jupiter-engined Southampton X. Southamptons were also used by the Argentine Navy (Lorraine engines, later used as trainers when re-equipped with American Consolidated PBY-3s), Imperial Japanese Navy and RAAF (joining Supermarine Seagulls); one was evaluated in Denmark, which subsequently chose the Dornier Wal.

Thomas Morse MB-3

USA

Purpose: Fighter
Makers: Thomas Morse Aircraft Corporation
In service: From 1922
Photo: MB-3A

Engine: See below
Span: 26ft 0in
Length: 20ft 0in
Height: 8ft 7in
Weight loaded: 2,540lb
Crew: One
Max speed: 141mph
Service ceiling: 19,500ft
Armament: Two 0.3in/0.5in machine guns

The Thomas Morse Aircraft Corporation was founded in 1916 on the strength of its contracts to licence-build aircraft for the US Army Air Corps. During this period it designed the S-4 as a low-powered single-seat fighter fitted with a 100hp Gnome rotary engine. Following the US Army's decision to select its fighters from proven foreign designs, the S-4 was modified into a single-seat advanced trainer, of which several hundred were built before the Armistice. With the end of World War 1, the Army sought indigenous-designed aircraft and once again Thomas Morse designed a fighter. The resulting prototype MB-3 first flew in February 1919. It was a straight-winged equal-span biplane with a cross-axle Vee undercarriage, and was powered by a 300hp

Wright (Hispano-Suiza type) engine. In fact, the MB-3 was a fairly unremarkable aircraft and was only marginally faster than the lower-powered SPAD XIII fighter it was built to replace, mainly because it was some 700lb heavier. Production of the MB-3A totalled 250 aircraft, most of which were built by the Boeing Company which had tendered the lowest estimate for construction. The final 50 Boeing-built MB-3As differed from all earlier aircraft in that the tail-fin was enlarged to form a more rectangular vertical surface. These were completed in 1923 and allowed Boeing to proceed with the production of a modified version of the DH4 and to ponder over the

failure of its large GA-2 ground attack aircraft. More importantly, the production and subsequent modification of the MB-3A had given Boeing the experience to design a fighter of its own, in the form of the PW-9, and this started the company along a path that lasted most of the period covered by this book, culminating with the P-26. MB-3As served as fighters until the latter part of the 1920s, after which time they were converted into trainers. As for Thomas Morse, the company had little success until the arrival of the O-19 armed observation aircraft of 1928.

Tupolev I-4 (ANT-5)   USSR

Purpose: Fighter
Makers: Soviet State Aircraft Factories
In service: From 1928

Engine: See below
Span: 37ft 5in
Length: 23ft 10.5in
Height: 9ft 2.75in
Weight loaded: 3,000lb
Crew: One
Max speed: 160mph
Service ceiling: 25,100ft
Armament: Two fixed forward-firing machine guns

Until the late 1920s the Red air force (VVS) relied heavily on military aircraft of foreign design. As well as those of British and American origin, Junkers and Fokker types were prominent. Indeed, in 1927 the Red air force had about 330 fighters, light bombers and armed reconnaissance aircraft in service of Junkers and Fokker design. But, although further numbers of Junkers aircraft were licence-built thereafter, the major change over to military aircraft of home design had already begun in accordance with the official view that the country should work intensively to catch up and outpace technically the most advanced Western countries. The Tupolev I-4

was conceived as part of this process, but clearly owed much to the Fokker DXI/DXIII fighters. Two great names of Soviet aviation were connected with the designing of this aircraft, those of P. Sukhoi as chief designer, and A. N. Tupolev as overall supervisor. Of Kolchugaluminium metal construction, the I-4 was a sesquiplane and the whole aircraft was covered with corrugated sheet. Power was provided by a 460hp M-22 (Jupiter) radial engine. First flown in 1927, the highly manoeuvrable I-4 was an immediate success and quantity production began in the following year. About 370 examples were built, production stepping up in the early 1930s to cater for the rapidly increasing size of the air force. It was reported at the time that in 1932 alone 242 of the total number were produced. Many experiments were carried out with I-4s, including the famous evaluation trials as parasite fighters, two being carried on the wings of a Tupolev TB-1 twin-engined bomber.

Tupolev R-3 (ANT-3)   USSR

Purpose: Reconnaissance
Makers: Soviet State Aircraft Factories
In service: 1926-31
Data: M-5-powered

Engine: See below
Span: 42ft 8.6in
Length: 31ft 2in
Height: 12ft 9.5in
Weight loaded: 4,691lb
Crew: Two
Max speed: 128.6mph
Service ceiling: 16,142ft
Normal range: 466 miles
Armament: Three 7.62mm machine guns (see below)

Andrei Tupolev's ANT-3 had the distinction of being the first two-seat aircraft of Soviet design to go into quantity production. It was also the first all-metal aircraft to achieve this distinction. First flight was made by factory pilot V. N. Phillipov in October 1925, and Mikhail Gromov completed official state testing successfully in May the following year. The new unequal-span biplane showed considerable innovation. The fuselage was of inverted triangle section, providing good downward visibility for the two crew members who sat in tandem open cockpits. Wing bracing was by means of V-struts either side. The fuselage was covered in KA sheeting (a Russian-developed aluminium alloy). One hundred and nine R-3s were produced, 30 at GAZ No 3 and the rest at GAZ No 1 (GAZ, an abbreviation for State Aircraft Factory), over the period 1927-1929, most for military use. Various power plants were utilised. Early machines had 450hp Lorraine Dietrichs installed, although most aircraft had M-5s of similar horsepower, while a 1929 development (designated R-4) had a 550hp BMW VI engine. Armament comprised a fixed forward-firing Vickers 7.62mm gun and twin rear-mounted 7.62mm Lewis guns. Bomb load was 441lb. Interestingly the Soviet air propaganda organisation Osoaviakhim operated a number of R-3s, while others were used as mail couriers. One experimental aircraft was fitted with additional fuel tankage and re-engined with a British 450hp Napier Lion. Registered RR-SOV, it was flown by Mikhail Gromov on a tour of European capitals from 31 August to 2 September 1926. The next year S. A. Shestakov and D. V. Fufayev flew an R-3M-5 (the designation of the M-5-powered version) from Moscow to Tokyo and back, a distance of some 13,700 miles, in 153hr flying time.

Tupolev R-6 (ANT-7)   USSR

Purpose: Long-range reconnaissance/Escort fighter
Makers: Soviet State Aircraft Factories
In service: 1932-41
Photo: KR-6

Engines: See below
Span: 76ft 1.4in
Length: 49ft 4.9in
Weight loaded: 14,268lb

Crew: Four
Max speed: 142.9mph
Service ceiling: 16,076ft
Normal range: 500 miles
Armament: Five 7.62mm machine guns. 1,102lb of bombs

This twin-engined cantilever low-wing monoplane looked like a smaller-scale TB-1. Wing area was just two-thirds that of the TB-1. Developed by Andrei Tupolev's design team under the designation ANT-7, a BMW VI-powered prototype flew for the first time on 11 September 1929 piloted by Mikhail Gromov. Its nose section was of totally new design and it had gunners' cockpits in nose and dorsal positions, each of which had twin 7.62mm DA-2 machine gun mountings. A fifth 7.62mm machine gun was operated from a retractable ventral turret. The pilot was seated in an open cockpit in line with the wing leading-edge. Wings and fuselage had a covering of corrugated KA aluminium alloy sheeting. Some 400 ANT-7s were built, all except 45 (which had main undercarriage legs identical to those on TB-1) with

undercarriages of new design. The ANT-7 had been designed to perform reconnaissance missions at greater ranges than could be achieved by single-engined machines. In this role the type served as the R-6, but the Soviet Command was anxious to develop a twin-engined escort fighter on the lines of French World War 1 Letord and Caudron types. Thus some ANT-7s were designated KR-6 (KR for 'Cruiser') and were operated alongside TB-3 bombers. All series aircraft were powered by twin 715hp M-17F inline engines. Transport conversions of the ANT-7 included the R-6 Limousine and the PS-7 (alternatively designated P-6). They flew with Aeroflot and Soviet Arctic Aviation, carrying passengers or freight. An R-6, piloted by P. G. Golovin, reconnoitred the North Pole in 1937 in preparation for the landing of the remaining aircraft in the Soviet Arctic Expedition of that year. A twin-float torpedo-bomber version was designated MR-6 (or KR-6P), while a passenger floatplane was known as the MP-6. R-6s and KR-6s still in service in 1936 were relegated to training duties. A number of all versions remained flying until 1944 as military transports.

Tupolev TB-1   USSR

Purpose: Bomber
Makers: Soviet State Aircraft Factories
In service: 1929-35 (as a bomber)

Engines: See below
Span: 94ft 1.9in
Length: 59ft 0.67in
Height: 19ft 11.75in
Weight loaded: 15,013lb
Crew: Six
Max speed: 128mph
Service ceiling: 15,847ft
Normal range: 621 miles
Armament: Six 7.62mm machine guns. Bomb load: 2,205lb

In the early 1930s Soviet units operating the TB-1 all-metal cantilever low-wing monoplane constituted the world's most potent contemporary heavy bombing force. Inspired by his mentor Zhukovsky, Andrei N. Tupolev had set about design of the large ANT-4 in 1923. First prototype was flown by test pilot A. I. Tomashevsky on 24 November 1925. After

protracted development, the original 450hp British Napier Lion engines were replaced by 730hp German BMW VIs in 1928. The following year Shestakov flew the ANT-4 *Stranya Sovietov* (Land of the Soviets) on a long distance flight from Moscow to New York, during some stages of which twin floats of British Short design were fitted. The flight achieved tremendous publicity in the United States. First series TB-1s, powered by 680hp M-17 engines, were delivered in June 1929, production continuing until 1932, when a total of c216 had been completed. A number of TB-1P floatplanes were also constructed for Soviet Naval Aviation. Armament comprised three twin DA-2 7.62mm machine guns, one in the nose and two in tandem amidships. The dorsal gun rings were on slides in cockpits which stretched the width of the fuselage. This enabled fire to be concentrated either to port or starboard as required. Pilot and co-pilot were seated side by side in open cockpits. Fuselage and wing covering consisted of corrugated Kolchugaluminium alloy sheeting. The large divided undercarriage had single main wheels. Passages inside the thick-section

wings provided access in flight. 'Parasite' fighter experiments with 'Zveno 1', a combination of a TB-1 with two I-4 fighters mounted on its wings, began in December 1931. A number of successful aerial 'launches' had been made when work was switched to the TB-3 and 'Zveno 2'. Several other ANT-4s were converted for use by Soviet Arctic Aviation (some with enclosed pilots' cockpits), one hitting world headlines in March 1934 when Lyapidevsky landed his ski-equipped aircraft on drifting ice to begin the rescue of scientists and crew from the abandoned polar research icebreaker *Chelyuskin*. When TB-1s were phased out of the heavy bombing units in 1936 surviving machines were redesignated G-1s and converted as military transports. They operated until the end of the war against Germany, some with equipment panniers between the main undercarriage legs.

Tupolev TB-3   USSR

Purpose: Heavy bomber
Makers: Soviet State Aircraft Factories
In service: 1931-43
Data: TB-3 M-34RN (1935 version)

Engines: See below
Span: 137ft 3.6in
Length: 82ft 7.33in
Height: 27ft 8.75in
Weight loaded: 41,617lb
Crew: Ten
Max speed: 179mph
Service ceiling: 25,394ft

Normal range: 597 miles
Armament: Eight 7.62mm DA-2 machine guns

First prototype ANT-6 (military designation TB-3) made its maiden flight on 22 December 1930, powered by four American 600hp Curtiss Conqueror engines. An all-metal cantilever low-wing monoplane derived from the TB-1, it went into production at the GAZ No 22 and GAZ No 39 factories in Moscow. First series aircraft (with 680hp M-17F engines) were delivered from January 1932. Armament comprised 10 7.62mm DA-2 twin-mounted machine guns. The nose gunner's cockpit

was in a 'balcony' and immediately behind was the amply glazed navigator/bomb aimer's cabin. Pilot and co-pilot were seated in an open cockpit side-by-side and behind the wing were two dorsal gunners' cockpits in tandem (on the lines of the TB-1). Two retractable 'dustbin' turrets were installed under the wings just inboard of the two outer engines. Fuselage and wing covering was corrugated light alloy sheeting. The fixed undercarriage had a tandem pair of wheels on each main leg. Production of an 830hp M-34-powered version lasted a few months in 1934 before it was phased out in favour of the M-34R-engined TB-3 with reduction gear. In this version the fuselage was extended aft of the tail fin and rudder to accommodate a tail gun position, protected by a large windshield. The previous huge tailskid was replaced by a tailwheel. Only one dorsal gunner's cockpit was provided. The underwing turrets had been deleted during the production run of the M-17F-powered version. Later in 1934 a version with supercharged M-34RN engines went into production. At that period the metal skin of the wings and tail unit were fabric covered and other aerodynamic refinements helped to improve performance. From 1935 the M-34RNF engine was fitted to production machines. A smooth skin covering was adopted and the main undercarriage legs had large single wheels with low-pressure tyres. A redesigned smoothly contoured nose had a manually-operated gun turret and another turret was usually installed amidships in place of the open position. Crew was reduced to six and machine guns to three 7.62mm ShKASs, which had greater total firepower than the 10 DA weapons on the original TB-3. Throughout the 1930s TB-3s flew in impressive mass formations over Red Square, the first such flight being by nine aircraft on May Day 1932. As well as equipping heavy bomber Brigades (of some 50 machines each) deployed in Europe and the Far East, TB-3s were widely employed in paratroop manoeuvres and participated in Zveno-2 parasite fighter experiments. Soviet Arctic Aviation used the ANT-6 civil version, including a variant of the later production aircraft with fully enclosed crew accommodation. During September 1936 a number of world load-to-height records were established by a TB-3. Normal bomb load of 4,410lb could be increased to a maximum 10,572lb (18×220lb bombs in the bomb bay plus six 1,100lb bombs on external racks) for short-range missions.

TB-3/ANT-6 production terminated in 1938 with the 818th machine. TB-3s took part in operations against the Japanese at Lake Hasan and Nomonhan during 1938-9 and against Finland in 1939-40. Interestingly, a long-range dive-bombing Zveno unit was established in 1940 in which TB-3s acted as mother ships to a pair of SPB single-seaters (I-16 conversions) each with two 550lb bombs. The unit was operational over the Ukraine and Romania during 1941, achieving some success. TB-3s were used widely for night bombing and transport duties (some G-2 transports carrying vehicles between the undercarriage legs) during the German invasion until attrition took its inevitable toll. And losses were not surprising, for although the original maximum speed of 133.6mph at sea level with the M-17F-engined version had risen to 143.5mph with the M-34R-powered version and to 179mph at 9,842ft with the M-34RN version, this was still well below an acceptable speed for a bomber in the 1940s.

Vickers Vildebeest   UK

Purpose: Torpedo bomber
Makers: Vickers (Aviation) Ltd
In service: 1933-42
Data: Mk IV

Engine: See below
Span: 49ft 0in
Length: 37ft 8in
Height: 14ft 8in
Weight loaded: 8,500-8,700lb
Crew: Two
Max speed: 156mph
Absolute ceiling: 19,000ft
Range: 630-1,250miles
Armament: One forward-firing Vickers machine gun and one Lewis machine gun in rear cockpit. One 18in torpedo or bombs.

During World War 1, the Vickers company established itself as a designer and manufacturer of successful combat planes with the Gunbus fighting scout, itself a development of the Destroyer prototype which had been exhibited at the 1913 Olympia aero show. Towards the end of the war the company produced the Vimy bomber, which began its successful pattern for huge aircraft that remained its hallmark until the early 1930s, and then again during World War 2 and beyond, taking in the series of Virginia bombers and Vernon/Victoria transports. The pattern temporarily changed with the introduction of the Vildebeest, a smaller (but not small) biplane of easily discernible shape. There had been other small Vickers aircraft — the Vixen, Vivid, Vendace, Vespa and others — but these proved unsuccessful in terms of orders. Designed from the outset as a torpedo-bomber, the Vildebeest was one of the best aircraft to serve in this role during the period covered by this book, and later formed the basis of another fine aircraft, the Vincent. The two-seat prototype (which was later civil registered) first flew in the spring of 1928, powered originally by a 460hp Bristol Jupiter VIII radial engine. Unusually for an aircraft of this size, the pilot was accommodated forward of the wings and so was afforded an excellent view, and sat well above the level of the rear-gunner. The standard prone bombing position was below the pilot's seat. Production started in 1932, and in the following year the first examples (which could be fitted with twin floats) were delivered to the RAF. The original production model was the Vildebeest Mk I, powered by the 620hp Pegasus IM3 radial engine. This model had a maximum speed of 141mph as a landplane at 6,560ft. This was followed by the Mk II, with a

650hp Pegasus IIM3 engine and wheel fairings (which were often removed). The next version, the Mk III of 1934, was powered by the same engine as the Mk II but had, as standard layout, a third crew member. The final production version was the Mk IV, which was powered by a moderately supercharged 810hp Bristol Perseus VIII engine, driving a three-blade propeller, and enclosed in a cowling. Total production of Vildebeest amounted to just over 200 aircraft, including two modified into Vincents at an early date, one modified into a long-range floatplane and one used as a test aircraft for the proposed Latvian model; of these, about half were operational

with the RAF at the outbreak of World War 2. Following demonstration of the type to Spanish officials, about 27 were built in Spain by the Construcciones Aeronauticas SA. These were powered by 595hp Hispano-Suiza 12 engines, enclosed in streamlined cowlings, giving them a much cleaner appearance than RAF examples, and were operated by the Spanish Naval Air Service as both land- and seaplanes. The fate of these aircraft is not certain after the beginning of the Spanish Civil War. The other major user of the type was the Royal New Zealand Air Force, which acquired over 30.

Vickers Vimy   UK

Purpose: Heavy bomber
Makers: Vickers Ltd
In service: 1918-29
Photo and Data: Mk IV

Engines: See below
Span: 68ft 0in
Length: 43ft 6.5in
Height: 15ft 7.5in
Weight loaded: 10,900-12,450lb
Crew: Three
Max speed: 103mph
Service ceiling: 10,000ft

Range: More than 835 miles
Armament: 0.303in Lewis machine guns in nose and aft cockpits. Up to 2,475lb of bombs

Best remembered as the aircraft flown by Captain John Alcock and Lieutenant Arthur Whitten Brown on the first non-stop crossing of the Atlantic during 14 and 15 June 1919, the Vimy was the first of the 'heavies' to be produced by Vickers. It was designed to carry out long range strategic bombing raids on German Industrial areas and would have undoubtedly proved itself in the task had the war in Europe continued into 1919. Generally similar in

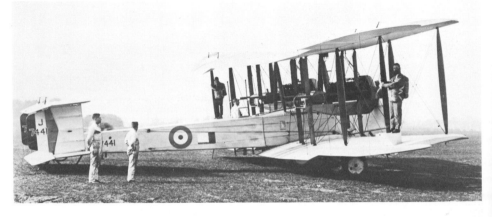

layout to the Handley Page 0/400, which it was expected to supplement in the Independent Force, it represented a slight improvement in performance and capability. This was fortunate as only three were in service by the Armistice and these had not been used operationally, and the government had little money to spend on new production aircraft postwar and even less enthusiasm. It is difficult to accurately assess how many Vimys were built for the RAF up to the mid-1920s, with so many huge orders cancelled after the war, others partially completed and a few aircraft being used for experimental purposes, including ditching trials in 1920. Three original prototypes were built, the first of these making its maiden flight on 30 November 1917, just four months after the Air Board had decided, temporarily, to stop further development of all heavy bombers. The third prototype had 305hp Fiat A-12 engines and it is probable that a few Vimys were produced with similar engines. However, the vast majority of production Vimys were powered by 360hp Rolls-

Royce Eagle VIIIs and are usually known as Vimy Mk IVs. Between 220 and 250 production Vimys were produced, first going to an RAF squadron in Egypt in July 1919. Aircraft of another squadron were used until mid-1926 for the Cairo-to-Baghdad mail services. It is interesting to note that only one flight of the RAF based in England was operational with the type until mid-1923, representing the entire home-based twin-engined heavy bomber force. In the following year Virginias began replacing Vimys in bomber squadrons and only the County of Ulster squadron retained Vimys for any length of time thereafter, these lasting until the end of the decade. As a bomber, the Vimy had served at a particularly mundane period of history, but there was consolation in that a large number were subsequently re-engined with Bristol Jupiter or Armstrong Siddeley Jaguar radials and were used as dual-control and parachute trainers, a fate that also awaited Virginias. The few Vimys still flying in the late 1930s ended life as targets.

Vickers Vincent   UK

Purpose: General purpose
Makers: Vickers (Aviation) Ltd
In service: 1934-41

Engine: One 650hp Bristol Pegasus IIM3
Span: 49ft 0in
Length: 36ft 8in
Height: 17ft 9in
Weight loaded: 8,100lb (of which 3,850 disposable)
Crew: Three
Max speed: 142mph at 4,925ft
Absolute ceiling: 19,000ft
Max range: 625-1,250 miles
Armament: One fixed forward-firing Vickers machine gun and one Lewis machine gun in rear cockpit. Up to 1,000lb of bombs

Vincents entered service with the RAF during the heyday of the developed biplane, when this type of aircraft reigned supreme in every military role. From

heavy night bombers to transports and trainers, the list was endless, including such familiar names as the Hyderabad, Hinaidi, Heyford, Hart, Sidestrand, Wallace, Audax, Wapiti, Demon, Fury, Gauntlet, Perth and Scapa. Yet, by 1936, the first monoplanes had taken over, initially in the form of the Hendon and Anson and in the following year as the Harrow, Whitley, Battle, Hurricane and Wellesley. The Silver Jubilee Review of the RAF at Mildenhall in 1935, in the presence of King George V, was virtually the last display of biplanes alone and marked the decline of an era, although still to come were such stalwarts as the Gladiator, Hector and Swordfish. Developed from the Vildebeest, the Vincent was designed essentially for tropical service and became the RAF's standard overseas general-purpose aircraft. Selection of the type followed trials in Egypt of a modified Vildebeest. Basically similar to the standard Vildebeest, the Vincent carried a streamlined long-range fuel tank under the centre-section of the lower wing which doubled its range, and other equipment included a

message retrieving hook, underwing bomb racks and special tropical and emergency items, including a water tank, rations, wireless, tool kit and Very pistol, the latter items considered expedient for the same reasons as those outlined under the DH9A entry. Accommodation for a third crew member was provided, as in the Vildebeest III. A converted Vildebeest was the first Vincent, and production lasted until the latter part of 1936, when other Vildebeests were converted. Just under 200 Vincents were produced, first entering RAF service in late 1934. A total of about 50 was later supplied to

the Royal New Zealand Air Force, already using Vildebeests. Subsequently, RAF Vincents equipped squadrons stationed in Aden, Egypt, India, Iraq, Kenya and the Sudan. The type remained in widespread use until the arrival of more modern monoplanes like the geodetic Vickers Wellesley. Even as late as the outbreak of war, a number of Vincents were still in service, and the last few remained operational overseas until 1941, despite such outdated performance as requiring over 9.5min to climb to 2,000m under ideal conditions, with an initial rate of climb of only 765ft/min.

Vickers Virginia
UK

Purpose: Heavy night bomber
Makers: Vickers Ltd
In service: 1924-37
Photo: Mk VII
Data: Mk X

Engines: Two 580hp Napier Lion Vs
Span: 87ft 8in
Length: 62ft 3in
Height: 18ft 2in
Weight loaded: 17,600lb
Crew: Four
Max speed: 108mph at 4,925ft
Service ceiling: 15,525ft
Range: 985 miles
Armament: One .303in Lewis Mk III machine gun in nose and two in tail. About 3,200lb of bombs (see below)

Developed as a replacement for the Vimy, the Virginia remained in service with the RAF for well over a decade as its principal heavy night bomber. It completely overshadowed its contemporary, the Avro Aldershot — which could carry a useful 2,000lb of bombs over a reasonable range — by virtue of having the favoured twin engines. Of wood or, later, metal construction, mostly fabric covered, the Virginia prototype first flew on 24 November 1922, powered by two 450hp Napier Lion engines, and was sent for evaluation trials. The first series production version was the Mk III, which incorporated minor refinements, and was followed by the Mks IV, V and VI, all with the original type of straight wings. The Mk Vs also featured a third vertical-tail surface. Many of these aircraft, together with Mk VIs, were subsequently converted into later

versions. The Mk VII differed considerably from its predecessors, having slightly swept outer wings and dihedral on the upper as well as the lower wings. Also, the nose was lengthened and modified — a feature found on both of the later production versions. The Mk IX followed the Mk VII in service, and took the rear gunner's cockpit from behind the wings to a 'dustbin' in the tail. The last version, the Mk X, was the only version with a fabric, plywood and aluminium covered duralumin and steel metal structure, and had Handley Page slots. Its bomb load was made up of nine 112lb bombs beneath the fuselage, and two racks beneath the lower centre plane each carried six 112lb, four 230lb, four 250lb, two 520lb or two 550lb bombs. A total of 126 Virginias was built, of which 50 were Mk Xs. They entered RAF service in late 1924, and were the first bombers of the RAF to have automatic pilots. But, however formidable a weapon during the 1920s, the Virginia was pretty poor compared with many types being flown operationally in Europe in the early 1930s. Nevertheless, the Virginia was still Britain's main bomber when Winston Churchill gave his first warning to Parliament about the increasing strength of Germany's Luftwaffe, in October 1933, a time when even the larger and heavier Handley Page airliners of Imperial Airways could fly faster. Following their final withdrawal from service in 1937, some Virginias were used subsequently for parachute training and air-to-air photography. It is worth noting that Vickers tried to keep the Virginia-type of bomber alive with a number of abortive prototypes, culminating in the four-engined Type 163. This aircraft, fitted with Rolls-Royce Kestrel engines, featured an enclosed cockpit for the flight crew and could carry a heavy bomb load or 21 fully-armed troops in the cabin as a transport.

Vickers Wellesley

UK

Purpose: Bomber
Makers: Vickers (Aviation) Ltd
In service: 1937-41
Data: Mk I

Engine: One 925hp Bristol Pegasus XX radial
Span: 74ft 7in
Length: 39ft 3in
Height: 12ft 4in
Weight loaded: 11,100lb
Crew: Two
Max speed: 228mph
Absolute ceiling: 35,250ft
Range: 1,110 miles
Armament: One .303in fixed forward-firing Vickers machine gun and one Vickers K machine gun in rear cockpit. Up to 2,000lb of bombs carried in two containers under the wings

The prototype Wellesley, built as a private venture, first flew on 19 June 1935. Although seemingly unlikely, it had as its most important feature a constructional innovation first developed by Barnes Neville Wallis for the Airship Guarantee Company's R-100 airship, one of the last two commercial airships developed in Britain. This was its geodetic construction, a lattice-work structure of intersecting geodetic duralumin members attached to four duralumin longerons, fabric covered. The Wellesley was a monoplane development of the earlier single Vickers Type 253, which had first flown in August 1934. The Type 253 had been designed to a 1931 specification and was a biplane with the upper wings attached to the top of the fuselage and lower wings of inverted-gull type. The undercarriage was fixed.

Following the conclusion of the flight trials — for which several aircraft including the Blackburn B-7, Fairey F-1 and Hawker PV-4 had also been built — many examples of the Type 253 were ordered. However, in September 1935 the order was cancelled in favour of the more modern Wellesley. When, in April 1937, the first Wellesley Mk Is entered RAF service, they became the first RAF aircraft of geodetic construction. The Mk I had an oval-section fuselage in which the crew of two were accommodated in separate cockpits, individually enclosed, with intercommunication between. Provision was made in the design for auxiliary flying controls for the observer/navigator. The later Mk II version featured a single long canopy, which extended from the pilot's cockpit to that of the observer/navigator. A total of 176 Wellesleys of both versions (not including the prototype) was built, serving before World War 2 with several home-based squadrons. By the outbreak of war, virtually all had been sent to the Middle East, where they served during 1940 as bombers, and as reconnaissance aircraft until 1941.

In 1938, Wellesleys of the Long-range Development Flight of the RAF broke the world long distance record held previously by a Russian ANT-25. The flight had been formed in 1935 in preparation for such an attempt. On 5 November 1938, three Wellesleys (each with a 1,000hp Pegasus XXII radial engine and an all-up weight of 18,400lb) took off from Ismailia, Egypt, in a bid for the record. One aircraft landed short of the goal, but the other two (one piloted by Sqn Ldr R. Kellett and the other by Flt Lt A. Coombe) landed at Darwin, Australia, two days later, having flown 7,162 miles non-stop.

Westland Wallace   UK

Purpose: General purpose
Makers: Westland Aircraft Ltd
In service: 1933-43
Photo: Mk II

Engine: See below
Span: 46ft 5in
Length: 34ft 2in
Height: 11ft 6in
Weight loaded: 5,750lb
Crew: Two
Max speed: 158mph at 5,000ft
Absolute ceiling: 25,700ft
Range: 470-1,120 miles
Armament: One forward-firing Vickers machine gun and one Lewis machine gun in rear cockpit. Up to 580lb of bombs as normal load or 1,130lb in overload condition

Still in service in small numbers as a target towing aircraft in 1943, the Wallace was designed as a rugged general purpose biplane suitable for bombing, reconnaissance, photography, army co-operation and other duties. Apart from its excellent service with the RAF, it made a name as one of two aircraft that achieved the first flights over Mount Everest on 3 April 1933, piloted by Flt Lt D. F. McIntyre. For the flight, all military equipment had been removed and replaced with electrical and photographic equipment needed for the survey. Because of the extreme altitude that had to be attained during the crossing, special alterations to the fuel and oil systems were made to ensure engine reliability. (The other aircraft was the

Westland PV-3, flown by the Marquess of Clydesdale, and also known as the Houston-Westland. It was reported at the time, and widely believed, that one of these aircraft set up an unofficial world height record of more than 35,000ft while on test. This, of course, was not the case as the official height record in 1932 was 43,976ft set by a Vickers Vespa.) The Wallace was a private venture development of the Wapiti and first appeared in prototype form in 1931. It was known originally as the Wapiti Mk VII, and successive refinements to this machine were carried out until it appeared with the lengthened fuselage of the late-model Wapiti, a new divided-type undercarriage, a tailwheel and a Bristol Pegasus radial engine. Following evaluation trials, 12 Wapitis were rebuilt to this standard, except that power was provided by a Pegasus IIM3 engine of 570hp. A further 51 Wapitis were converted subsequently to the same standard and, as Wallace Mk Is, first entered service with the RAF in 1933. One Wallace I was used as an experimental tanker. In 1935 there appeared the improved Mk II version. Fitted with a 680hp Bristol Pegasus IV engine, this had a sliding coupé canopy over the pilot's cockpit and a rounded lobster-type hood over the rear gunner's cockpit. The latter was formed by using segmental transparent windows which could be locked down to enclose the rear cockpit or folded back to give an unrestricted field of fire for the Lewis gun. In an emergency, the roof section of the pilot's canopy could be pushed out at the centre joint. Total production of the Mk II amounted to 107 aircraft, including three Wapitis converted to Wallace II standard, originally earmarked as Wallace Is.

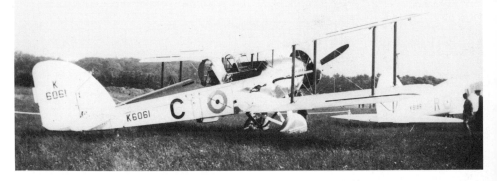

Westland Wapiti   UK

Purpose: General purpose
Makers: Westland Aircraft Ltd
In service: From 1928
Photo and Data: Mk IIA

Engine: See below
Span: 46ft 5in
Length: 32ft 6in

Height: 11ft 10in
Weight loaded: 5,400lb
Crew: Two
Max speed: 140mph at 5,000ft
Service ceiling: 20,600ft
Normal range: 360 miles
Armament: One forward-firing Vickers machine gun and one Lewis machine gun in rear cockpit. Up to 500lb of bombs

In common with other aircraft manufacturers in the latter 1920s, Westland produced several prototypes of military aircraft, of which only one was selected for service, the Wapiti. Non-successful machines included the Yeovil biplane bomber, Wizzard high-performance parasol-wing fighter and Witch short-range day bomber. Prior to these, Westland had been engaged in re-conditioning DH9As and it was this experience that put the company in a strong position to satisfy the RAF's need for a new general-purpose aircraft to replace the DH9A, which culminated in the Wapiti. To conform to Air Ministry requirements, the new aircraft had to embody as many DH9A parts as possible, while improving on general performance. A modified Armstrong Whitworth Atlas, the Bristol Beaver, the DH9AJ Stag, a modified Fairey IIIF, the Gloster Goral, the Vickers Valiant, the Vickers Vixen and the Wapiti were all contenders for the coveted production contracts. The Wapiti first flew in March 1927, powered by a 420hp Bristol Jupiter VI radial engine and embodying the wings, ailerons and interplane struts of the DH9A. It won the competition, and an initial order for 25 Mk Is was placed for the RAF (one built as Mk IA with a special rear cockpit for the Prince of Wales), followed by a contract for 10 460hp Jupiter VI-engined Wapiti Mk IIs — the first version with an all-metal structure. Next came 415 Wapiti Mk IIAs powered by 525hp Jupiter VIIIF or XFa radial engines, 35 Wapiti Mk Vs with lengthened fuselages, and 16 unarmed Wapiti Mk VIs, with dual controls for use as trainers. Wapiti Mk Is first entered RAF service in 1928 in Iraq, where they were used for air control duties. However, most Wapitis were operated at home or in India. (Between late 1928 and early 1929, Wapitis escorted Victorias during the Kabul evacuation — see Vickers Victoria.) Among the Wapitis produced were a number of specialised versions for specific tasks. These included an army co-operation version with a message retrieving hook, Wapitis fitted with float and ski undercarriages, and overseas patrol aircraft that could carry an extra fuel tank, a spare wheel, spare tail skid, fitter's tool box, engine spares, crew survival rations, water, bedding and other equipment. The Wapiti was finally withdrawn from Auxiliary Air Force squadrons in the UK in 1937; but a large number remained in service in India in 1939 (see Vickers Victoria). 64 Wapitis were converted to Wallaces during the early 1930s. Others were operated by the air forces of Australia (Jupiter VIII engines, and served alongside Bristol Bulldogs), Canada, India and South Africa (joining Avro Tutors and DH9s); and a small number were sold to China (Panther IIA engines, and joining a wide selection of American, French, Italian and British aircraft), and Hedjaz. A further 27 were licence-built in South Africa, at the Aircraft and Artillery Depot at Roberts' Heights, Pretoria. Those of the Indian Air Force formed its initial equipment when received in 1933, the force having been constituted in October 1932 and the officers trained at Cranwell.

Yokosuka B3Y1

Japan

Purpose: Carrier-borne torpedo bomber
Makers: Aichi Tokei Denki KK (Aichi Clock &
Electric Co Ltd)
In service: 1933-37

Engine: See below
Span: 44ft 3.7in
Length: 31ft 2in
Height: 12ft 2.8in
Weight loaded: 7,055lb
Crew: Three
Max speed: 136mph
Armament: Two 7.7mm machine guns. One
torpedo or up to 1,102lb of bombs

The Yokosuka Naval Air Arsenal built an improved
version of the B1M3 torpedo bomber as the Type
13KAI, utilising a 500hp V-12 engine. The
urgent need for a new carrier torpedo bomber led to a more
powerful production development being ordered
almost immediately. Designated B3Y1, series aircraft
were powered by an inline 750hp Type 91 V-12
liquid-cooled engine with a 'chin' radiator under the
nose. The type went into service as the Navy
Type 92 Carrier Torpedo Bomber. It was an equal-
span two-bay biplane. Wings were staggered and

swept back. Ailerons were fitted to both upper and
lower wings. The crew was accommodated in three
tandem open cockpits close together in the slim,
long fuselage. The wide-track undercarriage was of
divided type and a tailwheel replaced the traditional
tailskid. Offensive armament could include a 1,764lb
torpedo or one 1,102lb bomb. Alternative loads
included two 511lb bombs or six 66lb bombs.
Defensive armament comprised one fixed 7.7mm
machine gun in the engine cowling and another gun
of the same calibre on a ring mounting over the
rearmost cockpit. 130 B3Y1s were built between
1933 and 1936, all at the Aichi factory. The B3Y1
saw operational service when the Sino-Japanese
Incident led to fighting between Japan and China in
July 1937. Six of the type were embarked on the
carrier *Hosho* commanded by Captain Ryunosuke
Kusaka and attached to the Imperial Navy's First
Carrier Division. The carrier cruised off Shanghai and
the bombers operated over the adjoining mainland
area. In the early days of fighting a further 12 B3Y1s
moved from their base at Omura to the Shanghai
area to fly with the 12th Air Corps (attached to the
Second Combined Air Flotilla). The B3Y1 proved
singularly unsuccessful in action, being slow and
cumbersome in flight and difficult to manoeuvre on
board aircraft carriers.

Part Two

Aero A30 Series
/ Czechoslovakia

Purpose: Reconnaissance-bomber
Photo: A230

Engine: One 450hp Skoda L
Span: 50ft 2.25 in
Max speed: 146mph
Armament: Fixed forward-firing Vickers and two rear-mounted Lewis machine guns. Up to 1,323lb of bombs

First appearing in 1926, the A30 was basically a scaled-up and streamlined development of the earlier A11. It had unequal-span single-bay wings of wooden structure, fabric covered, with ailerons on the upper planes only. The rectangular section fuselage was constructed of steel tubes, again fabric covered, and a cross-axle Vee undercarriage was fitted. The engine was installed on a quickly detachable mounting, fed by fuel from tanks in the fuselage and the raised upper wing centre section. Production began in 1927, and in August of that

year an A30 set-up a world speed-with-payload record, averaging more than 132mph over a 500km circuit. Included in the total of 79 production aircraft built were a number of improved A230s, the first of which appeared in 1930. The A230 was powered by an Avia-built 450hp Lorraine engine and had a number of refinements including a new frontal radiator, differently shaped lower wings, a divided undercarriage and new bomb racks under the lower wings, and fuselage. Aircraft of the series remained in first-line service until the latter 1930s, when they were replaced by the faster A100/101.

Aero MB-200 Series
/ Czechoslovakia

Purpose: Bomber

Engines: Two 850hp Walter-built Gnome-Rhône K-14 radials
Span: 73ft 8in
Max speed: 152mph
Armament: Three Mk30 machine guns. Up to 3,086lb of bombs

The Aero MB-200 high-wing bomber was a licence-built version of the French Marcel Bloch MB-200 BN4. A total of 124 Aero (and Avia)-built MB-200s

went into Czech Air Force service from 1936 and these slow and poorly armed bombers served alongside the far better Avia B-71s right up to March 1939, when Germany occupied Czechoslovakia to make the country a so-called German Protectorate.

Aichi D3A / Japan

Purpose: Carrier-based dive bomber

Engine: One 1,075hp Mitsubishi Kinsei 44 radial
Span: 47ft 1.25in
Max speed: 242mph
Armament: Three 7.7mm machine guns. Up to 816lb of bombs

This was Japan's first all-metal low-wing monoplane dive-bomber. It was one of the main types used by the Japanese during the attack on Pearl Harbor in December 1941 and production of 'Vals' continued until 1944, latterly in the D3A2 version. It was conceived after exhaustive studies of German

Heinkel aircraft and entered production as the Aichi D3A1 in 1937. Production of this version was completed in 1942 after 478 had been built for the Imperial Japanese Navy.

Amiot 122-BP3 / France

Purpose: Bomber/Escort

Engine: One 650hp Lorraine 18Kd
Span: 70ft 6in
Max speed: 128mph
Armament: Five machine guns (see below). Normal
bomb load 1,300lb; Max bomb load 1,764lb

This very large single-engined three-seat biplane was
designed by the Société d'Emboutissage et de
Constructions Mécaniques (Société Genérale
Aéronautique) (SECM) and appeared in 1928. The
prototype undertook demonstration flights in several
countries in a bid to win production orders.
Production aircraft, of which 80 were built from
1929, had a greater wing span than the prototype
and served with the Armée de l'Air. The pilot's
cockpit was behind the trailing-edge of the upper
wing, and tandem cockpits were provided for the
gunner and navigator/bomber. The fuselage had two
floors which connected all crew positions. Armament
comprised two fixed Vickers guns firing forward, two
Lewis guns on a flexible mounting in the gunner's
position and a further Lewis gun firing downward
through the floor of the fuselage. Five Amiot 122s
were exported to Brazil.

Arado Ar95 and Ar196
/ Germany

Purpose: Reconnaissance-bomber
Photo: Ar196
Data: Ar95A-1

Engine: One 880hp BMW 132Dc radial
Span: 41ft 0.25in
Max speed: 171.5mph (seaplane)
Armament: Two 7.9mm machine guns, forward-
firing and rear-mounted, and six 110lb bombs, one
bomb up to 1,102lb weight or one torpedo

The Ar95 was a reconnaissance and bombing
biplane capable of being operated as the Ar95See
seaplane or as a landplane with heavily trousered
main undercarriage legs (with oleo-pneumatic shock
absorbers) and a faired tailwheel. The land version
had a maximum speed of over 200mph. Six
prototypes were built and these were sent to Spain
in August 1938 to serve with the Condor Legion
fighting with the Nationalists in the civil war. A few
Ar95 land and seaplanes were also exported to Chile
just before the outbreak of World War 2 and others
built for Turkey were retained for Luftwaffe use. The
Arado Ar196 was a development of the Ar95 and
appeared in 1938. It was probably the most
successful seaplane used by the German Navy air
forces during World War 2 and was for several years
the standard catapult seaplane. Up to four Ar196s
could be carried on board larger German battleships.
Production began with the Ar196A-1, of which some
20 were built before production changed to later
wartime variants.

Avia B-71 / Czechoslovakia

Purpose: Bomber

Engines: Two 760hp Avia-built Hispano-Suiza
12 Ydrs
Span: 66ft 8.5in
Max speed: 267mph
Armament: Three Mk 30 machine guns in nose,
dorsal and ventral positions. Up to 1,323lb of bombs

Between 1937 and 1938 a total of more than 50
SB-2 (ANT-40) medium bombers were acquired
from the USSR by the Czechoslovak Air Force, which
designated them B-71s. (See SB-2.)

Avro Anson / UK

Purpose: Reconnaissance/Trainer

Engines: Two 350hp Armstrong Siddeley Cheetah IX radials
Span: 56ft 6in
Max speed: 170mph
Armament: Two .303in machine guns. Up to 360lb of bombs

Developed from the six-seat Avro 652 commercial aircraft, the prototype of what became known as 'Faithful Annie' first flew on 24 March 1935, powered by two Armstrong Siddeley Cheetah VI engines. 174 modified examples were ordered, the first of these entering service in March 1936, equipping a Squadron of RAF Coastal Command. 1,500 Anson trainers were also ordered, and began to enter service in early 1939. In December the type was selected as part of the equipment for the Commonwealth Air Training Plan. Production of the Anson finally ceased in May 1952, after many thousands of British-built aircraft had been completed. Canadian factories produced a further 2,882.

Blackburn Skua / UK

Purpose: Fighter/Dive bomber

Engine: One 830hp Bristol Perseus XII radial
Span: 46ft 2in
Max speed: 225mph
Armament: Four forward-firing Browning machine guns and one rear-mounted Lewis gun. Up to 500lb bomb

The Skua was the first monoplane to enter service with the Fleet Air Arm and was the first FAA type to bring down a German aircraft in World War 2. This action began when Swordfish from *Ark Royal* spotted three Dornier Do18s. Skuas were launched to intercept them and one Do18 was brought down and the crew captured. The first prototype Skua had flown on 9 February 1937; but before this an order for 190 production aircraft had been placed and these were to be designated Skua Mk IIs. The first entered service with the FAA in November 1938 on board HMS *Ark Royal* and three squadrons were equipped by the outbreak of World War 2. In 1941 they were replaced in first line service, but remained flying as target tugs and trainers. Design features worthy of note include the all-metal watertight fuselage, to enable the aircraft to remain buoyant in an emergency, and all-metal folding wings.

Blackburn Swift/Dart/Velos / UK

Purpose: Carrier-borne torpedo bomber
Data: Dart

Engine: One 450hp Napier Lion IIB or Lion V
Span: 45ft 6in
Max speed: 108mph
Armament: One 18in torpedo or two 520lb bombs

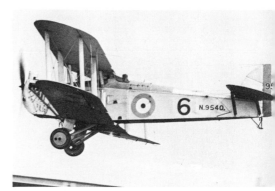

The Swift prototype was built in 1919, with a divided undercarriage to facilitate torpedo dropping. The only production examples built went for export. From the Swift was developed the Dart, which entered FAA service in 1923. By the end of production nearly 120 had been built, and Darts remained on FAA strength until 1933. One of them made the first landing at night on board an aircraft carrier, HMS *Furious*, on 1 July 1926. The Velos was a twin-float version of the Dart and was used by the RAF to train reserve pilots. A few also served in Greece and Spain, being constructed at the Phaleron Aircraft Factory, near Athens, in the former case. Spanish aircraft served alongside Dornier Wals and Macchi 18s.

Blériot 127/2 / France

Purpose: Bomber

Engines: Two 550hp Hispano-Suiza 12s
Span: 76ft 1.5in
Max speed: 124mph
Armament: One or two forward-firing Lewis machine guns on a flexible mount in nose and two machine gun positions in tail of nacelles. Up to 2,205lb of bombs

The prototype 127 monoplane, constructed of wood and fabric, appeared in 1928. It had been developed from the earlier Blériot 117 multi-seat monoplane, which had not entered production and had been one of a few aircraft produced by Blériot during the mid-1920s not to bear the SPAD name (the company having taken over SPAD and produced its designs). Designed specifically for high-altitude fighting and escorting day bombers, the 117 made its preliminary flight tests at Buc. Power was provided by 400hp Lorraine-Dietrich engines. Estimated maximum speed was 118mph. The standard model 127/2

entered production in 1929 and more than 40 were built for the French Air Force. These aircraft embodied several modifications over the prototype 127, including a switch to more powerful engines. Unfortunately, their greater take-off weight caused reduced maximum speed and distortion of the wings in flight, leading to their rapid withdrawal from service. Blériot also produced an all-metal version as the 137, differing also from the 127 in having shoulder-mounted wings, repositioned pilot's cockpit, jutting out gun positions on the fuselage sides for the rear-gunners and a shallower fuselage. However, no production orders were placed for the 137.

Bloch 131 / France

Purpose: Reconnaissance-bomber

Engines: Two 950hp Gnome-Rhône 14N radials
Span: 66ft 3in
Max speed: 217mph
Armament: Three machine guns. Up to 1,765lb of bombs

The Bloch 131 prototype first flew on 16 August 1936 and, after modifications were incorporated into the second prototype, the type entered production at the close of 1937. The first production Bloch 131 RB4s were delivered in mid-1938. Unfortunately, the performance of the aircraft did not match expectations and therefore it was considered too vulnerable to fighter attack to be used as a day bomber. Because the excellent LéO 451 twin-engined bomber was about to go into production, with a maximum speed nearly 100mph faster than

that of the Bloch 131, the latter was produced only as an armed reconnaissance aircraft with bombing capability and 139 aircraft were built.

Bloch 151 and 152 / France

Purpose: Fighter
Photo and Data: MB-152

Engine: One 1,080hp Gnome-Rhône 14N-25 radial
Span: 34ft 7in
Max speed: 316mph
Armament: Four 7.5mm machine guns or two 7.5mm machine guns and two 20mm cannon

The Bloch 150 (MB-150) first flew in October 1937. Following modification of the design, into the MB-151, production started in May 1938. Only 140 MB-151 fighters were built for the Armée de l'Air before production changed to the Bloch 152. Later aircraft of this series had a 1,100hp Gnome-Rhône

14N-49 engine and redesigned fin. However, during this period the French aircraft industry was having considerable difficulty in matching the expected output of combat aircraft and, more importantly, actually completing those aircraft three-quarters

built. Consequently, at the outbreak of World War 2 only 92 MB-151/152 fighters were in service, all of which lacked either a propeller or gunsight. With the war in Europe started, Bloch fighters began coming off the production lines at a much improved rate, subsequent production including the MB-155 version. A prototype MB-157 flew during the German occupation and achieved a speed of over 440mph, powered by a 1,700hp Gnome-Rhône 14R-4 engine.

Boulton Paul Overstrand / UK

Purpose: Medium bomber

Engines: Two 580hp Bristol Pegasus IIM3
Span: 72ft 0in
Max speed: 153mph
Armament: Three Lewis machine guns, situated in nose, dorsal and ventral positions. 1,600lb of bombs

The Overstrand was the first RAF bomber to have a power-operated enclosed gun turret when it entered service with No 101 Squadron in 1934. Power for operating the turret — which had a Lewis gun projecting through a vertical full-depth slot — was provided by an engine-driven air compressor which kept a set of compressed air bottles under pressure. In the event of engine failure, pressure in the bottles could turn the turret up to 20 times at a normal rate of 12 revolutions a minute, thus not leaving the aircraft undefended from the front. The prototype was a converted Sidestrand, first flown in 1933 and was followed by three other converted Sidestrands. 24 production aircraft, originally designated Sidestrand Vs, were then constructed. Overstrands served as bombers with the RAF until 1937, after which they were used as gunnery trainers. Notable features of the Overstrand included an enclosed cockpit for the pilot and a windshield for the dorsal gunner.

Boulton and Paul Sidestrand / UK

Purpose: Medium bomber
Photo and Data: Mk III

Engines: Two 460hp Bristol Jupiter VIIIF radials
Span: 71ft 11in
Max speed: 140.5mph
Armament: Three Lewis machine guns. Up to 1,050lb of bombs

The Sidestrand prototype first flew in 1926. Production Mk IIs entered service in April 1928 with No 101 Squadron RAF, the only squadron to receive the type, and proved to be excellent bombers. 18 Sidestrands were built, including the Mk II version with direct-drive Jupiter VI engines (later modified to Mk III standard) and the Mk III incorporating several refinements. All were withdrawn from service in late 1934. Notable feature of the Mk III was the hinged window in the nose of the fuselage, provided so that the bomb aimer had an unrestricted downward view when on a bombing run. Tandem cockpits, forward of the biplane wings, were provided for the pilot and navigator/bomber (with easy access to the nose cockpit), while a fourth cockpit, aft of the wings, was for the rear gunner armed with dorsal and ventral guns.

Breguet 14 and 16 / France

Purpose: Bomber
Photo: Breguet 14A2
Data: Breguet 14B2

Engine: One 300hp Renault 12Fe
Span: 48ft 9in
Max speed: over 112mph
Armament: One fixed forward-firing Vickers machine gun and two or three Lewis machine guns. Normal bomb load of 520lb

The Breguet 14 was the best bomber/reconnaissance aircraft of French design built during

World War 1. The prototype, designated Breguet AV, first flew in November 1916. Production started in 1917, and the type entered service as the 14A2 reconnaissance and 14B2 bomber aircraft in September of that year. By the end of 1918, Breguet 14s had been supplied to 55 French bomber squadrons, while others equipped Belgian and American units. The Breguet 14 remained in production until 1926, several thousand examples being built in many versions. The 14B2 served with the French Air Force until 1930 (used in the same

way as Britain operated the DH9A) and examples were purchased after World War 1 by Finland, Poland, Romania and Spain (which also obtained a licence for manufacture). Japan received a licence for the type, designating its aircraft Nakajima B6s. The Breguet 16 entered production late in 1917, and was basically an enlarged version of the 14. Too late for service during the war, the 16BN2 version served with the French and Czechoslovak forces until the late 1920s.

Breguet 690 and 691 / France

Purpose: Light bomber/Dive bomber/Fighter/Reconnaissance
Data: Br691

Engines: Two 680hp Hispano-Suiza 14Ab radials
Span: 50ft 4.75in
Max speed: 289mph
Armament: (Br691-B2) One 20mm cannon and one 7.5mm machine gun. Eight 110lb bombs

The Breguet 690 first flew in March 1938 as a multi-purpose aircraft for the French Air Force and the type entered production the same year as the Breguet 691. The production aircraft were more

streamlined than the prototype and had a greater all-up weight. Four versions of the 691 were produced: the 691-B2 light bomber; 691-AB2 dive bomber; 691-A3 reconnaissance aircraft; and 691-C3 fighter. All but the dive bomber were flown operationally during the early stages of World War 2.

Breguet 521 Bizerte / France

Purpose: Long-range reconnaissance-bomber
Data: Standard model

Engines: Three 900hp Gnome-Rhône 14Kirs radials
Span: 115ft 3in
Max speed: 158.5mph
Armament: Five 7.5mm Darne machine guns. Four 165.3lb bombs on under-wing racks

The Bizerte prototype first flew in September 1933. The first production aircraft was similar to the prototype, but the following examples differed in having an extended T-shaped fully enclosed cockpit in the nose for the bomb aimer/navigator and the two pilots (with dual controls and seated side by side), revolving gun positions on each side of the hull immediately aft of the pilot's cockpit, two midship guns and a tail gun. Production ended in 1940, by

which time over 30 examples had been built. Bizertes served with French Navy squadrons from 1935-40, replacing CAMS 55s. A similar civil variant of the design was the Breguet Saigon, a 19-passenger long-range flying-boat.

Bristol Blenheim / UK

Purpose: Bomber/Night fighter
Data: Mk I
Photo: Mk IV

Engines: Two 840hp Bristol Mercury VIII radials
Span: 56ft 4in
Max speed: 260mph
Armament: One .303in fixed forward-firing Browning machine gun (in port wing) and one Vickers machine gun in hydraulically-operated dorsal turret. Up to 1,000lb of bombs

136

Developed from the six-passenger Type 142 'Britain First', the Blenheim proved to be faster than the fighters then operating when it entered squadron service early in 1937, and so followed the traditions of the Fairey Fox and Hawker Hart. The Air Ministry had ordered 150 Blenheim Mk Is in 1935, and the first two production aircraft served as prototypes, the first flying on 25 June 1936. Final production of the Mk I eventually reached a total of over 1,400 aircraft. The Blenheim I was also exported and licence-built in other countries. Those of Finland were the only

modern aircraft to face the invading Russians on 30 November 1939, with the exception of Fokker DXXIs. Some 200 Mk Is were later converted into Mk IF night fighters, with a four-abreast machine gun pack under the bomb bay and AI radar. The first Mk IFs entered service at the end of 1938. Also in 1938 the Mk I was superseded in production by the Blenheim IV. This had a modified enlarged nose and entered RAF service in early 1939. Bomb load of the Blenheim IV was normally 1,000lb. Some Mk IVs were converted to night fighters in 1939.

CAMS 55 / France

Purpose: Bomber/Reconnaissance

Engines: Two 500hp Gnome-Rhône 9Kbr Mistral or similar radials
Span: 66ft 11in
Max speed: 121.25mph
Armament: Four Lewis machine guns and two 165lb bombs

Four prototype CAMS 55s appeared in 1928. The first version to enter production in 1929 was the CAMS 55[1], powered by two 600hp Hispano 12Lbr 12-cylinder engines. More than 40 of this version were built, followed in the next year by the CAMS 55[2], powered by 480hp Gnome-Rhône 9Akx engines. The last version was the CAMS 55[10], produced from 1934, bringing the total of CAMS 55[2]/55[10]s built to more than 60 in roughly equal quantities. CAMS 55s first entered service in 1930, subsequently, from 1935, being transferred for reconnaissance duties. Some CAMS 55[10]s

remained in operational squadron use until August 1940. These were the last production aircraft built by CAMS, the company being divided between two nationalised groups during the mid-1930s. The final CAMS design to be built as a prototype was the CAMS 110 overseas reconnaissance flying-boat.

CANT Z506B Airone (Heron) / Italy

Purpose: Torpedo bomber/Reconnaissance
Data: Early production aircraft

Engines: Three 750hp Alfa Romeo 126 RC34 radials
Span: 86ft 11in
Max speed: 217mph
Armament: Two 12.7mm and one 7.7mm Breda-SAFAT machine guns. Up to 1,984lb of bombs or a torpedo. Number of guns and bomb load increased in later production aircraft

Developed from the CANT Z506 12-passenger transport seaplane, intended for Mediterranean service, the Z506B entered production in 1937. Named Airone, it had a dorsal turret for two machine guns and an under-fuselage fairing accommodating

the bomb aimer at the front, a bomb bay and a rear-mounted machine gun. In the latter part of 1938, Z506Bs took part in the Spanish Civil War, equipping the Aviazione Legionaria. At the time of Italy's entry into World War 2, two groups of the Regia Aeronautica were equipped with the type, amounting to 97 aircraft. One example was exported to Poland. The last Z506 in Italian Air Force's service was retired from air-sea rescue duties in 1960.

Caproni Ca101 and Ca102 / Italy

Purpose: Bomber/Transport
Photo and Data: Ca101D2

Engines: Three 240hp Alfa Romeo D2s
Span: 64ft 6.75in

Max speed: 129.5mph
Armament: Two/four machine guns. Up to 3,750lb of bombs and fuel

The Ca101 entered service with the Stormi de Bombardamento in the mid-1930s. The most notable design features of the aircraft were its high-mounted thick strut-braced monoplane wings and bulky fuselage. Although Alfa Romeo engines were standard on Ca101s, versions existed with 370hp Piaggio Stella VIIs and other engines. Bombs were

carried either in containers inside the fuselage or externally. Ca101s were used during the Abyssinian hostilities, as bombers and supply aircraft. They could also be used as troop transports and ambulance aircraft. The name Colonial was often associated with Ca101s used as civil transports, as distinct from military bombers and transports. A modified version of the design was the Ca102, which was powered by two 500hp Jupiter VII radial engines.

Caproni Ca111 / Italy

Purpose: Reconnaissance/Support
Photo: Ca111*bis*

Engine: One 970hp Isotta-Fraschini Asso 750 RC
Span: 64ft 6.75in
Max speed: 186mph
Armament: Machine guns in dorsal, ventral and aft positions. Small bomb load carried internally or externally

Derived from the Ca101, the larger Ca111 was also used during Italy's invasion of Abyssinia in October 1935 and during World War 2, mostly in the support of ground forces. However, the type had virtually

disappeared from Regia Aeronautica service by 1943. The Ca111 was operated as a landplane on a fixed divided undercarriage and as the Ca111*bis* Idro twin-float seaplane. It is believed that a number of Ca111s were also exported to Peru before the war.

Caudron C23 / France

Purpose: Bomber

Engines: Two 260hp Salmson 9Zs
Span: 80ft 0in
Max speed: 84mph
Armament: One forward-firing machine gun. Three large bombs carried under bottom wing

Caudron aircraft built during World War 1 have the distinction of being some of the most ugly produced during this period, although they performed well. The C23 two-seat night bomber appeared at the end of World War 1 and continued this tradition, although it

was somewhat slow and underpowered. Of wood and fabric construction, more than 50 were produced for the French Air Force. The type was withdrawn from first-line service in February 1920.

Consolidated PB-2A / USA

Purpose: Fighter

Engine: One 700hp Curtiss V-1570-61
Span: 43ft 11in
Max speed: 275mph
Armament: Two .303in Browning fixed forward-firing machine guns and one rear-mounted machine gun

With the exception of a few N4Y biplane trainers built for the US Navy and Coast Guard around 1934, the PB-2A was the last production landplane produced by the Consolidated Aircraft Corporation to go into US military service prior to the wartime Liberator — the aircraft produced between all being flying-boats. The PB-2A had its origins in the Lockheed Altair, a high-speed commercial monoplane with a retractable undercarriage.

Lockheed produced a fighter variant in 1931 but, despite USAAC interest, eventually dropped the project. The Consolidated Aircraft Corporation adopted the basic design and produced fighter and attack versions, the latter as the unsuccessful A-11. Following a few evaluation fighters which were subsequently designated PB-2s, the USAAC purchased 50 PB-2A production fighters. These remained operational in the pursuit role right up to the end of the period covered by this book.

Consolidated PBY Flying-boat (Catalina) / USA

Purpose: Maritime patrol/Reconnaissance

Engines: Two 900hp Pratt & Whitney R-1830-64 radials
Span: 104ft 0in
Max speed: 177mph
Armament: Four machine guns. Up to 4,480lb of bombs

The Catalina became famous before and during World War 2, in civil and military roles respectively. Civil Model 28s made news with their prewar exploration missions and PBY Catalinas for their outstanding war record with the US and Allied air forces, proving tough, dependable and adaptable. First flight of the prototype took place in 1935, and an initial order for 60 aircraft was placed for the US Navy. By the time the first PBY-1 flew, on 5 October 1936, orders had been placed for 116 PBY-2s and PBY-3s, the latter with R-1830-66 radial engines. The only other version to appear before the war was the PBY-4 in 1938. This was longer and heavier than the earlier versions and was powered by R-1830-72

Twin Wasp engines, later examples introducing transparent side blisters for the gun positions. The name Catalina was first used by the RAF and was later adopted by the US Navy. 'Cats' were also built in Canada and Russia. Excluding those produced in Russia, 2,140 Catalinas were built as flying-boats and amphibians, and eventually served with air forces and airlines of more than 25 countries. Interestingly, the last U-boat sunk by RAF Coastal Command during World War 2 was destroyed by a Catalina on 7 May 1945.

Consolidated P2Y / USA

Purpose: Maritime patrol
Photo: P2Y-2
Data: P2Y-1

Engines: Two 575hp Wright R-1820E Cyclone radials
Span: 100ft 0in
Max speed: 126mph
Armament: One .303in Browning machine gun in nose and two rear-mounted machine guns aft of wings

Derived from the PY-1 Admiral monoplane flying-boat of 1928, which was powered by 425hp Pratt & Whitney engines and had open cockpits for the crew, the prototype P2Y first flew in 1932. (Interestingly, a commercial version of the PY-1 was produced as the Commodore for Pan American Airways). The P2Y differed from the earlier Navy prototype in having three more powerful engines enclosed in low-drag cowlings, the addition of short-span lower wings

with stabilising floats, and an enclosed cockpit for the flight crew. A total of 46 production P2Ys was built for the US Navy, split evenly between P2Y-1s and P2Y-3s, powered by two 575hp Wright and 700hp Wright R-1820-90 Cyclone engines respectively. Most P2Y-1s were subsequently converted to P2Y-2s with the engines mounted on the upper wings (as for the P2Y-3s). Delivery of production aircraft began in 1933. The only country which received more than one export P2Y was Argentina, which received six P2Y-3s to replace Supermarine Southamptons as navy patrol aircraft.

Curtiss A-8 and A-12 Shrike / USA

Purpose: Attack
Photo and Data: A-12

Engine: One 690hp Wright R-1820 Cyclone radial
Span: 44ft 0in
Max speed: 177mph
Armament: Four .303in Browning fixed forward-firing machine guns and one rear-mounted machine gun. Up to 488lb of bombs

The A-8 was the Curtiss Aeroplane and Motor Company's first successful attempt to sell a low-wing monoplane combat aircraft to the US forces. The prototype A-8 was selected over the Atlantic-

139

Fokker XA-7 as a possible production aircraft for the USAAC in 1931 and, following a number of evaluation aircraft, 46 A-8Bs were ordered, to be powered by 600hp Curtiss Conqueror engines. Tandem cockpits were provided for the pilot and gunner, the latter having a sliding canopy to allow free use of the track-mounted gun. Dual flying controls were provided. Following refinement of the design to include a radial engine in a Curtiss cowling ring and redesigned cockpits in which the gunner's semi-cabin was brought closer to the pilot's cockpit and the two were joined by a new upper deck fairing, and other changes, production aircraft were redesignated A-12s. A-8 elevation aircraft were retired from front-line service in 1936 but A-12s remained in service until the war.

Curtiss CS/SC / USA

Purpose: Torpedo bomber
Data: SC-2

Engine: One 585hp Wright T-3
Span: 56ft 6.75in
Max speed: 105mph
Armament: Aft-mounted machine gun. One 1,618lb torpedo

The Curtiss CS-1 appeared in 1923, powered by a 525hp Wright T-2 engine, and had an interchangeable wheel or float undercarriage. Six CS-1s were delivered to the US Navy, together with examples of a version with the T-3 engine, designated CS-2. When the Navy placed a repeat order for the type in 1924, production was undertaken by the Martin Company, which built 35 T-2-powered examples under the revised

designation SC-1, and 40 SC-2s as detailed above. All were delivered by the beginning of 1926, replacing Douglas DT-2s. Three were later modified into SC-6s and an SC-7.

Curtiss F9C Sparrowhawk
/ USA

Purpose: Airship parasite fighter
Data: F9C-2

Engine: One 420hp Wright R-975-22 Whirlwind radial
Span: 25ft 6in
Max speed: 177mph
Armament: Two .303in Browning forward-firing machine guns

Intended for use by the US Navy as parasite fighters from the airships, USS *Akron* and *Macon,* a total of only eight Sparrowhawks were produced, but their significance to aviation history is great. The prototype, designated XF9C-1, first flew on 12 February 1931. It was followed by the improved XF9C-2 second prototype, which was also bought by the Navy. In 1931 an order for six production aircraft designated F9C-2s was placed; all were delivered in the following year and attached to the *Akron* unit, where the first aircraft to airship 'hook on' was achieved in June. Following the crash of the *Akron* in April 1933, the production aircraft and the second

prototype were allocated to the *Macon* until its loss in February 1935. These were the first and only US fighters to serve operationally from airships and, although the concept had been successful, subsequent development of the parasite fighter involved the use of bombers and 'mother planes'.

Curtiss P-36 Mohawk and
Hawk 75 / USA

Purpose: Fighter
Photo: P-36
Data: P-36A

Engine: One 1,050hp Pratt & Whitney R-1830-13 Twin Wasp radial
Span: 37ft 4in
Max speed: 300mph
Armament: One .30in and one .50in machine guns

The P-36 was the first Curtiss low-wing monoplane fighter with retractable undercarriage to go into USAAC service, of which 210 were produced for home use, becoming operational from the spring of 1938. Most were P-36As, powered by Pratt & Whitney R-1830-13 Twin Wasp radial engines and poorly armed with just one .30in and one .50in machine gun each (the same armament as fitted to

US fighters of 1924), although a small number of P-36Cs were built with four .30in machine guns and powered by 1,200hp R-1830-17 engines. Many fighters were also exported as Hawk 75s, going to several countries before World War 2, including Argentina, Canada, China, France, Iran, the Netherlands East Indies, Siam and UK. By September 1939 about 165 Hawk 75s had been delivered to France, becoming one of the main types used by the French air force during the following months because of the failure of the French aircraft industry to produce sufficient fighters. French Hawk 75s met Luftwaffe Bf109s for the first time on 8 September 1939, downing two German aircraft.

Curtiss SBC Helldiver / USA

Purpose: Scout/Dive bomber

Engine: See below
Span: 34ft 0in
Max speed: 220mph
Armament: Two .30in machine guns, one forward-firing and one rear-mounted. One 500lb bomb

Developed from the F8C Helldiver of 1928, the prototype first flew in 1933 as a parasol-winged naval fighter. A change of role subsequently led to its modification to biplane configuration with a multi-section cockpit canopy streamlined into the rear fuselage. The US Navy received 83 production SBC-3s from mid-1937, powered by 750hp Pratt & Whitney R-1535-94 radial engines. The main production version of the design was the later SBC-4, powered by the 950hp Wright R-1820-34

Cyclone radial engine and able to carry a 1,000lb bomb. The first SBC-4 entered US Navy service in 1939. Helldivers could be found on board several US aircraft carriers by September 1939. Five SBC-4s found their way to Britain via France and were named Cleveland Is by the RAF.

Curtiss SOC Seagull / USA

Purpose: Observation/Scout
Data: SOC-1

Engine: One 550hp Pratt & Whitney R-1340 Wasp radial
Span: 36ft 0in
Max speed: 165mph
Armament: Two .30in Browning machine guns, one forward-firing and one rear-mounted. Two 116lb or 325lb bombs could be carried

The dependable Seagull served with every carrier, battleship and cruiser of the US Navy and outlasted the modern Seamew built to replace it. The prototype first flew in 1934 as a seaplane with a central amphibious main float. More than 260 production aircraft were subsequently built for the US Navy and a few for the US Coast Guard,

designated SOC-1 to SOC-4 (including a batch of SOC-3s built by the Naval Aircraft Factory as SON-1s), of which nearly half were of the original production version. Most could be fitted with float or wheeled undercarriages, but the SOC-2s had only the single-strut wheeled undercarriage with legs and wheels faired by aluminium-alloy casings.

Dewoitine D19 and D21 / France

Purpose: Fighter
Photo and Data: D21

Engine: One 575hp Hispano-Suiza 12Gb or 450hp Lorraine

Span: 42ft 0in
Max speed: 166mph with H-S engine
Armament: Two 7.5mm Vickers and two 7.5mm Darne fixed forward-firing machine guns

The D19 single-seat fighter of 1925 was a development of the earlier D9, powered by the larger 450hp Hispano-Suiza engine. Three slightly modified fighters were built in Switzerland, of which one was put on display at an aero exhibition held in Geneva in

1929. The D21 followed and, although none were built for French service, a fair number became operational with foreign air forces. Argentina licence-built 58 D21s with modified wide-track undercarriages and Lorraine engines. These formed the fighter component of the air force for several years, although some were later transferred to Paraguay. The other major user was Czechoslovakia, where 25 were licence-built with Hispano-Suiza engines at the Skoda works.

Dewoitine D37 / France

Purpose: Fighter
Photo: D373
Data: D372

Engine: One 870hp Gnome-Rhône 14Kfs
Span: 36ft 9in
Max speed: 248.5mph
Armament: Two 20mm cannon or four machine guns

The Dewoitine D37 was basically a les Établissements Lioré et Olivier development of the unsuccessful D53, and first flew in August 1932. Production began with the D371, of which 18 were built for the Armée de l'Air and others modified to serve with the Republican forces in Spain during the civil war, making up a small proportion of the 70 Dewoitine D37, D500 and D510 fighters sent to that country as part of the French contribution of over

100 fighters. Subsequent versions for French service were the D373 and D376 carrier-based fighters for the Navy (with deck arrester gear fitted), entering service in 1936 and differing only in the latter having wings that folded for easy stowage. 44 naval fighters were built and these served on the *Béarn* until 1940, armed with a Hotchkiss 13.2mm machine gun from 1938. 14 D372s were built for Lithuania.

Dornier Do17 / Germany

Purpose: Medium bomber/Reconnaissance
Photo: Do17P
Data: Do17E-1

Engines: Two 745hp BMW VIs
Span: 59ft 0.5in
Max speed: 220mph
Armament: One forward/downward firing and one rear-mounted 7.9mm MG15 machine gun. Up to 1,653lb of bombs

Nicknamed 'Flying Pencil' and 'Eversharp' because of the slim fuselage shape, the Do17 started life as a fast mail-carrier and passenger aircraft for Deutsche Luft Hansa and as such first flew in 1934. Unwanted by the airline, a fourth prototype was built as a bomber with a twin tail assembly, shorter fuselage and military modifications. Following more prototypes, the Do17 entered production as the Do17E-1 bomber and Do17F-1 photo-reconnaissance aircraft, these versions entering Luftwaffe service in 1937. Early Do17s were very

poorly armed and so subsequent versions increased the number of machine guns available for defence and the bomb load. Also in 1937 the first Do17s were sent to Spain to fight with the Nationalists in the Civil War. Yugoslavia ordered export Do17Ks and these were delivered the same year. During 1938 and 1939 the Luftwaffe received Do17M and Do17Z bombers, Do17P and Do17Z reconnaissance aircraft, Do17U pathfinders, training and rescue aircraft. Armament on the Do17Z-2 bomber had been increased to six 7.9mm machine guns and 2,200lb of bombs. By the outbreak of World War 2 the Luftwaffe had in operational service Do17M and Z bombers, Do17Ps and a few Do17Fs.

Douglas T2D/P2D / USA

Purpose: Torpedo bomber
Photo and Data: P2D-1

Engines: Two 575hp Wright R-1820 Cyclone radials

Span: 57ft 0in
Max speed: 138mph
Armament: Machine guns in nose and rear cockpit. One 1,620lb torpedo or bombs

In 1926 the Naval Aircraft Factory produced a prototype torpedo bomber. Douglas redesigned the aircraft and produced 12 examples in 1927 suitable for bombing, torpedo bombing and scouting, for use from aircraft carriers. This version was designated T2D-1 and was powered by two Wright R-1750 engines. Either a twin-float or wheeled undercarriage could be fitted. Most of these were allocated as seaplanes to USS *Aroostook*, although one served on board the first US aircraft carrier proper USS *Langley*. Accommodation provided for a bomber/ gunner in the nose of the fuselage, with tandem cockpits in front of the wing leading-edge and under the centre-section for two pilots with dual controls, and a rear gunner's cockpit and wireless operator's compartment aft of the wings. Particular attention had been paid to the placing of the crew positions to facilitate landing on board ship. In 1930, 18 more aircraft were ordered, designated P2D-1s, and these remained operational as armed patrol aircraft with bombing capability until 1937.

Fairey Battle / UK

Purpose: Light bomber/Trainer

Engine: One 1,030hp Rolls-Royce Merlin I, II, III or V
Span: 54ft 0in
Max speed: 241mph
Armament: One .303in Browning fixed forward-firing machine gun and one rear-mounted Vickers K machine gun. Up to 1,000lb of bombs

Although in production in one form or another until December 1940, by which time about 2,400 had been built, the Battle was already obsolete by the time war started. Designed as a replacement for the Hawker biplanes, the prototype first flew on 10 March 1936, 10 months after 155 had been ordered. The first RAF squadron received Battles in 1937 and within two years there were 17 squadrons so equipped. A Battle gunner claimed the first German aircraft shot down during World War 2, and two of the RAF's first VCs of the war were won by Battle pilots during the attack on the Maastricht bridges. However, Battles suffered heavy losses because they were underpowered and under-armed and were soon transferred to training and target towing duties. Battles were exported to Belgium, Turkey and South Africa.

Fairey Hendon / UK

Purpose: Heavy night bomber
Photo and Data: Hendon II

Engines: Two 600hp Rolls-Royce Kestrel VIs
Span: 101ft 9in
Max speed: 155mph
Armament: Three Lewis machine guns in nose, dorsal and tail positions. Up to 1,660lb of bombs carried internally

The prototype Hendon, known originally as the Fairey Night Bomber, and with open cockpits for the crew, first flew in November 1931, powered by Bristol Jupiter X radial engines. Production Hendon IIs entered RAF service in late 1936, the 14 aircraft remaining operational until superseded by Wellingtons just prior to the outbreak of World War 2. Hendons were the RAF's first low-wing monoplane heavy bombers.

Fairey Seafox / UK

Purpose: Reconnaissance

Engine: One 395hp Napier-Halford Rapier VI
Span: 40ft 0in
Max speed: 124mph
Armament: One rear-mounted Lewis machine gun on a Fairey mounting. Small bombs could be carried

The first of 64 Fairey Seafox light reconnaissance biplanes entered FAA service in April 1937 and by

the outbreak of World War 2 they equipped several British cruisers as catapult seaplanes. In December 1939, a Seafox, used as a spotter for naval guns, contributed to the defeat of the German battleship *Admiral Graf Spee* during the Battle of the River

Plate. An unusual feature of the aircraft was that the pilot sat in an open cockpit below the trailing-edge of the wing while the observer's cockpit had a transparent hood in which the rear part was hinged to allow free firing of the machine gun.

Fiat BR20 Cicogna (Stork) / Italy

Purpose: Medium bomber
Data: BR20M

Engines: Two 1,000hp Fiat A80 RC41 radials
Span: 70ft 8.75in
Max speed: 267mph
Armament: One 12.7mm and three 7.7mm machine guns in nose, dorsal and ventral positions. Bombs carried internally

The BR20 appeared in 1936, and served in the Spanish Civil War with the Aviazione Legionaria. Others were exported, including a number to the Japanese Army Air Force. Combat experience during the 1930s revealed shortcomings in the initial version, and in 1939 the BR20M appeared. This had

a modified nose, to improve visibility, and other refinements. A total of about 600 BR20s, including the later BR20*bis* version, was built, of which less than one-third were in service with the Regia Aeronautica when Italy entered the war.

Fokker CX / Netherlands

Purpose: Reconnaissance/Bomber

Engine: One 650hp Rolls-Royce Kestrel V
Span: 39ft 4.25in
Max speed: 199mph
Armament: One or two forward-firing 7.9mm machine guns and one in rear cockpit. Two underwing racks, each for up to 440lb of bombs

The prototype Fokker CX first flew in 1934 and followed closely the successful configuration of the earlier CV. A total of 30 production aircraft was built for Dutch service, most going to the LVA but a number to the Netherlands and East Indies Army Air Service from 1937, about half of which had an enclosed cockpit for the pilot, made of Plexiglas windows and which could be jettisoned in an emergency. The seat in the observer's cockpit could

be used in two positions or folded back when not in use to allow room for other military equipment. The Finnish Air Force received 34 Bristol Pegasus XXI-engined CXs, the majority licence-built in Finland in 1938. A small number of CXs were still in LVA service when Germany invaded Holland on 10 May 1940.

Fokker DVII / Netherlands

Purpose: Fighter

Engine: One 185hp BMW IIIa inline
Span: 29ft 2.33in
Max speed: 124mph
Armament: Two fixed forward-firing Spandau machine guns

DVIIs began to reach German operational units in April 1918 and proved to be the finest German fighters of World War 1. Following the end of hostilities, it was specified in the Armistice Agreement that all DVIIs were to be surrendered to the Allies. Anthony Fokker, however, managed to get into Holland a large number of DVII aircraft and parts, and formed the Dutch Fokker Company. DVIIs of this vintage were sold to Belgium and Switzerland.

In Holland the type re-entered production for service with the Royal Netherlands Air Force and for operations in the East Indies, where they remained flying into the 1930s. Ironically the Dutch were so happy with their DVIIs that the company had considerable difficulty in selling its later products for home use.

Fokker TIV / Netherlands

Purpose: Torpedo bomber/Reconnaissance
Data: TIVa

Engines: Two 770hp Wright SR-1820-F2 Cyclone radials
Span: 85ft 11.5in
Max speed: 161.5mph
Armament: Three 7.9mm FN-Browning machine guns. Up to 1,960lb of bombs or a torpedo

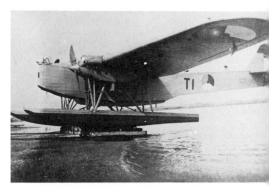

The TIV prototype seaplane first flew in 1927. 11 were ordered the same year, each powered by two 450hp Lorraine-Dietrich engines, and were used mainly by the Royal Netherlands East Indies Navy. A very small number also served with the Portuguese Navy, powered by Rolls-Royce Eagle engines, and joined in service a small selection of French, Italian and British seaplanes and flying-boats. In 1935 the Dutch ordered a further 12 aircraft, designated TIVas. These were updated to take into account the age of the basic design, and incorporated more powerful engines, an enclosed rotating gun turret at the nose with bomb aiming glazed panels below and a wireless compartment, an enclosed cockpit for the pilot (which falred the upper fuselage to make the aircraft a mid-wing instead of high-wing monoplane), a dorsal gun turret and a ventral gun position. TIVs still operational at this time were similarly modified. TIVas were still operational with the Royal Netherlands East Indies Navy, on reconnaissance and rescue duties, in 1941.

Gourdou-Leseurre B2, B3 and ET1 / France

Purpose: Fighter (B2/B3)
Photo and Data: B3

Engine: One 180hp Hispano-Suiza 8A
Span: 29ft 7.75in
Max speed: 143mph
Armament: Two forward-firing machine guns

The ET1 was a parasol-wing advanced trainer of attractive appearance that was powered by a 180hp Hispano-Suiza 8Ab engine and went into French Army and Navy service. The B2 and B3 were similar to the ET1 and appeared as lightweight export fighters. B2s and B3s were sold to Czechoslovakia, Estonia, Finland and Latvia. Others were licence-built in Yugoslavia.

Great Lakes BG-1 / USA

Purpose: Dive bomber

Engine: One 750hp Pratt & Whitney R-1535-82 Wasp radial
Span: 36ft 0in
Max speed: 188mph
Armament: One .30in fixed forward-firing machine gun and one .30in machine gun in rear cockpit. One 1,000lb bomb

The BG-1 was the product of a company that had not managed previously to interest the US forces in its prototype military aircraft and had worked mainly in producing licence-built aircraft and civil types. It is ironic, therefore, that the only successful military product of its own design should have marked the closedown of the company and, more importantly, have been the last biplane torpedo bomber to go into US Navy service. The BG-1 was the culmination of many years of work in the torpedo bomber field, and the prototype first flew in 1933. It was quickly followed by 60 production examples, delivered to the Navy between 1934 and 1936. A large number were later handed over to the US Marine Corps. They served on board aircraft carriers until replaced by modern low-wing Douglas Devastators from 1938, after which time they continued to operate from land only until finally retired a couple of years later.

Grumman JF/J2F Duck / USA

Purpose: Utility transport (including photographic reconnaissance, observation, rescue, target towing)
Photo: JF
Data: J2F-2

Engine: One 775hp Wright R-1820-F52 Cyclone radial
Span: 39ft 0in
Max speed: 180mph

The JF/J2F Duck series of utility transport amphibious biplanes were in service with the US Navy from 1934 and US Coast Guard from 1935 until well after the end of World War 2, a record of durability and dependability virtually unsurpassed by any aircraft designed during the interwar period. The prototype flew in 1933. Initial production JF-1s were powered by Pratt & Whitney Twin Wasp engines,

but the powerplant changed to a Wright Cyclone for the later JF-2 (US Coast Guard version) and JF-3. Argentina also purchased a small number of JF-2s. The name Duck was adopted by the Navy with the J2F-1 to J2F-6 series, each equipped with deck arrester gear and catapult points in the main central float. Production totalled 55 JFs and more than 560 J2Fs, the majority of the latter produced after the war in Europe had started.

Haefeli DH-3 / Switzerland

Purpose: Reconnaissance

Engine: One 150hp Saurer-built Hispano-Suiza 41 8Aa
Span: 41ft 0in
Max speed: 90mph
Armament: One 7.45mm machine gun in rear cockpit

The two-seat DH-3 first entered production in 1917, a total of 100 being completed for the Swiss Air Force, followed by 10 more in the mid-1920s. Early aircraft were powered by the SLM-built 120hp Argus As-II engine, but later examples were usually fitted with a Saurer-built Hispano engine. About half were converted for other duties from 1930, remaining in

service for several more years, probably making the DH-3 the most out-of-date aircraft to be in use with any air force in the latter 1930s.

Haefeli DH-5 and DH-5A
/ Switzerland

Purpose: Reconnaissance
Photo and Data: DH5

Engine: One 200hp Winterhur
Span: 37ft 10in
Max speed: 106mph
Armament: Two fixed forward-firing machine guns and one rear mounted machine gun. Light bombs

Developed from the earlier DH-3, the DH-5 first flew in 1919. The first of the quantity production aircraft were delivered in 1922. A total of 60 DH-5s was built, most of which were converted for other duties

from 1930, remaining in service for many more years. In 1928 the DH-5A appeared with a fuselage constructed of steel tubing instead of wood, and powered by the 220hp LFW engine. About 20 examples were built by the Eidgenössische Kondstruktions Werkstätte.

Handley Page Hinaidi / UK

Purpose: Heavy night bomber
Data: Mk 117

Engines: Two 440hp Bristol Jupiter VIII radials
Span: 75ft 0in

Max speed: 122mph
Armament: Nose, dorsal and ventral positions each with one Lewis machine gun. Up to 1,450lb of bombs

The last of the traditional biplane heavy bombers built by Handley Page for the RAF — the later Heyford being a somewhat unusual biplane — the prototype Hinaidi was a converted Hyderabad and

first flew in March 1927. In the following year, this aircraft took part in the Kabul airlift (see Vickers Victoria). Altogether a total of 12 Hinaidi Is was built (including six ordered as Hyderabads), followed by 33 metal structure production Hinaidi IIs. A further three Hinaidis were produced by converting Hyderabads. Hinaidis entered service with the RAF in 1929, but from 1933 Heyfords began to replace them.

Handley Page Hyderabad / UK

Purpose: Heavy night bomber

Engines: Two 450hp Napier Lions
Span: 75ft 0in
Max speed: 109mph
Armament: Nose, dorsal and ventral positions each with one Lewis machine gun. Up to 1,100lb of bombs

Developed from the Handley Page W8 airliner, the Hyderabad prototype first flew in 1923 and was known originally as the Handley Page W8d. A total of 39 Hyderabads was built, first entering RAF

service in 1925. They were withdrawn from first-line service at the end of 1930, after which they served with Auxiliary Air Force squadrons until 1933.

Hawker Hector / UK

Purpose: Army co-operation

Engine: One 805hp Napier Dagger III
Span: 36ft 11.5in
Max speed: 191mph
Armament: One forward-firing Vickers machine gun and one Lewis machine gun in rear cockpit. 225lb of bombs or other stores

Unlike the earlier Armstrong Whitworth Atlas and Hawker Audax army co-operation biplanes, the Hector never served at one of Britain's overseas bases, and indeed only went overseas after the outbreak of World War 2 to raid German positions in occupied France. The prototype Hector first flew in February 1936, and this aircraft was later converted into a dual-control trainer. Production totalled 178 aircraft, the first entering RAF service in early 1937, so becoming the last Hawker biplane to be delivered

to the RAF. Most were replaced by modern monoplanes before the war.

Heinkel He111 / Germany

Purpose: Medium bomber
Data: He111E

Engines: Two 1,050hp Junkers Jumo 211s
Span: 74ft 1.75in
Max speed: 261mph
Armament: Three 7.9mm MG15 machine guns in nose, dorsal and ventral positions. Up to 4,409lb of bombs

The He111 was designed ostensibly as an airliner, but prototypes appeared simultaneously as bombers and 10-passenger civil transport aircraft. The first bombers built in series were He111A pre-production

types, but these were underpowered and were sold to China. The first series-built bombers to enter Luftwaffe service were delivered from 1936 as

He111Bs, the final B-2 version powered by 910hp supercharged DB600CG engines. A number were sent to Spain in 1937 to fight with the Nationalists in the civil war. Subsequent production versions that entered Luftwaffe service before the outbreak of World War 2 included the He111E with 1,050hp Jumo engines, He111F (some also going into Turkish service), He111J, He111P and He111H, the final two versions in 1939. The 'P' and 'H' were the first versions with the symmetrically-placed highly-glazed 'bubble' nose which housed the machine gun and incorporated the flight crew's cockpit. By the

beginning of the war, nearly 1,000 He111s had been built. After its early successes in the war, the He111 suffered greatly at the hands of the RAF during the Battle of Britain. The rush to fit extra armour plating and defensive gun power helped little, leading to its relegation to night bombing, minelaying and torpedo-carrying duties. Interestingly, two He111s were among the first three aircraft shot down over Britain during World War 2, brought down on the same day (16 October 1939) but later than a Junkers Ju88A-1, all of which had been raiding the Firth of Forth.

Ilyushin DB-3 / USSR

Purpose: Bomber

Engines: Two 765hp M-85 radials, on early aircraft
Span: 70ft 2in
Max speed: 253mph
Armament: One 7.62mm ShKAS machine gun in each of the nose, dorsal and ventral positions. Up to 5,500lb of bombs

The DB-3 was the first combat aircraft to go into Russian service to bear the Ilyushin name, a name which remains synonymous with Soviet bombers. It was the result of several years of design work and prototype testing, and production DB-3s began to enter air force service in 1937. Development of the aircraft continued during the production run, later

production aircraft having more powerful M-86 engines. The bomber remained the backbone of the long-range bomber force into the war years, and was flown against Finland during the 'Winter War', that began on 30 November 1939, and against German forces from June 1941.

Junkers H-21
/ USSR/Germany

Purpose: Reconnaissance/Fighter

Engine: One 185hp BMW IIIa
Span: 35ft 4in
Max speed: 136mph
Armament: One forward-firing machine gun, plus one rear-mounted gun. Light bombs could be carried

Because of the Versailles Treaty, which limited the aircraft Germany could produce, German aircraft companies established factories abroad in which to develop new types. Junkers built a factory in Fili, near Moscow, and subsequently produced over 100 H-21s before concentrating its foreign activities in Sweden. Of all-metal construction, with the famous

corrugated sheet metal covering, H-21 parasol-wing monoplanes entered Russian service from 1924 as R-2s. A single-seat fighter version was designated H-22 and three were completed experimentally (maximum speed over 150mph).

Junkers Ju86 / Germany

Purpose: Bomber/Reconnaissance/Trainer
Photo: Ju86K
Data: Ju86D-1

Engines: Two 600hp Junkers Jumo 205s
Span: 73ft 9.75in
Max speed: 202mph
Armament: Three 7.9mm MG15 machine guns in nose, dorsal and ventral positions. Normal bomb load 1,764lb

The Ju86 was intended as a modern bomber to serve with the Luftwaffe, but proved disappointing in this role and was used during the war mainly as a trainer and reconnaissance aircraft. Indeed special very high altitude reconnaissance versions, designated Ju88p/Ju86R with pressurised cabins, were the only really successful model and allowed important information to be gained (especially during the Russian campaign) without the menace of fighter interception. The first Ju86 prototype flew in 1934 and, like the He111, was suitable for use as a

bomber or civil transport. The Luftwaffe received its first production Ju86As in 1936, followed by Ju86Ds. Evaluation of a handful of Ju86s in Spain proved correct the Luftwaffe's fears that it wasn't a good bomber, although Ju86Es and Gs were subsequently delivered for this role before the war. From 1938, Ju86s were gradually withdrawn as bombers and converted into trainers and transports. Many Ju86s were exported, Sweden, South Africa, Chile, Portugal and Hungary all receiving examples.

Letov S-1 and S-2
/ Czechoslovakia

Purpose: Reconnaissance/Light bomber
Photo: S-2
Data: SH-1

Engine: One 230hp Hiero L
Span: 43ft 5in
Max speed: 121mph
Armament: Three 7.7mm machine guns. Up to 265lb of bombs

In 1919 the Smolík S-1 appeared as the first military type to originate in Czechoslovakia. The first

production version was the SH-1, followed by the SM-1 and S-2, both of the latter types powered by 260hp Maybach MbIVa engines. A total of 90 aircraft were produced.

Letov S-20 / Czechoslovakia

Purpose: Fighter

Engine: One 300hp Skoda-built Hispano-Suiza 8Fb
Span: 31ft 10in
Max speed: 160mph
Armament: Two Vickers machine guns

The early production S-20s for the Czech Army Air Force had a wide and deep section portly fuselage sandwiched between the upper and lower wings. Later production aircraft were modified by having a new, slimmer fuselage and as such were designated

S-20M. 140 aircraft of the S-20 series were built, which included a small number of fighters for Lithuania and S-21 unarmed advanced trainers.

Levasseur PL7 / France

Purpose: Torpedo bomber

Engine: One 600hp Hispano-Suiza 12Lbr
Span: 54ft 1in
Max speed: 106mph
Armament: Two rear-mounted Lewis machine guns. One torpedo or bombs

The PL-7 was an extremely sturdy-looking long-range torpedo bomber of the late 1920s, but, despite its appearance, actually suffered structural weakness which resulted in its withdrawal from service between 1931 and 1932. It had been derived from the PL-4 reconnaissance aircraft which was powered by a 450hp Lorraine-Dietrich W engine. The French Navy received about 55 pre-production and production PL-7s, and these served on board the aircraft carrier *Béarn* until the outbreak of World

War 2, by which time they were totally obsolete. An interesting feature of the design was the use of an undercarriage that could be dropped in an emergency sea landing so that the fuselage could be used as a hull, further aided by the small wing floats.

Levasseur PL14 / France

Purpose: Torpedo bomber/Reconnaissance

Engine: One 650hp Hispano-Suiza 12Nb
Span: 59ft 1in
Max speed: 105mph
Armament: Two rear-mounted machine guns. One 1,477lb torpedo or 904lb of bombs

The PL-14 was a twin-float seaplane version of the PL-7. 28 production aircraft were ordered in 1931 to serve on the catapult seaplane carrier *Commandant Teste*, and in the following year these were

strengthened. They were temporarily withdrawn from operational service in 1933 after the discovery of engine mounting distortion, and were used subsequently only as landplanes. All PL-14s were retired from service in 1937.

Lioré et Olivier 206 / France

Purpose: Bomber

Engines: Four 320hp supercharged Gnome-Rhône 7 Kds engines
Span: 80ft 6in
Max speed: 143mph
Armament: Machine guns in nose, dorsal and ventral positions. Approximately 2,205lb of bombs

In 1933 the first of 40 LéO 206 production bombers entered French Air Force service. They were very similar to the earlier LéO 20 bombers but had four engines in tandem pairs on the centre section of the lower wings. All-up weight was reported to be 18,630lb. By the mid-1930s the type was obsolete by foreign standards and by the standard of French high-wing monoplane bombers, but remained in service in Algeria and Tunisia until 1939. Experimental developments of the LéO 206 also appeared as the LéO 207 and 208, the latter with a retractable undercarriage (which retracted into the engine nacelles) a nose gun turret and a long fully enclosed cabin for the flight crew of two and wireless operator/rear gunner in tandem. A high-wing monoplane development of the LéO 206 also appeared in 1933/34 as the LéO 30, with an enclosed cockpit for the pilot and a very strange double divided-type undercarriage. The four engines were still mounted in tandem pairs, but were incorporated into the wing leading- and trailing-edges.

Martin BM/T5M / USA

Purpose: Dive bomber
Photo and Data: BM-1

Engine: One 575hp Pratt & Whitney R-1690-44 Hornet radial
Span: 41ft 0in
Max speed: 143mph
Armament: 0.30in machine guns, forward-firing and in rear cockpit. Bomb rack for one 1,000lb bomb under fuselage

The Martin BM began a line of Navy dive bombers which subsequently led, prior to the outbreak of war, to the Douglas Dauntless of World War 2 fame. The prototype BM first appeared in 1930 and, following evaluation, was ordered into production. The US

Navy ordered a total of 16 BM-1s and an equal number of modified BM-2s, the first of which entered service on board USS *Lexington* in 1932. Despite the appearance of the much better Great Lakes BG-1, BMs continued in their designed role until 1937, thereafter serving as land-based hacks.

Mitsubishi 1MT / Japan

Purpose: Torpedo bomber

Engine: One 450hp Napier Lion
Span: 42ft 6in
Max speed: 130mph

Armament: One 1,765lb torpedo

The Mitsubishi 1MT1 was a naval single-seat triplane torpedo bomber. 20 production aircraft, designated 1MT1Ns, were built from 1923 and these served on board the new aircraft carrier *Hosho* (the first Japanese carrier; completed in 1922 and scrapped after World War 2).

Mitsubishi A5M / Japan

Purpose: Fighter
Photo and Data: A5M4

Engine: One 710hp Nakajima Kotobuki 41 radial
Span: 36ft 1in
Max speed: 273mph
Armament: Two 7.7mm fixed forward-firing machine guns. Light bombs could be carried

The A5M was the Japanese Navy's first operational low-wing monoplane fighter, and first flew in prototype form in 1935. Production began with the A5M1 or Type 96 carrier-based fighter, powered by a 585hp Kotobuki 2Kai-1 engine, followed in 1937 by the A5M2a and A5M2b with more powerful Kotobuki 2Kai-3A and Kotobuki 3 engines respectively. Aircraft of the last variant appeared with and then without cockpit canopies. The A5M4 was built in greatest numbers and remained in production until 1940. These began to reach operational units fighting in China (during the Sino-Japanese hostilities) in 1938, joining earlier production fighters. The A5M4 was also the standard type at the time of the Pearl Harbor attack in 1941. Total production amounted to nearly 1,000 aircraft.

Mitsubishi 2MB1 / Japan

Purpose: Light bomber

Engine: One 450hp Hispano-Suiza
Span: 48ft 7in
Max speed: 115mph
Armament: One 7.7mm fixed forward-firing machine gun, two in rear cockpit and one in ventral position. Up to 1,102lb of bombs

The Mitsubishi 2MB1 was designed as a fast light bomber, and first flew in prototype form in 1926. 48 production aircraft were completed between 1927 and 1929 as 2MB1s or Army Type 87 bombers, although by then their performance was low

compared with the latest foreign types. 2MB1s were operated by Japanese forces when they attacked China in September 1931, helping in the eventual occupation of Manchuria.

Morane-Saulnier 225 / France

Purpose: Fighter

Engine: One 500hp supercharged Gnome-Rhône 9Kbrs radial
Span: 34ft 8in
Max speed: 204mph
Armament: Two forward-firing Vickers machine guns

The MS225 and the Nieuport-Delage 629 were the first operational French fighters with supercharged engines. Following the parasol-wing configuration of the earlier MS trainers of the 1920s, but improved upon, the MS225 prototype first flew in 1932, and production aircraft were delivered to the Armée de l'Air in the following year. A total of 74 production MS225s was completed, 12 of which served with the French Navy and a few went to China. Several

experimental aircraft were also evolved from the design, the most significant being the MS275 which was powered by a 600hp Gnome-Rhône 9K engine. Although it could match the performance of later-designed aircraft, it was discarded in favour of low-wing monoplane fighter designs, such as the MS325 (a fairly unpleasant-looking aircraft with heavily-braced wings and a very tall fairing aft of the open cockpit, built as a contender for another fighter competition).

Naval Aircraft Factory PT-1 and PT-2 / USA

Purpose: Torpedo attack
Data: PT-1

Engine: One 400hp Liberty
Span: 74ft 0in
Max speed: 96mph
Armament: One torpedo

The NAF was outdated virtually before it went into service, being a hybrid of the wartime Curtiss R-6 torpedo bomber and the Curtiss MS flying-boat. The result was a particularly slow and antiquated twin-float seaplane. A total of 33 production aircraft was produced as PT-1s and slightly refined PT-2s, first

entering Navy service in late 1921. These were soon replaced by Douglas DTs.

Nyeman R-10 / USSR

Purpose: Light bomber

Engine: 750hp M-25V radial
Span: 47ft 3in
Max speed: 224mph
Armament: Three 7.62mm ShKAS machine guns, two in wings and one in rear gunner's turret. Normal bomb load of 880lb

Developed from a civil airliner of 1932, the R-10 (KhAI-5) entered production in 1937 as a modern and fast low-wing light bomber with retractable

undercarriage. About 500 were produced for the Soviet Air Force, becoming operational in time to be used against the Japanese in Mongolia in 1938 and then against Poland, Finland and subsequently Germany in 1941.

Potez XV / France

Purpose: Reconnaissance/Bomber

Engine: 400hp Lorraine-Dietrich 12Db
Span: 41ft 7.25in
Max speed: 126mph
Armament: One forward-firing 7.92mm Vickers machine gun and one Lewis machine gun in rear cockpit

This two-seat reconnaissance aircraft of the 1920s was widely used by the Armée de l'Air (300) and was also operated by the air services of Denmark, Poland, Romania, Spain and Yugoslavia. Poland alone operated 245 as reconnaissance and bombing aircraft. Thirty examples of a derivative, the Potez

XVIII, were operated by Bulgaria. The fabric-covered fuselage accommodated a crew of two in tandem.

Potez 39 / France

Purpose: Reconnaissance
Data: Potez 390

Engine: A variety of engines could be fitted of 500/800hp including a 580hp Hispano-Suiza 12Hb
Span: 52ft 6in
Max speed: 143mph
Armament: Two forward-firing Vickers machine guns and two Lewis guns in rear cockpit. Fifth gun fired through floor

The Potez 39 was a two-seat high-wing monoplane of the early 1930s, which served as a reconnaissance aircraft with the Armée de l'Air alongside the Potez 25 and Breguet 27. The wings and fuselage were covered in a corrugated duralumin sheet, the former being supported by large Vee-type struts. A divided undercarriage was fitted with the wheels enclosed in streamlined fairings. 244 were built including 12 for Peru.

PZL P-23 and P-43 Karas
/ Poland

Purpose: Bomber/Reconnaissance
Photo and Data: P-23B Karaś

Engine: One 680hp licence-built Pegasus VIII radial
Span: 45ft 9.5in
Max speed: 198mph
Armament: Three 7.7mm machine guns, one forward-firing and one each in dorsal and ventral positions. Up to 1,543lb of bombs

First flown in prototype form in 1934, the P-23 was a low-wing light bomber and reconnaissance aircraft accommodating a pilot and observer in enclosed cockpits and a rear-gunner in an open cockpit, all in tandem. Like so many monoplane bombers of the 1930s, it had been developed from a civil aircraft. Production began with the P-23A Karaś A, but this version subsequently became an operations trainer. In 1936 the major production version, the P-23B

Karaś B, went into production, 210 being completed for the Polish Air Force. At the height of deployment, the PAF had 17 Karaś squadrons, but the number had been reduced by the time of the German invasion. A further 54 P-23Bs were built between 1937 and 1938 for Bulgaria, under the designation P-43, all powered by more powerful Gnome-Rhône 14 engines.

PZL P-24 / Poland

Purpose: Fighter
Photo: P-24G
Data: P-24F

Engine: One 970hp Gnome-Rhône 14N7 radial
Span: 35ft 1in
Max speed: 267mph
Armament: Two Oerlikon cannon and two machine guns

The P-24 was generally similar to the P-11, the main external differences being a spatted undercarriage and an enclosed cockpit for the pilot. It was never employed on a squadron basis by the Polish Air Force, although when it appeared it was one of the finest fighters in the world, but was produced solely as an export fighter and licence-built in other

countries. Recipients included Turkey (40 P-24As and Cs, and licence), Romania (six P-24Es and licence), Greece (36 P-24Fs and Gs) and Bulgaria (54 P-24Bs and Fs). Turkey built the greatest number under licence, eventually producing about 100, which served alongside its Bristol Blenheim and Heinkel He111 bombers.

PWS 10 / Poland

Purpose: Fighter

Engine: One 450hp Skoda-built Lorraine W
Span: 36ft 1in
Max speed: More than 150mph
Armament: Two forward-firing machine guns

Eighty PWS 10 parasol-wing fighters were ordered for the Polish Air Force as interim aircraft until PZL P7s could enter service. Deliveries began in 1932. Unfortunately for the PWS fighters, the P7s began to be delivered that year and the former aircraft were withdrawn to be used as trainers.

However, PWS 10s got a taste of action when 15 were sold to the Spanish Nationalists and these were used during the initial stages of the civil war.

Saro London / UK

Purpose: Maritime patrol
Photo and Data: London II

Engines: Two 920hp Bristol Pegasus X radials
Span: 80ft 0in
Max speed: 155mph
Armament: Three Lewis machine guns. Up to 2,000lb of bombs or depth charges

Despite the appearance of the Saro Cloud in 1931 as a monoplane flying-boat, the London was produced as a biplane (the later Lerwick reverting to high-wing monoplane design). 10 production London Is were built for Coastal Command, RAF, powered by Bristol Pegasus III engines, the first being delivered in 1936. Production continued with London IIs. Some

Londons were still in front-line service when World War 2 began; they remained operational until replaced by Catalinas in 1941, thereafter going to the Royal Canadian Air Force.

Savoia-Marchetti SM79 Sparviero (Hawk) / Italy

Purpose: Medium bomber
Data: SM79-II

Engines: Three 1,000hp Piaggio PXI RC40 radials
Span: 69ft 6.75in
Max speed: 270mph
Armament: Three 12.7mm Breda-SAFAT and one 7.7mm Lewis machine guns. Up to 2,750lb of bombs

First appearing as a commercial transport aircraft in 1934, the SM79 was put in production as a bomber and, later, as a torpedo bomber; as such it was thought by many to be the best aircraft of its kind to serve during World War 2. Total production of the SM79 amounted to about 1,200 aircraft, of which about half were in service when Italy entered World War 2. As the SM79-II, and powered by three 780hp Alfa Romeo 126 radial engines, it entered production for the Regia Aeronautica. The type was blooded

during the Spanish Civil War, when SM79s were operated in support of the Nationalists, alongside SM81s from April 1937. Meanwhile, the Italian Air Ministry had sponsored trials of the aircraft as a torpedo bomber, and the SM79-II entered production to serve in this role a month after the war in Europe had started. SM79-Is were exported to Yugoslavia in 1938, and twin-engined SM79Bs — with a streamlined 'glasshouse' nose section and modified fin and rudder — were exported to Brazil, Iraq and Romania (and licence).

Seversky P-35 / USA

Purpose: Fighter
Photo: P-35A
Data: P-35

Engine: One 950hp Pratt & Whitney R-1830-9 Twin Wasp radial
Span: 36ft 0in
Max speed: 282mph
Armament: One .50in and one .30in machine guns. Small bombs could be carried

The prototype of this fighter was built originally as a two-seater, before being converted into a single-seat aircraft and evaluated by the USAAC. 76 production aircraft were built for this service, deliveries starting in 1937 as P-35s. A wartime P-35A version also appeared, comprising hastily requisitioned export fighters. Exports made before the war included a

number to Japan, Sweden and the USSR, the latter also receiving a licence and building the aircraft as the 2PA-L, powered by the 1,000hp Wright Cyclone engine. Interestingly, this reverted to two-seat layout, the rear gunner being armed with a .30in machine gun.

Short Singapore III / UK

Purpose: Maritime reconnaissance-bomber

Engines: Two 560hp Rolls-Royce Kestrel IIIMS engines (tractor) and two 560hp Rolls-Royce Kestrel IIMS engines (pusher) mounted in tandem pairs
Span: 90ft 0in
Max speed: 145mph
Armament: Three Lewis machine guns in bow, dorsal and tail positions. Up to 2,000lb of bombs.

The series of Singapore flying-boats originated with the Singapore I of 1926, becoming world-famous after Sir Alan Cobham's round-Africa flight. This version was followed in 1930 by the Singapore II and, although it did not go into production, it was from this aircraft that the Singapore III was developed. 37 Singapore IIIs were built for the RAF, becoming operational in 1935. Singapores were operated at home, in the Middle East and Singapore.

For a short while in 1937 they were also stationed in Algeria to offer a measure of protection to British shipping in the Mediterranean and through the Strait of Gibraltar to the Atlantic Ocean. At the outbreak of World War 2, a few remained in limited service with the RAF, and a number were later acquired by the Royal New Zealand Air Force.

SPAD XX / France

Purpose: Fighter

Engine: One 300hp Hispano-Suiza 8Fbc
Max speed: 143mph
Span: 31ft 10in
Armament: Two forward-firing Vickers machine guns and one Lewis machine gun aft.

Ninety-five two-seat SPAD XXs were built for service in France, production aircraft appearing at the end of 1918. Japan also acquired a licence to produce the type. The majority of SPAD XXs built were subsequently modified for other work. Variants of the type included the SPAD XX*bis* 5, built for the Gordon-Bennett Cup race, and the SPAD XX*bis* 6, which on 9 October 1920 set up a world speed

record of 181.83mph, only to be bettered the next day by a Nieuport-Delage 29. On 4 November a SPAD regained the record with a speed of 191.98mph, but N-D29s increased this with four consecutive new records between 1920 and 1922.

SPAD 81 / France

Purpose: Fighter
Photo: SPAD 81C1

Engine: One 300hp Hispano-Suiza 8Fb
Span: 31ft 6in
Max speed: 146mph
Armament: Two forward-firing Vickers machine guns

Often recorded as the Blériot-SPAD 81C1 (as Blériot held interests in the SPAD Company), this aircraft was virtually a lower-powered version of the SPAD 61C1. The prototype first flew in March 1923. Of mixed construction with a cross-axle vee-type

undercarriage, 80 production aircraft were produced in 1924 for the French Air Force, remaining operational until 1929.

Supermarine Scapa / UK

Purpose: General reconnaissance

Engines: Two 525hp Rolls-Royce Kestrel IIIMS
Span: 75ft 0in

Max speed: 142mph
Armament: Three Lewis machine guns, mounted in bow and two dorsal positions. Up to 1,000lb of bombs

Built as a modern development of the Southampton, the Scapa was a biplane flying-boat of metal construction, with only the wings and twin-tail unit fabric covered. It also featured an enclosed cockpit for the flight crew. Like the Southampton it carried a crew of five, the two pilots sitting side-by-side in the cockpit and the other crew members doubling roles when necessary to man nose and two dorsal open gun positions, navigator's and engineer's compartment. Full domestic arrangements were provided in the hull for crew comfort, including a stove, ice chest and lavatory. 15 Scapas were built, first becoming operational with the RAF in 1935 and remaining in service until 1938. The same basic and successful configuration was further retained with the Supermarine Stranraer.

Supermarine Seagull III and Walrus / UK

Purpose: Spotter-reconnaissance
Data: Walrus

Engine: One 775hp Bristol Pegasus IIM2 or VI radial
Span: 45ft 10in
Max speed: 135mph
Armament: Two or three Vickers K machine guns in nose and dorsal positions. Up to 760lb of bombs or other stores

The success of the Seagull/Walrus class of light amphibious flying-boat can be measured by the fact that the last biplane to go into RAF service in 1943 was a similar but more modern development of the aircraft, named the Sea Otter, such was the competence of the basic design. Production started with six wooden Seagull IIIs for the FAA, which served on board Britain's third aircraft carrier HMS *Eagle* (completed in 1920, but sunk by a U-boat in 1942) from 1923 to 1925, later being transferred to the Royal Australian Air Force, where they were used to continue the aerial surveys of Australia started in

1924 by Fairey IIIDs. These had open cockpits for the crew and were powered by 450hp Napier Lion V engines. The later Seagull V featured a metal hull and enclosed cockpit for the flight crew and, most importantly, it could be catapult-launched from battleships and cruisers. It was ordered by the RAAF, FAA and RAF. In Britain it was called the Walrus, and production aircraft entered service from 1936. By 1944, a total of over 740 Walrus flying-boats had been built, the majority as wooden-hulled Saro Walrus IIs, powered by Pegasus VI engines.

Supermarine Spitfire / UK

Purpose: Fighter
Photo and Data: Mk I

Engine: One 1,030hp Rolls-Royce Merlin II or III
Span: 36ft 10in
Max speed: 355mph at 19,000ft
Armament: Early examples had four .303in machine guns. Changed in Mk IA and IB versions as noted below

Rated as one of the greatest combat aircraft ever built and undoubtedly recognisable to more people than any other military aircraft, the Spitfire was, with the Hawker Hurricane, a hero of the Battle of Britain. Testimony to its design potential was that during its production, its maximum speed was raised by 100mph. By the outbreak of World War 2, RAF Spitfires equipped nine full Fighter Command squadrons. The design had been evolved by Reginald Mitchell via the Supermarine F7/30 or Type 224, itself embodying features of the S6B racing seaplane which had won the Schneider Trophy outright for Britain in 1931, at an average speed of about 340mph. The Type 224 was a Rolls-Royce

Goshawk-powered, cranked wing, monoplane fighter, with a fixed trousered undercarriage and open cockpit. The prototype Spitfire, an improved fighter built as a private venture and powered by a Merlin C engine (incorporating a cockpit canopy reminiscent of that of the German Bf109), first flew on 5 March 1936. Deliveries of the Spitfire Mk I began in 1938, replacing Gauntlets. Initial Mk Is were powered by Merlin II engines and were boldly claimed at the time to be the fastest military aircraft in the world. Later production Mk Is were powered by Merlin III engines driving de Havilland three-blade variable-pitch propellers and had the familiar bulged canopies. The Mk IA version introduced the 'standard' RAF armament of eight machine guns, and the Mk IB of 1939 was armed with two British Hispano 20mm cannon and four machine guns. A total of just over 1,580 Mk Is was built, some of which were subsequently converted into Mk Vs and other versions.

Supermarine Stranraer / UK

Purpose: General reconnaissance

Engines: Two 920hp Bristol Pegasus X radials
Span: 85ft 0in
Max speed: 165mph
Armament: Three Lewis machine guns. Up to 1,000lb of bombs

A slightly larger and more powerful development of the successful Scapa, the Stranraer was the last twin-engined biplane flying-boat built for the RAF by Supermarine. 23 were completed, entering service with Coastal Command RAF in 1936. 15 remained operational in September 1939. A further 40 Stranraers were built by Canadian-Vickers for the Royal Canadian Air Force between 1938 and 1941.

Tupolev SB-2 (ANT-40) / USSR

Purpose: Medium bomber

Engines: Two 750hp M-100 engines on early production aircraft
Span: 66ft 8in
Max speed: 255mph
Armament: Four 7.62mm ShKAS machine guns in nose, dorsal and ventral positions. Up to 2,205lb of bombs

The SB-2 entered production in 1936, this original version being superseded by a version with 860hp M-100A engines and then by the SB-2*bis* with 960hp M-103 engines, which attained a speed of 280mph. SB-2s served with the Republican forces in Spain during the civil war, fought the Japanese in China, were used by the Red Air Force against the Japanese in Mongolia, against Finland in 1939 and then during World War 2. Interestingly, it is thought that of 210 SB-2s sent to Spain, about 178 were lost during the fighting. Also, the first aerial victory claimed during the Winter War between Finland and Russia was made by a Finnish pilot in a Fokker DXXI over an SB-2. Total SB-2 production is believed to have been well over 6,600 aircraft. A variant of the bomber was also built in Czechoslovakia as the B-71. A four-engined experimental development of the SB-2 also appeared in 1937, powered by supercharged M-34 engines and with a semi-retractable undercarriage incorporating large trousered legs. This was used on an unsuccessful attempt to fly over the North Pole from Moscow to North America.

Vickers Valentia / UK

Purpose: Transport
Data: Standard version

Engines: Two 650hp Bristol Pegasus IIL3 radials
Span: 87ft 4in
Max speed: 120mph
Accommodation: 22 troops. Bombs could be carried

Developed from the Victoria of 1926 the Valentia entered service with the RAF in the Middle East from 1934. A total of 28 Valentias was built and 54 more were produced by converting Victorias. A Pegasus IIM3-engined version of the Valentia subsequently served in India. Valentias remained in RAF service, in decreasing numbers, until late 1943.

Vickers Vernon / UK

Purpose: Transport

Engines: Two 360hp Rolls-Royce Eagle VIIIs or

450hp Napier Lion IIs or Napier Lion IIIs
Span: 68ft 1in
Max speed: 118mph
Accommodation: 12 troops. Bombs could be carried

Derived from the Commercial Vimy, the Vernon was

Vickers Victoria / UK

Purpose: Transport
Data: Mk V

Engines: Two 570hp Napier Lion XIs
Span: 87ft 4in
Max speed: 110mph, 134mph (MkVI)
Accommodation: 22 troops. Bombs could be carried

The Victoria was one of the most successful aircraft to serve with the RAF during the interwar period, and was derived from the Vickers Virginia bomber. Production of the type totalled some 94 aircraft, made up of wooden-structure Mk IIIs with 570hp Napier Lion V engines, composite construction Mk Vs and composite Mk VIs, with 620hp Bristol Pegasus IM3 radials. Victorias were mostly used in the Middle East and India, first entering service in 1926. They were employed on the first large-scale

Vought O2U, O3U and SU Corsair Series / USA

Purpose: Scout/Observation
Photo: O2U-4 seaplane
Data: SU-1

Engine: One 600hp Pratt & Whitney R-1690-42 Hornet radial
Span: 36ft 0in
Max speed: 171mph
Armament: Forward-firing and rear-mounted .30in machine guns. Bombs could be carried

Aircraft of the Corsair series were used by the US Navy and US Marine Corps from 1926, operating as landplanes, seaplanes and amphibians. Starting with orders for O2U-1s (powered by 450hp Pratt & Whitney Wasp engines), a total of well over 600 aircraft was built in many versions, a figure which

Vought SBU-1 and SBU-2 / USA

Purpose: Scout/Bomber
Data: SBU-1

Engine: One 750hp Pratt & Whitney R-1535-82 Twin Wasp Junior radial
Span: 33ft 3in
Max speed: 205mph
Armament: One .30in forward-firing machine gun and one in rear cockpit. Up to 500lb of bombs

The SBU was the last of the Vought biplanes of the

the first specially-designed troop-transport aircraft to serve with the RAF. A total of 55 was produced, made up of Vernon Mk Is with Eagle engines, Vernon Mk IIs with Lion III engines and Vernon Mk IIIs with Lion II engines. They entered RAF service in 1922, serving mainly in Iraq and operating the Cairo-Baghdad air mail services.

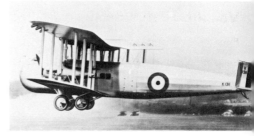

air-lift evacuation of civilians between December 1928 and February 1929. Some 586 persons and 24,193lb of baggage were transported from Kabul, Afghanistan, during tribal hostilities, by RAF aircraft which included eight Victorias, escorted by Westland Wapitis. Valentias replaced them in service from late 1934, some 54 Victorias subsequently being converted into Valentias.

does not include single and two-seat export versions sold to other countries, including Argentina, Brazil, China, Mexico and Peru. Mexico and Thailand also received licences to manufacture Corsairs, the latter country building over 70 aircraft.

Corsair type, which during the 1930s served as observation, scouting and bombing aircraft on board US aircraft carriers, battleships and cruisers. The SBU was not actually named Corsair, but was of the same general type. However, those delivered to Argentina were known as 'Corsarios'. The SBU-1 initial production version first entered service with the US Navy in 1935; a total of 84 was built. A further order brought about production of 40 Pratt & Whitney R-1535-98-engined SBU-2s for the Navy and reserve units, plus a number of export V-142s for the Argentine Navy with some of the special equipment removed. US Navy SBUs were superseded by Vought Vindicator monoplanes from 1938.

Vought UO-1 / USA

Purpose: Observation

Engine: One 200hp Wright J-3 Whirlwind radial
Span: 34ft 1in
Max speed: 122mph

Production of this type started in 1923, about 140 eventually being constructed. Capable of being operated as a landplane or seaplane, the UO-1 became the standard observation aircraft of the US Navy for many years, serving as a catapult aircraft from battleships and cruisers and being flown from land bases and aircraft carriers. Examples were exported to Peru (see Vought FU-1).

Wibault 7 Series / France

Purpose: Fighter
Data: Wibault 72

Engine: One 420hp Gnome-Rhône 9 Ac Jupiter radial
Span: 36ft 0in
Max speed: 156mph
Armament: Two Vickers and two Darne machine guns

The Wibault 7 followed the classic French layout for a fighter of the 1920s and early 1930s in being a strut-braced parasol-wing monoplane with a radial engine. A small number of Wibault 7s entered French Air Force service in 1926. These were followed by 60 improved Wibault 72s for the air force — a number of these remaining on strength nearly a decade later — and 32 Wibault 74 and 75 fighters for service with the French Navy on board the carrier *Béarn*, with 480hp engines and arrester gear. Export fighters were sold to Bolivia, Brazil and Paraguay, the latter as Wibault 73s with 450hp Lorraine engines. Chile also received Wibault 7s, licence-built in Britain by Vickers as Type 121s. Poland licence-built about 30 Wibault 72/73s, but these were used mainly as trainers.

Yokosuka B4Y1 / Japan

Purpose: Torpedo bomber

Engine: One 700-840hp Nakajima Hikari radial
Span: 49ft 2.5in
Max speed: 173mph
Armament: One 7.7mm machine gun in rear cockpit. One 1,765lb torpedo or 1,100lb of bombs

The Yokosuka B4Y1 entered production in 1936 as the Type 96 carrier-borne attack aircraft; 200 of the biplanes were eventually produced. They served on board all five of Japan's aircraft carriers of the time — the *Hosho*, *Akagi*, *Kaga*, *Ryujo* and *Soryu* (all but the *Hosho* sunk in 1942) — but were operational only as trainers in reduced numbers by the time Japan attacked Pearl Harbor in 1941.

Part Three

Less important aircraft, non-combat types, and those serving mainly during the two world wars and fully covered in the *Aircraft of World War I* and *Aircraft of World War II* companion books of this series.

Argentina

Military Aircraft Factory AeC3 Two-seat cantilever low-wing monoplane trainer of the latter 1930s, powered by a 140hp Armstrong Siddeley Genet Major engine. Operated by the Army Air Force.
Military Aircraft Factory AeMB2 Light bomber, powered by 712hp Wright CR-1820-F3 Cyclone engine. 15 built up to mid-1930s, able to carry 880lb of bombs, although some used as observation aircraft.

Military Aircraft Factory AeMO1 Two-seat trainer of similar configuration to AeC3, powered by a Wright Whirlwind engine.
Military Aircraft Factory AeT1 Five-passenger low-wing cabin monoplane, powered by a 450hp Lorraine engine. Operated by the Army Air Force as a transport aircraft.

Austria

Phönix DIII First delivered to Austro-Hungarian naval fighter units in late 1918. After the war, 17 DIIIs acquired by the Swedish Army Air Service as J1s. A further 10 were built in Sweden.

Belgium

Stampe et Vertongen SV4 Two-seat biplane trainer, first flown in 1933. The SV4B was the major pre-World War 2 version.

Canada

Vickers Vancouver II Following the prototype Vancouver I flying-boat, five production Vancouver IIs were built. In the mid-1930s, these were taken over by the Royal Canadian Air Force as Vancouver II/SW coastal patrol aircraft.

Czechoslovakia

Aero A12 Two-seat reconnaissance and light bombing biplane of 1923. 93 built for Czech Army Air Force. Powered by a 240hp Maybach Mb IVa engine and featured Aero patented side radiators. Wing span 42ft, length 27ft 2.75in and maximum speed 124mph.
Aero A14 Czech-built version of Hansa-Brandenburg C1.
Aero A18 Biplane fighter of which 20 served with Czech Army Air Force from 1923.

Aero A24 Unsuccessful prototype twin-engined biplane bomber of 1924.
Aero A25 Training aircraft, powered by a 185hp Walter engine. Operated from latter 1920s by Czech Army Air Force.
Aero A304 Three-seat light bombing and reconnaissance aircraft of 1938. Also used as aircrew trainer. 15 built, incorporating minor alterations from A204 airliner from which it was developed.
Avia B-34 Fighter of 1932, the airframe used as an engine test bed (see Avia B-534).
Avia B-35 and B-135 First prototype B-35 low-wing monoplane fighter flew September 1938. B-135 prototype, derived from B-35, appeared mid-1939. 12 delivered to Bulgarian Air Force in 1940, after German occupation.

Left: *Aero A18*

Avia BH-3 Low-wing monoplane fighter of 1921, powered by either a 180hp BMW IIIa or 240hp Walter W-IV engine. 10 built for Czech Army Air Force.

Avia BH-10 Single-seat braced low-wing monoplane trainer, powered by a 60hp Walter engine. Used during 1920s by the Czech Army Air Force.

Avia BH-11 Two-seat version of BH-10 for the Czech Army Air Force, powered by a 85hp Walter Vega engine. Built under licence in Switzerland.

Avia FIX Avia-built Fokker FIX bomber, 12 built in 1932, each powered by three 450hp Walter-built Jupiter engines and carrying up to 3,306lb of bombs. Two exported to Yugoslavia as F39s and licence acquired by Yugoslavia.

Letov S-18 Two-seat biplane trainer, powered by a 60hp Walter engine. Used from latter 1920s by Czech Army Air Force and Bulgarian Air Force.

Letov S-228 General purpose single-engined biplane, used by the Estonian Air Force.

Praga BH-41 Two-seat biplane advanced trainer, powered by a 300hp Hispano-Suiza engine.

Denmark

Hawker Dankok 12 Hawker Woodcock IIs built under licence in Denmark from 1927 as Dankoks. In service up to late 1930s. Maximum speed 146mph. One set new Scandinavian height record.

Finland

IVL Kotka Two-seat maritime reconnaissance, light bombing and photographic biplane. Entered service with Finnish Air Force at end of 1920s. Could be powered by any radial engine of 450-600hp, but built with Bristol Jupiters.

State Aircraft Factory Smolik S-218A Two-seat biplane basic trainer, powered by 120hp or 145hp engine. Of Czech design, it was licence-built in Finland for Finnish Air Force in early 1930s.

France

Amiot 120 and 120S Renault-engined predecessors of Amiot 122.

Amiot 350 Series Amiot E6/E7 twin-engined bomber prototype appeared in 1934. Developed into 340 and 350, and later into major production versions 351, 353 and 354. First 351 flew January 1940; 86 aircraft delivered by fall of France.

Blanchard Brd 1 Bomber flying-boat, powered by two pusher engines. 14 entered service with the French Navy in 1923.

Bloch 174 Twin-engined light bomber and reconnaissance aircraft.

Bloch 175 Three-seat monoplane bomber, developed from the 174, capable of carrying up to 3,416lb of bombs. 21 built by the fall of France. Others built during occupation and sent to Germany.

Breguet 27 Two-seat sesquiplane observation and light-bombing aircraft of 1929, powered by a 500hp Hispano-Suiza 12 engine. Of unusual configuration, with boom between rear fuselage and tail unit. 130 operated by the Armee de L'Air, serving throughout the 1930s. Exported to Brazil, China and Venezuela.

CAMS 33B Twin-engined biplane maritime reconnaissance flying-boat, first flown in 1923. French Navy operated 12. Others flown in Yugoslavia. Could carry light bomb load.

CAMS 37 Biplane flying-boat, powered by a 450hp Lorraine pusher engine and accommodating a crew of three. Used as a coastal patrol aircraft from the latter 1920s.

CAMS 51R-3 Three-seat bombing and reconnaissance flying-boat, powered by two 380hp Gnome-Rhône-built Jupiter engines in tandem.

Caudron C-59 Designed as a two-seat naval training biplane, powered by a 180hp Hispano-Suiza engine.

Caudron 714 303mph lightweight fighter, powered by one 450hp Renault Rol inline engine and armed with four 7.5mm machine guns. Appeared in summer 1938 and entered production in mid-1939. 90 built in February 1940, six going into Finnish Air Force service and the rest to Armée de l'Air squadrons.

Above: *Caudron 714*

Caudron Goeland Twin-engined monoplane transport and training aircraft. Appeared 1934; several versions produced before World War 2, principally C445 military aircraft.

Dewoitine D520 First of three fighter prototypes flew on 2 October 1938. Production started early 1939, deliveries later that year. Approximately 430 completed before France's capitulation, after which German authorities allowed production to continue. Over 600 built in total.

Above: *Dewoitine D520*

Farman F50B2 Large biplane bomber, powered by two 265hp Lorraine-Dietrich engines. Appeared 1918. Small number built. After World War 1, two used by French Navy. Maximum speed 87mph.

Gourdou-Leseurre 810 HY Series. Armed reconnaissance and attack seaplane of 1927. 86 built as 810HY-813HY, powered by 420hp Gnome-Rhône 9Ac engines. Flew from warships. Max speed 121mph.

Gourdou-Leseurre 832HY Light catapult seaplane, powered by 230hp Hispano-Suiza 9Qb engine. Operated by two navy escadrilles.

Hanriot HD-1 Single-seat fighter of 1917, powered by a 120hp Le Rhône 9Jb rotary engine. Used for a brief time after World War 1.

Latécoère 28/9 Single-seat three-engined high-wing monoplane bomber. Three operated by Venezuelan Air Force in early 1930s.

Latham 42 Three-seat twin-engined biplane flying-boat of 1924. Small number operated in France and Poland for armed maritime patrol duties.

Latham 47 Twin-engined naval reconnaissance and bomber biplane flying-boat. Latham 47 R3B4 production aircraft entered service 1929. Withdrawn 1930.

Levasseur PL2 PL2 AT1 prototype biplane torpedo bomber appeared 1921. Nine production aircraft built as two-seaters. Entered service on the aircraft carrier *Béarn* in 1926; used from 1928 as trainers.

Levasseur PL4 Coastal-reconnaissance biplane of French Navy, powered by a 450hp Lorraine engine.

Levasseur PL10 Three-seat shipboard reconnaissance biplane, powered by a 600hp Hispano-Suiza engine.

Levasseur PL15 Single-engined attack seaplane of biplane configuration. 16 served on board *Commandant Teste* in 1934-8, later being relegated to training duties. Small number became operational at outbreak of war.

Levasseur PL101 Development of the PL10, powered by similar engine and of similar size and performance.

Levy GL40 Two-seat single-engined pusher seaplane bomber, able to carry 550lb of bombs. First flew November 1917, 100 built during 1918. Two GL 40s bought by Finland and six by Belgium. Some still in service after war.

Lioré et Olivier 5 and 7 The LéO 5 appeared in 1919 as an armoured aircraft for ground attack/infantry support duties. Production examples were built with 170hp Le Rhône 9R engines. It was followed into service by the LéO 7/2 bomber and 7/3 amphibious torpedo bomber, of which 20 and 12 were built from 1922 respectively. The latter was powered by two 300hp Hispano 8Fb engines and could carry a warload of up to 1,100lb.

Above: *LeO 7/2*

Lioré et Olivier 12 Twin-engined two-seat biplane night bomber. Five built and entered experimental service from 1924.

Lioré et Olivier 451 Twin-engined cantilever low-wing monoplane bomber. 10 serving with French Air Force by September 1939. Many others built up to French capitulation and during German occupation.

Loire 70 and 130 Three-engined and single-engined reconnaissance flying-boats of the mid-1930s.

Loire 210 Low-wing fighter seaplane. Prototype first flew on 21 March 1935 and first production aircraft in November 1938. 20 ordered, entering service 1939. Quickly withdrawn because of wing failure.

Morane-Saulnier 35 Two-seat parasol-wing trainer, powered by an 80hp Le Rhône engine. Became a standard type with the French Air Force.

Morane-Saulnier 138 Similar to MS35 but slightly larger and heavier, although marginally faster with a maximum speed of 84mph. Also became a standard type with the French Air Force.

Morane-Saulnier 130 Similar to MS35 but powered by a 230hp Salmson Ab-9 engine and used as an advanced trainer.

Morane-Saulnier 230 Two-seat parasol-wing advanced trainer, powered by a 250hp Salmson 9Ab radial engine. Operated by the air forces of France and Portugal.

Morane-Saulnier 405 and 406 Cantilever low-wing monoplane fighters, powered by 860hp Hispano-Suiza 12Y-31 engines. MS405 was the first

French monoplane fighter with retractable undercarriage and enclosed cockpit. 15 MS405s built, followed by more than 1,080 MS406s. The first production MS406 flew in January 1939 and deliveries began that year. About 527 were in service in September 1939. Others delivered to Finland, Switzerland and Turkey. Maximum speed 303mph. Armed with one 20mm cannon and two 7.5in machine guns.

Morane-Saulnier Parasol Name given to a series of trainers, including the MS315 which was powered by a 135hp Salmson 9Nc engine. The MS315EP2, and the previously mentioned MS230, formed the backbone of French Air Force training units in the 1930s.

Potez 29 Five-passenger cabin biplane, powered by a 450hp Lorraine-Dietrich engine. Some used as utility aircraft by the French Air Force, including the 'Sanitaire' ambulance version, accommodating three stretchers and an attendant. Last aircraft delivered as late as 1934.

Potez 63 and derivatives Multi-purpose low-wing monoplane, produced as a fighter, attack aircraft, light bomber, dive bomber and reconnaissance type. First prototype flew April 1936. 80 Potez 630 three-seat fighters built for French Air Force and delivered in 1938, each powered by two 640hp Hispano-Suiza engines. Followed by 214 Potez 631s (with 670hp Gnome-Rhône 14M3/4 radials), 115 Potez 633 two-seat attack, 61 Potez 637 observation and 717 Potez 63-II three-seat reconnaissance aircraft. Potez 633s exported before the war to Greece and Romania and Potez 630s to Switzerland. By September 1939, about 360 aircraft of the series operational with French Air Force. By May 1940 more than 1,200 delivered of which perhaps 500 were operational.

Above: *Romanian Potez 635*

Potez 65 Twin-engined shoulder-wing transport aircraft, of which several squadrons served with the French Air Force until the outbreak of war.

Nieuport 24 Prototype fighter appeared 1916. Used by France, Belgium and Italy; 121 with American Expeditionary Force. Nieuport 24*bis* appeared 1917, used by France and Britain; 140 with AEF. Some 24s built by Nakajima of Japan in 1919 as KO-4s.

Nieuport-Delage 42 Single-seat fighter. Appeared 1924 and 25 aircraft ordered as Ni-D42C1s. Between 29 August and 16 October 1924, 16 world records were gained by an Ni-D42.

Above: *Morane-Saulnier 406*

Other variants included the unsuccessful Ni-D42H seaplane, and experimental Ni-D44, Ni-D46, Ni-D47 and Ni-D48.

Salmson 2A2 Two-seat reconnaissance biplane, powered by a 260hp Salmson-Canton-Unne radial engine. Pilot sat under leading-edge of upper wing. Armament comprised one forward-firing Vickers and two rear-mounted Lewis machine guns. By end of war, 530 in French service, plus others with American Expeditionary Force. Remained in service into the 1920s.

SPAD VII Single-seat biplane fighter, first flown April 1916. Served with air forces of many countries. Two derivatives produced in 1923 were the SPAD 72 single-seat trainer and SPAD 62 two-seat trainer with dual controls.

SPAD XIII Over 8,400 SPAD XIII biplane fighters were built. Production aircraft began to enter service in May 1917. Remained in French service until 1923, and exported after war to Belgium, Czechoslovakia, Japan and Poland.

SPAD 510 Biplane fighter, powered by one 690hp Hispano-Suiza 12Xbrs engine. Armed with four machine guns. Maximum speed 236mph. Last biplane fighter to equip French Air Force. 60 operational in France from 1937 to 1940. 27 flown by Republican forces in Spain.

Above: *SPAD 510*

Tellier T4 and T5 Two-seat flying-boat bomber. T4 appeared December 1918 with folding biplane wings and more powerful engine than earlier T3 of World War 1, followed by twin-engined T5 with metal wings.

Germany

Albatros DI and DII DI entered service autumn 1916, followed by DII a few months later. Both types produced after World War 1, as L15 and L17 respectively.

Albatros DIII Single-seat biplane fighter. Served operationally from early 1917. By end of year nearly 450 aircraft in service. After war continued in production as L20.

Albatros DV and DVa Single-seat biplane fighters. DV entered service mid-1917; joined and superseded by DVa; 1,059 DVs and DVas serving by May 1918. Several DVs built after war as L24s.

Arado Ar76 Single-seat parasol-wing monoplane fighter and trainer, powered by a 240hp Argus As10C engine. First flown in 1935. Only a small number built, armed with one or two 7.9mm machine guns. Maximum speed 165mph.

Arado Ar96 Began to enter service 1939, becoming standard trainer for Luftwaffe in 1940.

Blohm und Voss Bv138 Reconnaissance, convoy patrol and U-boat co-operation flying-boat. Prototype first flew 15 July 1937. First production version was Bv 138A-1, in 1939.

Bucker Bu131 Jungmann Prototype trainer flew April 1934, deliveries to Luftwaffe starting end of that year. Also licence-built in Japan as Nippon Ki-86 (1,254 completed).

Bucker Bu133 Jungmeister Jungmeister trainer of 1935 was produced in large numbers, also being exported and licence-built.

Dornier Do18 Reconnaissance flying-boat. Developed from civil version, first military variant was Do18D which entered service 1938. Major production version was Do18G of 1939. Do18H was unarmed dual control trainer version of Do18G, and Do18N was converted Do18G ASR version. Production ended 1940, totalling over 100 aircraft.

Above: *Dornier Do18G*

Dornier Do22 Three-seat torpedo bomber and reconnaissance parasol monoplane. First appeared as Do22/See seaplane. Ordered by Greece, Latvia and Yugoslavia. First production aircraft flew 15 July 1938. Do22/Land aircraft flew 10 March 1939. Armament consisted of a torpedo or bombs, and four machine guns.

Dornier Do24 Designed as a patrol flying-boat for the Royal Netherlands East Indies Naval Air Service and first flown in 1937. 11 Do24K-1s delivered from Germany and 26 Do24K-2s licence-built for the service, operated from 1938. Others built mainly for the Luftwaffe during World War 2. Powered by two 760hp Wright Cyclone radial engines. Maximum speed 211mph. Armed with cannon and machine guns.

Above: *Dornier Do24*

Dornier Do217 First prototype Do217 bomber flew August 1938. First major production series, Do217E, appeared in Luftwaffe squadrons in 1941.

Dornier DoC, D and T Produced from earlier civil variants, the DoC was a single-engined parasol-wing trainer of 1925. The DoD was a twin-float version of the DoC, a torpedo bomber variant being built in 1927 for the Yugoslav Navy. The DoT appeared as an ambulance version. DoCs were used as light bombers with the Fuerza Aérea de Chile around 1930.

Focke-Wulf Fw44 Stieglitz First flown in late summer 1932, several hundred Stieglitz trainers were built and some exported.

Focke-Wulf Fw56 Stösser Advanced parasol-wing fighter trainer. Appeared 1934. Many built for Germany and also exported.

Focke-Wulf Fw58 Weihe Communications, transport and training aircraft. First flown 1935; built for Luftwaffe and exported.

Focke-Wulf Fw61 First fully-successful helicopter to fly, on 26 June 1936. Powered by one 160hp Siemens-Halske Sh14A engine, driving two rotors on outriggers. Established a world's closed-circuit distance record for helicopters in mid-1937 of over 76 miles. Not produced for the military or commercially, but led to development of Focke-Achgelis Fa223.

Focke-Wulf Fw189 Uhu Designed as a twin-engined close support and light bombing aircraft. Production started 1939 and FW189 entered service late 1940. Initially used mainly as reconnaissance aircraft.

Focke-Wulf Fw190 Prototype fighter first flown

on 1 June 1939, with deliveries beginning late 1940. Total production amounted to 20,051 aircraft, of which 6,634 were fighter bombers.

Gotha Go145 Two-seat biplane trainer of 1934, powered by a 240hp Argus As10C engine. Equipment was available to allow its use as a pilot, single or two-seat aerobatic, armament, wireless, aerial photography, blind-flying and night-flying trainer. About 10,000 Go145s produced by four German companies for civil and military use and was licence-built abroad.

Halberstadt CV Long-range photographic reconnaissance aircraft of 1918, armed with one fixed Spandau and one free-firing Parabellum machine gun. Some used after the war, including a small number operated by the Swiss Air Force as trainers between 1920 and 1921.

Hansa-Brandenburg W29 and W33 Seagoing monoplane fighters operated from April 1918 by German coastal patrol units. Versions of W29 operated by Danish Air Force after war, and 310 built in Japan by Nakajima and Aichi. W33 licence-built in Finland as A-22 and in Norway.

Above: *Hansa-Brandenburg W29*

Heinkel aircraft up to the He45 were sometimes designated HE for monoplanes and HD for biplanes.

Heinkel He1 Three-seat low-wing twin-float seaplane, powered by a 240hp Armstrong Siddeley Puma engine. First product of the postwar Heinkel company, and built in Sweden by Svenska Aero AB. First flown May 1923. Used as a trainer by the Swedish Navy, as the S1.

Heinkel He2 Improved version of the He1 with larger wings and powered by a 360hp Rolls-Royce Eagle IX engine. Built in Sweden, and these served as reconnaissance aircraft with the Swedish navy, as the S2. Also used by Finland. Remained operational until 1928.

Heinkel He4 and He5 Developments of the earlier He1/2 seaplanes, powered by Eagle and 450hp Napier Lion engines respectively. Users included the Swedish Air Force.

Heinkel He7 Similar to the earlier seaplanes, but powered by two 450hp Bristol Jupiter VI engines. Used as a reconnaissance and torpedo-carrying aircraft.

Heinkel He8 Development of He5, powered by a 450hp Armstrong Siddeley Jaguar engine. 22

acquired for the Danish Naval Flying Corps, which used them for reconnaissance and survey work from the latter 1920s until 1940. Sixteen of the Danish He8s were licence-built in that country by the naval shipyards.

Heinkel He9 Two- or three-seat seaplane, powered by a 660hp BMW VIa engine. Achieved 161mph and established six world seaplane records in 1929.

Heinkel He3 and He18 Three-seat (He3) and two-seat (He18) low-wing monoplane training aircraft, both powered by the 75hp Siemens-Halske engine. Twin-float or wheel landing gears could be fitted. He18 had a conventional steel tube fuselage (instead of the monocoque fuselage of the He3) to ease production, and foldable wings and tail unit.

Heinkel He19 and He30 Two-seat biplanes, both powered by the 450hp Bristol Jupiter VI engine. He30 an enlarged version of He19. Suitable for liaison, training and transport duties.

Heinkel He21, He29 and He32 Two- or three-seat biplane basic trainers of 1924-5, powered by 120hp Mercedes (He21) or 100hp Siemens engines. Available with wheel or twin-float landing gears. Large numbers built.

Heinkel He22 Advanced trainer version of He21 series, powered by a 230hp BMW IV engine or similar engines.

Heinkel He24 Two-seat seaplane trainer, powered by a 230hp BMW IV engine.

Heinkel He25 Large two-seat reconnaissance biplane, powered by the 450hp Napier Lion engine. Designed to a Japanese Navy requirement and as such was strengthened for catapulting from ships. Fitted with a twin-float landing gear.

Heinkel He26 Single-seat reconnaissance seaplane, powered by a 300hp Hispano-Suiza engine. Also built for the Japanese Navy for shipboard operation.

Heinkel He28 Three-seat twin-float seaplane, powered by a 650hp Lorraine engine. Designed as a larger development of the He17.

Heinkel He36 Two-seat biplane trainer of 1928, powered by a 160hp Mercedes DIII engine. Unsuccessful, but a small number were built.

Heinkel He42 Two-seat twin-float biplane reconnaissance and training aircraft, first flown in March 1931. Built in several versions, mainly for German naval training schools and the Luftwaffe. Last version was the He42C-2 reconnaissance aircraft, which could be catapult-launched. This was powered by a 380hp Junkers L-5-Ga engine and was armed with one MG15 or MG17 machine gun. Large number built, some remaining operational as trainers until 1944.

Heinkel He45 Two-seat general purpose biplane, used mainly for training, reconnaissance and light bombing duties. Powered by a 750hp BMW VI engine and possessing a maximum speed of 180mph. Production started in 1932 for the Luftwaffe. Total of over 500 He45s built of all versions.

Heinkel He46 Two-seat armed reconnaissance and army co-operation parasol-wing monoplane, powered by a 650hp Siemens Bramo SAM 322B radial engine. Total of 478 production aircraft built, some being exported to Bulgaria, Hungary and Spain. Initial production version for Luftwaffe was He46C-1, with internal provision for a camera mounted in a position beneath observer's cockpit or 20 22lb bombs. Production closed in 1936. Although He46s began to be replaced from 1938, some remained flying until 1943.

Heinkel He50 Biplane reconnaissance-bomber, powered by a 600hp BMW Bramo SAM 322B engine. Small number used by the Luftwaffe but unsuccessful. Exported to Japan, where it was developed into the Aichi D1A (qv).

Heinkel He60 Two-seat armed reconnaissance (one MG15 aircraft gun) and unarmed seaplane trainer, powered by a 660hp BMW VI engine. Some equipped for catapulting from cruisers of the German Navy, delivered from 1934. Maximum speed 140mph.

Above: *Heinkel He60C*

Heinkel He70 Developed from the He70 high-speed mailplane of 1932, military versions were the He70C and He70F. The He70F equipped Spanish forces as a light bomber. Hungary also operated 20 of a developed version designated He170A for reconnaissance duties.

Heinkel He112 Single-seat fighter and fighter bomber. Prototype flew mid-1935 and 30 built for Luftwaffe evaluation. 17 sent to Spain in 1938 and 12 sold to Imperial Japanese Navy. 24 built for Romanian Air Force.

Heinkel He114 Two-seat twin-float sesquiplane, used mainly as the He114A-2 shipboard reconnaissance aircraft, powered by a 960hp BMW 132K engine. Initial armament comprised one rear-mounted machine gun. Small number specially-built as He114C-2 unarmed trainers, powered by BMW 132N engines.

Heinkel He115 Twin-engined maritime reconnaissance and anti-shipping aircraft. Designed in 1937, prototype gained eight world seaplane speed records in March 1938. By outbreak of war, German Naval air arm was equipped with 10 evaluation He115A-Os and a number of He115A series aircraft. He115B series entered production

1939. Export version, designated He115A-2, ordered by Norway and Sweden. Total of well over 300 built.

Henschel Hs126 Two-seat reconnaissance and artillery observation parasol-wing monoplane, first flown in 1936. BMW 132Dc-powered Hs126A-1 production aircraft delivered to the Luftwaffe from 1938, a few subsequently serving in Spain during the late stages of the civil war. Armament comprised one MG17 forward-firing and one MG15 rear-mounted machine gun, plus provision for up to 330lb of bombs carried in two internal containers and under fuselage. Small number of Hs126s exported to Greece in 1939. Production changed to Hs126B-1 version in 1939, powered by an 850hp BMW Bramo Fafnir 323 engine. Approximately 250 Hs126s in operational status by the outbreak of war.

Henschel Hs129 Twin-engined anti-tank and close support aircraft. First prototype flew early 1939. Production aircraft delivered 1941. 841 Hs129s built.

Junkers DI and CLI DI appeared October 1917 as single-seat fighter. Used after war against Bolshevik forces. CLI two-seat development of DI. 47 built by end of war, some later serving in Estonia, Finland and Lithuania.

Junkers K39 and K59 Evolved from the A32 and A35 postal aircraft of 1926, as a three-seat light bomber and two-seat reconnaissance-fighter respectively. K39 powered by a 600hp Junkers L-55 engine and armed with two forward-firing, one ventral (operated by the observer in the lower middle cockpit which was also used for bomb aiming) and two rear-mounted machine guns, plus underwing and under-fuselage bombs. K59 powered by a 310hp Junkers L-5 engine and armed with two forward-firing and two rear-mounted machine guns. Built in Germany and Sweden.

Junkers K47 Two-seat high-performance low-wing monoplane fighter of 1928, powered by a 420hp Bristol Jupiter VII engine. Maximum speed was 180mph at 10,000ft. Armament comprised two forward-firing and one rear-mounted machine gun. Small number built in Sweden for China.

Above: *Junkers Ju87*

Junkers Ju87 The famous 'Stuka' dive bomber. First production Ju87A-1 delivered to the Luftwaffe in early 1937, powered by 600hp Jumo 210Ca engine. Maximum speed of 199mph. Armed with one 7.9mm machine gun forward and one in rear cockpit, plus one 550lb or 1,100lb bomb. Few sent to Spain for evaluation by Condor Legion in 1937. Ju87B, with 1,100hp Jumo 211D engine, new cockpit canopy, redesigned undercarriage and tail fin appeared in 1938. Total of more than 330 Ju87s, mostly Ju87Bs, in Luftwaffe service by outbreak of World War 2.

Junkers Ju88 Twin-engined medium bomber. Ju88V1 prototype first flew 21 December 1936. Ten pre-production Ju88A-0s and early Ju88A-1s in service by outbreak of war. Over 9,000 bomber aircraft built and about 6,000 non-bomber types by the end of the war.

Junkers Ju90 40-seat commercial transport prototype, Ju90V1, flew 28 August 1937. Following three more prototypes, small number of Ju90Bs delivered to Luftwaffe.

Junkers R42 Developed from the G24 commercial airliner, this monoplane medium bomber was built in the Soviet Union, Sweden and Turkey (military version known as the K30). Powered by three 310hp Junkers L-5 engines. Armament comprised machine guns aft of the cockpit and in mid-dorsal and ventral positions, plus underwing bombs. R-42s in Red Air Force service designated G-1s, while others were fitted with twin floats for the Soviet Navy. Small number of aircraft were delivered to Chile.

Above: *Junkers R42*

Junkers RO2 Evolved from the A20 postal aircraft and freighter of 1923, about 25 RO2 low-wing monoplane reconnaissance aircraft served with the Red Air Force in the latter 1920s, having been produced at the Fili works, near Moscow. Others

Italy

Ansaldo A-1 Balilla Biplane fighter of 1917. 150 built during World War 1 for Italian Air Force. Poland ordered 75 aircraft, 20 arriving in 1920 and the remainder in 1921. Some used in Russo-Polish war. 50 other aircraft licence-built in Poland, serving in fighter defence role until 1925. One, re-engined with a Curtiss K-12 in America, flown in 1921 Pulitzer race.

Ansaldo SVA5, 9 and 10 Fighter, reconnaissance and light bombing biplane. Single-seat SVA5 entered production 1917. SVA9 unarmed two-

were built in Sweden for the air forces of Iran and Turkey.

LVG CVI Two-seat armed reconnaissance and light bombing biplane of 1918, powered by a 200hp Benz BzIV engine. Many in operational use by August 1918. Some remained in military service after the war with other countries, including Switzerland.

Messerschmitt Bf108 Taifun Four-seat cabin monoplane of 1933, used before and during World War 2 as a communications and light transport aircraft. Powered by a 240hp Argus As10C engine.

Messerschmitt Bf110 Fighter and fighter bomber, operated by the Luftwaffe throughout World War 2. First flown in May 1936. Bf110C-1 entered operational service with the Luftwaffe in 1939, and followed a number of pre-production and Bf110B-1 production aircraft. Powered by two 1,100hp Daimler-Benz DB601A1 engines. Maximum speed 348mph. Armed with two 20mm cannon and five machine guns. About 250 Bf110s in service at outbreak of war.

Above: *Messerschmitt Bf110*

Rumpler CIV and CVII Two-seat reconnaissance aircraft of 1917. Used after the war by other air forces, including the Swiss which used a very small number for training pilots in high-altitude flying and for training observers.

Zeppelin LZ CII 2 Two-seat long-range reconnaissance aircraft, built in 1918 but not used operationally during war. 19 purchased by the Swiss Air Force in 1920 and used until 1927, although proving dangerous to fly.

seater and SVA10 armed two-seater. 1,248 aircraft built by Armistice. Remained in service for more than a decade after war.

Breda Ba19 Single or two-seat advanced biplane trainer.

Breda Ba25, Ba26, and Ba28 Appeared early 1930s. Ba25 and BA26 were basic trainers. The Ba28 was a single-seat advanced trainer.

Breda Ba27 Single-seat fighter monoplane of 1935. Small number ordered by China and used during Sino-Japanese war. No order from Regia Aeronautica.

Breda Ba64 Fighter, light bomber and reconnaissance aircraft, produced during 1933-4. Moderate number built for the Regia Aeronautica.

Breda Ba88 Lince Twin-engined fighter-bomber/reconnaissance aircraft. Appeared 1937, and small number built for Regia Aeronautica.

Caproni Ca36 Large biplane bomber put into production in 1923 as Ca36M. Served with Italian Air Force for four years.

Caproni Ca135 Twin-engined medium bomber. Prototype first flew 1 April 1935. Regia Aeronautica ordered small number for evaluation in 1936, but relegated them to secondary duties. 32 acquired by Peruvian Air Force and others by Hungarian Air Force during 1939-40.

Caproni Ca164 Two-seat aerobatic biplane trainer of the 1930s, operated by the air forces of Italy and France (latter assembled in that country).

Caproni Ca309 to Ca312 Ca309 Ghibli designed 1936 as 'police' and general duties aircraft; Ca310 Libbacio reconnaissance aircraft, not used by Regia Aeronautica but by Spanish Nationalist forces, Croatia, Hungary, Norway (where licence-built by Navy Aircraft Factory) and Yugoslavia; Ca311 and Ca311M reconnaissance and bomber types; Ca312 and Ca312M for communications, training and other duties, some exported to Norway; Ca312*bis* twin-float version.

Caproni-Vizzola F5 Single-seat fighter, first flown 1939. Construction of pre-production aircraft started 1940, equipping one Regia Aeronautica squadron.

CANT Z1007*bis* Alcione Three-engined medium bomber. First prototype flew end of 1937. Production started 1939 to equip several Regia Aeronautica squadrons.

Fiat A120 and R22 Two-seat parasol-wing monoplane and two-seat biplane armed reconnaissance aircraft respectively, built in late 1920s.

Fiat CR25 Three-seat twin-engined low-wing aircraft. Two prototypes flew 1938 and 10 pre-production aircraft ordered. Entered service 1941; used mainly for maritime reconnaissance and later transport.

Fiat CR42 Falco Developed from CR41, the prototype CR42 single-seat biplane fighter first flew early 1939 and was ordered for Regia Aeronautica. 34 ordered by Belgian Air Force and some exported to Hungary late 1939. 72 acquired by Sweden during World War 2.

Fiat G50 Freccia Single-seat fighter monoplane, first flown 26 February 1937. Initial order for 45 aircraft, which entered production 1938. Some used in last months of Spanish Civil War and another 200 ordered. Entered service proper with Regia Aeronautica from 1939.

Fiat RS14 Italy's last operational floatplane torpedo-bomber. Two prototypes first flown 1939. Production deliveries started 1941; used primarily as maritime reconnaissance aircraft.

IMAM Ro43 and Ro44 Ro43 two-seat reconnaissance floatplane: 105 in service when Italy entered war and usually operated from warships. Ro44 single-seat floatplane fighter, first flown 1936; about 30 in service by war, usually operated from coastal stations.

Jona J-6/S Two-seat sesquiplane biplane trainer, powered by a 240hp Alfa D2C30 engine.

Macchi C200 Saetta Single-seat monoplane fighter, prototype first flown 24 December 1937. 156 in service with Regia Aeronautica by Italy's entry into the war.

Macchi M5 Single-seat flying-boat fighter biplane. Entered production 1917; 240 built. Remained in service for some years after war.

Macchi M7 and M8 Flying-boat fighter biplanes. Three of 17 M7s ordered were operational by end of World War 1. Remained in service until 1928. M8 appeared late 1917; 57 completed by end of war and used mainly for coastal patrol and anti-shipping duties. Used after war as trainers.

Piaggio P-6 and P-10 Two-seat reconnaissance seaplanes built for catapulting, powered by a 420hp Fiat A20 and Piaggio-built Jupiter engine respectively.

Piaggio P-11 Version of Blackburn Lincock, built as a two-seat trainer. Powered by an Alfa-Romeo-built Lynx engine.

Piaggio P108B Italy's largest aircraft and only heavy bomber of World War 2. Prototype first flew 1939. Entered service with Regia Aeronautica 1942, production eventually totalling 163 P108Bs.

Reggiane Re2000 Falco I Monoplane fighter; first appeared 1938. Not ordered by Regia Aeronautica, but eventually operated by Italian Navy and exported to Sweden and Hungary. Also produced in Hungary in small numbers.

Savoia-Marchetti S55 Tandem-engined twin-hulled monoplane flying-boat, capable of carrying bombs or torpedo. Best remembered for first

Above: *Savoia-Marchetti S55*

Left: *Fiat CR42*

formation flight across the South Atlantic in January 1931 and first formation flight across North Atlantic in July 1933.

Savoia-Marchetti S62 Three-seat armed reconnaissance flying-boat, powered by one 500hp Isotta-Fraschini engine.

Savoia-Marchetti SM72 Developed from SM71 eight-seat passenger airliner, the SM72 was a three-engined monoplane bomber. Prototype first flew 1934; 20 ordered by China.

Savoia-Marchetti SM85 Single-seat twin-engined monoplane dive bomber. First flown 1938; 32 pre-production aircraft entered service with Regia Aeronautica.

Japan

Aichi E10A1 and E11A1 Biplane flying-boats, the latter powered by a 620hp Hiro 91 pusher engine. Operated from Japanese warships as reconnaissance aircraft, each armed with a single 7.7mm machine gun. E11A1 superseded E10A1 from 1938, although both types were operational when Japan entered war.

Aichi E13A Single-engined reconnaissance floatplane. Designed 1938 and entered production 1941.

Hiro G2H1 Twin-engined monoplane medium bomber. Prototype first flew 1933 and entered production 1935 as Navy Type 95. Eight built and used during Sino-Japanese war. Most G2H1s destroyed by fire at their Cheju Island base.

Kawanishi H3K2 Biplane flying-boat of Short Brothers design. Small numbers built for Imperial Japanese Navy as reconnaissance and training aircraft, serving between 1932 and 1936.

Kawanishi H6K Four-engined maritime patrol flying-boat. First of five prototypes flew July 1936. Three entered JNAF service as Type 97 in January 1938. Fifth prototype became first H6K2. Used during Sino-Japanese war; by outbreak of World War 2 the main version in service was H6K4.

Kawasaki E7K Three-seat twin-float reconnaissance biplane, powered by a 500-600hp Hiro 91 or 870hp Mitsubishi Zuisei engine (E7K1 and E7K2 respectively). First flown in 1933, production aircraft remained in service until 1942-3 as land- and carrier-based seaplanes.

Kawasaki Ki-32 Single-engined monoplane bomber. First of eight prototypes appeared March 1937. Ordered into production July 1938 as Type 98 Army light bomber. 846 built and used mainly in China.

Kawasaki Ki-48 Twin-engined monoplane light bomber. First prototype flew July 1939 and entered production for JAAF in November 1939, as Type 99 Model 1.

Kawasaki Type 87 High-wing tandem twin-engined bomber of the Japanese Army. Designed by Dornier of Germany; 28 built by Kawasaki. First flown 1926. Used operationally in Manchuria in 1931.

Mitsubishi B5M1 Conceived as a rival to the Nakajima B5N. Total of 125 production aircraft built as Type 97 Model 2s, and operated against China during Sino-Japanese hostilities.

Mitsubishi A6M Zero-Sen Single-seat monoplane fighter and fighter-bomber. First prototype flew 1 April 1939 and entered production in 1940 as A6M2 Model 11 or Type 0 carrier-based fighter.

Mitsubishi F1M Two-seat reconnaissance and general-duties biplane. First prototype flew June 1936. Entered production for JNAF October 1939 as F1M2 or Type 0 Model 11 observation floatplane.

Mitsubishi G3M Medium bomber, powered initially by two 840hp Mitsubishi Kinsei 3 engines as G3M1. Majority of about 1,000 G3Ms built as G3M2s, with 1,000hp Kinsei 45 engines and armed with one 20mm cannon, two 7.7mm machine guns and 2,205lb of bombs or a 1,760lb torpedo. Maximum speed 238mph. G3Ms formed backbone of Japanese Naval Air Force when Japan entered World War 2, with more than 250 in service.

Above: *Mitsubishi G3M*

Mitsubishi G4M Twin-engined monoplane bomber. First prototype flew October 1939.

Mitsubishi K3M Adaptation of Fokker Universal, first appearing in 1931-32. Powered by a 580hp Nakajima Kotobuki II-Kai-I radial engine. Used as a radio and navigational trainer.

Mitsubishi Ki-1 Twin-engined low-wing monoplane bomber of 1933. Powered by 700hp Ha-2 engines; about 118 built. Used during Sino-Japanese war.

Mitsubishi Ki-20 Multi-engined monoplane heavy bomber. Similar to K51 bomber development of Junkers G-38 civil transport, the first Ki-20 was built

Left: *Mitsubishi B5M1*

Above: *Mitsubishi Ki-20*

Nakajima E4N1 (Type 90) Reconnaissance floatplane, predecessor of the 48N. Powered by a 450hp Nakajima-built Jupiter engine. Wing span 39ft 4in; max speed 137mph; range 560 miles. Served on ships of the Imperial Japanese Navy.

Nakajima E8N Single-engined reconnaissance floatplane. Designed 1933; 550 E8N1 two-seat biplanes built by Nakajima and Kawanishi. Usually catapulted from warships; saw operational service during early war years.

in 1931. Five others completed between 1932 and 1934. Adopted for Army service as Type 92 heavy bomber in 1932, but never used in action.

Mitsubishi Ki-21 Medium bomber, known to the Allies as 'Sally' during World War 2. First production version (Ki-21-Ia) powered by two 850hp Nakajima Zuisei Ha-5-Kai radial engines and armed with three 7.7mm machine guns and up to 1,650lb of bombs. Entered service with Japanese Army Air Force in 1938 and used during Sino-Japanese war. Improved Ki-21-Ib version had five or six machine guns and increased bomb load. Ki-21-IIa, powered by Ha-101 engines, was major wartime version, followed by Ki-21-IIb.

Above: *Nakajima E8N1*

Above: *Mitsubishi Ki-21*

Mitsubishi Ki-30 Two-seat single-engined monoplane light bomber. First flown February 1937 and entered production 1938. Used during Sino-Japanese war and served with JAAF during first years of World War 2.

Mitsubishi Ki-51 Single-engined monoplane, developed from Ki-30. Entered production June 1939 as Ki-51a reconnaissance and Ki-51b ground attack aircraft, becoming operational early 1940.

Nakajima A1N Nakajima-built Gloster Gambet single-seat carrier-based fighter. Two versions built: A1N1 with Bristol Jupiter VI engine and, later, A1N2 with uprated engine and enclosed cockpit. Could carry four 20lb bombs for ground attack.

Nakajima B5N Carrier-borne low-wing monoplane torpedo bomber, first flown in 1937. B5N1 version became operational as light bomber in China, but most later converted into trainers. B5N2 entered service from late 1939. More than 1,200 B5Ns built, used during Pearl Harbor attack and subsequently (B5N2s) as anti-submarine aircraft. Known to Allies during war as 'Kate'.

Nakajima Ki-27 Japanese Army Air Force's first low-wing monoplane fighter and the first to have an enclosed cockpit. First production version (Ki-27a) produced as Type 97 Model A fighter. Became operational in Manchuria from 1938. Powered by one 710hp Nakajima Ha-1b radial engine. Maximum speed 286mph. Armed with two 7.7mm machine guns and could carry 220lb of bombs. Ki-27s also operated by Manchurian Air Force. Refined Ki-27b version entered production in 1939. Known to Allies as 'Nate' during World War 2.

Above: *Nakajima Ki-27*

Below: *Nakajima B5N1*

Above: *Yokosuka K4Y1*

Nakajima Ki-43 Hayabusa Single-seat monoplane fighter. First prototype flew January 1939, followed by the first of 10 evaluation aircraft in November. Production started March 1941 as Type 1 Model 1 Army fighter.

Nakajima Ki-49 Donryn Twin-engined monoplane medium bomber. Designed to JAAF specification of 1938, first prototype flew August 1939. Production started 1940.

Nakajima Koshiki Type 4 Licence-built version of Nieuport-Delage 29C1, in service until replaced from December 1931 by Nakajima Type 91s.

Tachikawa Ki-9 Two-seat biplane basic trainer, powered by a 350hp Hitachi Ha-13a engine. First flown 1935 and remained in service until the end of World War 2.

Tachikawa Ki-17 Two-seat biplane primary trainer, powered by a 150hp Hitachi Ha-12 engine. First flown 1935 and remained in service until 1944.

Yokosuka K2Y Two-seat naval biplane trainer, first used in late 1920s as the K2Y1. Later supplemented by the K2Y2, powered by a 160hp Hitachi Kamikaze engine. About 350 production aircraft built.

Yokosuka K4Y1 Two-seat twin-float biplane trainer, operated by the Japanese Navy from 1933. Total of over 200 built, remaining in service during World War 2. Powered by a similar engine to that of the K2Y.

Yokosuka K5Y Two-seat biplane trainer of 1933, powered by an Hitachi Amakaze 11 engine. Operated as a land or twin-float seaplane, as the K5Y1 and K5Y2 respectively. More built than any other trainer of Japanese origin. Remained in service during World War 2.

Lithuania

Anbo II, III, IV, V and VI Anbo II and V two-seat parasol-wing trainers; III and VI two-seat advanced trainers; IV two-seat reconnaissance/general purpose type.

Netherlands

Fokker CI Two-seat fighter biplane, developed from Fokker DVII. Powered by a 180hp BMW or 185hp Armstrong Siddeley Lynx, and with rear-mounted machine gun. Developed in Germany during World War 1 but not operated during war. Used for many years after war by Royal Netherlands Air Force as artillery spotter and trainer.

Fokker CII/III Further developments of CI, built for passenger carrying. A number of CIIIs purchased by America in early 1920s.

Fokker CIV Fighter, reconnaissance and light bombing biplane, powered by a 450hp Napier Lion or Liberty, or 360hp Rolls-Royce Eagle engine. First two-seater built in the Netherlands after World War 1. Used by air force (and others including Russia) from latter 1920s, mainly as long-range reconnaissance aircraft.

Fokker CVI Artillery spotting aircraft used by the air force from the late 1920s. Powered by either a 350hp Hispano-Suiza or 385hp Armstrong Siddeley Jaguar engine.

Fokker CVII-W Two-seat reconnaissance or training twin-float seaplane, powered by a 220hp Armstrong Siddeley Lynx engine. Used mainly as an unarmed trainer by the Naval Air Service.

Fokker CVIII and CVIII-W Three-seat long-distance reconnaissance parasol-wing monoplane, powered either by a 450hp Lorraine engine in the Dutch naval twin-float version or a 600hp Hispano-Suiza engine in the air force version. Armament comprised one forward-firing and two rear-mounted machine guns.

Fokker CIX Reconnaissance and training aircraft, powered by a 600hp Hispano-Suiza 12Lb engine. Used during 1930s by the Royal Netherlands Air Force.

Fokker CXIV-W Twin-float two-seat biplane, powered by a 425hp Wright Whirlwind engine. Used by Naval Air Service during latter 1930s as a training and reconnaissance aircraft. In latter role armed with one forward-firing and one rear-mounted 7.9mm machine gun.

Fokker DIX One of the first fighters designed by Fokker after World War 1. Prototype only, but helped with the development of later designs such as the Fokker DXI.

Fokker DX Parasol-wing fighter. 10 sold to Spain in early 1920s.

Fokker DXII Biplane fighter, first flown on 21 August 1924. Only prototype built.

Fokker DXIII Single-seat biplane fighter. First flown 12 September 1924; gained four world speed records in 1925. Fifty production aircraft ordered and built for Russia, on Germany's behalf, serving from 1927 alongside about 300 other German fighters, bombers and armed reconnaissance aircraft.

Fokker DXVI and DXVII Prototype DXVI single-seat sesquiplane fighter first flown 1929. Fifteen ordered by LVA, one by China and four by Hungary. Prototype DXVII flew 1931. Eleven ordered by LVA and deliveries began 1933. Last biplane fighter produced by Fokker.

Fokker DXXI Single-seat cantilever low-wing monoplane fighter with fixed and spatted undercarriage. Prototype first flew March 1936. Thirty-six entered service with the LVA from 1938, powered by the 830hp Bristol Mercury VII or VIII radial engine. Maximum speed 286mph and armed with four forward-firing 7.9mm FN-Browning machine guns. 38 built in Finland and a few purchased by Denmark before World War 2. A DXXI was the first Finnish aircraft destroyed during the Finnish-Russian Winter War (shot down by 'friendly' anti-aircraft guns), while a similar aircraft claimed the first Finnish aerial victory, a Russian SB-2 bomber.

Above: *Fokker DXXIs*

Fokker DCI Short-span fighter version of Fokker CIV. Ten production aircraft delivered to Netherlands East Indies Army Air Service in 1925.

Fokker FVII-3m/M and FIX/M FVIIA-3m/Ms and FVIIB-3m/Ms ordered by LVA. Three used in Holland as bombing and night flying trainers or transports; seven used as bomber-transports by Netherlands East Indies Army Air Service. Several acquired by Spanish Air Force and a number built under licence in Poland. FIX/M built under licence by Avia as F-39 bomber for Czechoslovakian and Yugoslav Air Forces.

Fokker GI Twin-boom fighter and ground attack aircraft, powered by two 830hp Bristol Mercury VIII radial engines. Maximum speed 295mph. Armed with nine 7.9mm machine guns and capable of carrying 880lb of bombs. 36 GIAs delivered to LVA in 1938. GIB export aircraft, with Pratt & Whitney Twin Wasp Junior engines, retained in Holland after German invasion.

Left: *Fokker GIB*

Fokker SII, SIII and SIV Two-seat biplane trainers, powered by 110hp Le Rhône, 120hp Mercedes or 120hp Armstrong Siddeley Mongoose engines respectively. SII and SIV used by the Royal Netherlands Air Force and SIII by Naval Air Service from 1920s to end of 1930s.

Fokker SIX Two-seat biplane trainer, powered by a 165hp Menasco Buccaneer or Armstrong Siddeley Genet Major radial engine. First flown 1937; 24 acquired by the Royal Netherlands Air Force and 27 by Naval Air Service during following year.

Fokker TV Twin-engined monoplane medium bomber. 16 ordered by LVA, the first flying 16 October 1937. Deliveries began 1938. Nine still serviceable when Germany invaded the Netherlands in May 1940.

Fokker TVIII-W Twin-engined torpedo bomber and reconnaissance float-plane. First flown 1938, the Naval Air Service received 11 by the time of the German invasion of Holland. Few of these escaped to the UK. Others completed for the Luftwaffe under occupation.

Koolhoven FK31 Parasol-wing two-seat fighter and reconnaissance aircraft, powered by one 400hp Bristol Jupiter radial engine. Entered service with LVA in 1925, but maximum speed of 146mph was disappointing and some were transferred to Netherlands East Indies Air Service. Withdrawn 1930. Few built in France.

Above: *Koolhoven FK31*

Koolhoven FK51 Two-seat biplane trainer, of which 68 in service with the Royal Netherlands Air Force and Naval Air Service at outbreak of World War 2. Used also for artillery spotting duties.

Koolhoven FK56 Cantilever low-wing monoplane training and reconnaissance aircraft, powered by a 420hp Wright Whirlwind radial engine. Accommodation for two under sliding hoods. Two forward-firing and two rear-mounted machine guns. Used by the air force from late 1930s.

Koolhoven FK58 Single-seat monoplane fighter. First prototype flew 22 September 1938. Fifty ordered by France at end of 1938. The Netherlands ordered 36 aircraft March 1939, but none in service with LVA by German invasion. Deliveries to Armée de l'Air started 17 June 1939.

Norway

Marinens Flyvebåtfrabrik MF9 Single seat floatplane fighter biplane. Appeared 1925; about 20 built for Norwegian Naval Air Force. Withdrawn from squadron service after five years.

Poland

Bartel M4 Two-seat biplane primary trainer, powered by a 80hp Le Rhône, 100hp Walter Junior or 120hp de Havilland Gipsy engine. First ordered in 1928 for the Polish Air Force and operated in reasonable numbers.

Bartel M5 Two-seat biplane basic trainer, powered by a 220hp Daimler, Spa, licence-built Wright Whirlwind or 300hp Hispano-Suiza engine. Ordered for the Polish Air Force in 1928.

LWS4 and LWS6 Zubr Twin-engined monoplane bomber. First flew March 1936. Polish Air Force ordered 16 LWS4s and Romania 24. In September 1937 prototype broke up in air and Romania withdrew order. Modified LWS4 few end of 1937. Second Zubr fitted with twin-tail assembly and designated LWS6. Remaining 14 LWS4s delivered 1939.

LWS RWD-14 Czapla Two-seat parasol-wing army co-operation aircraft, powered by a 420hp PZL G1620B Mors II radial engine. First flown in 1935, the type was put into production in 1938, and by early 1939 65 had been built. Armament comprised two 7.7mm machine guns.

Plage and Laskiewicz Lublin RVIII Five RVIII biplane reconnaissance-bombers built, plus prototypes. Four later converted into seaplanes for the Polish Naval Wing.

Plage and Laskiewicz Lublin RX Small batch of RX two-seat parasol-wing monoplanes operated by the Polish Air Force from 1930 as army co-operation aircraft, powered by licence-built 220hp Wright Whirlwind engines.

Plage and Laskiewicz Lublin RXIII Development of RX incorporating many refinements. Between 1932 and 1936 a total of 300 built in several versions, of which about half remained in service at the outbreak of war. Principal version was RXIIID, powered by a licence-built 200hp Wright Whirlwind engine and possessing a maximum speed of just 121mph. Armament comprised a single rear-mounted 7.7mm machine gun. Small number served with twin-floats with Polish Navy.

Plage and Laskiewicz Lublin RXIV Two-seat trainer development of RX. Large number operated by the Polish Air Force from 1930.

PWS 14 Two-seat biplane basic trainer, developed from the unsuccessful PWS 12 (itself a two-seat development of the single-seat PWS 11 fighter trainer). Small number built for the Polish Air Force in early 1930s, powered by licence-built 220hp Wright Whirlwind engines.

PWS 18 Polish licence-built version of the Avro 621 Tutor, powered by a 220hp Wright Whirlwind engine.

PWS 16 Small number of PWS 16 and 16*bis* two-seat biplane trainers built for the Polish Air Force from 1933. Type later developed into the PWS 26.

PWS 26 Two-seat armed training and liaison biplane of 1936, powered by a licence-built 220hp Wright Whirlwind engine. 240 acquired by the Polish Air Force. A few were used in reconnaissance and light bombing roles during World War 2.

PWS RWD-8 Two-seat parasol-wing monoplane trainer, of which several hundred were built for the Polish Air Force from 1934 by PWS, powered by 110hp PZInz Junior or Major engines. Total RWD-8 production, including those built for civil use and those licence-built in Yugoslavia, amounted to about 650 aircraft. Late in their career small number of RWD-8s were used for liaison duties, sometimes carrying a single machine gun.

PZL P-37 Lós (Elk) Mid-wing monoplane bomber with retractable undercarriage. Prototype flew mid-1936. 100 production aircraft built for Polish Air Force, 70 as Lós Bs each with two 925hp licence-built Bristol Pegasus XX radial engines and armed with three 7.7mm machine guns and between 4,900lb and 5,685lb of bombs. Maximum speed 273mph. 61 Lós Bs in service with PAF at the time of the German invasion, nearly 50 escaping to Romania.

Above: *PZL P-37B Los*

PZL 46 Sum Bomber and reconnaissance monoplane. First flew October 1938. Production started mid-1939, but stopped at outbreak of war.

Romania

Fabrica de Avione SET XV Single-seat biplane fighter, with enclosed cockpit. Maximum speed 211mph. Comparatively small number built in early 1930s for Romanian Air Force.

IAR 37, 38 and 39. Bomber/reconnaissance biplanes, the IAR 37 powered by one 870hp IAR-built Gnome-Rhône 14K radial engine. Max speed 208mph. One forward-firing and one rear-mounted machine gun, plus up to 1,325lb of bombs. Entered service from 1938.

IAR 80 Single-seat monoplane fighter. First prototype flew end of 1938, embodying components of Polish PZL P-24E fighter (built in Romania under licence). Production started 1941; delivered from early 1942.

Right: *IAR 39*

Spain

Loring R1, R2, R3 Two-seat reconnaissance aircraft. R1 built in latter 1920s and became first of the line to enter Spanish Army service, when 30 were delivered. R3 remained in service until latter 1930s, despite a maximum speed of only 146mph, achieved with a 600hp Hispano-Suiza engine. Armament comprised machine guns and racks for light bombs.

Sweden

Svenska/Heinkel He17 Two-seat reconnaissance biplane, powered by a 450hp Napier Lion engine. Built in Sweden by Svenska Aero AB and in the USA as the Cox-Klemin CO-2.

Svenska J6 Jaktfalk J5 single-seat fighter prototype built 1929 and purchased by Flygvapnet in January 1930. Two more prototypes bought as J6s.

Five more ordered mid-1930, followed by three J6As in 1931 and seven J6Bs in 1934. Last aircraft withdrawn from service 1941.

Thulin Type K Single-seat fighter monoplane. 18 built between 1917 and 1919, of which two served with Swedish Army and 12 sold after war to Royal Netherlands Naval Air Service.

Switzerland

D-3800 Licence-built Morane-Saulnier 406 monoplane fighter. Production, under designation D-3800, began 1939, deliveries to Swiss Air Force beginning early 1940.

EKW C-35 Two-seat reconnaissance and close support biplane, powered by one 860hp Hispano-Suiza 12Ycrs (Moteur canon). 80 built for Swiss service, replacing Fokker CV-Es from 1937. Maximum speed 211mph. Armed with one 20mm cannon (Moteur canon), three 7.5mm machine guns and light bombs.

EFW C-3603 Two-seat close support monoplane. First prototype (C-3601) flew spring 1939 and second prototype (C-3602) November 1939. First production C-3603 flew 1941.

Wild WT-1 and WT-1S Two-seat biplanes, each powered by a 120hp Argus As11 engine. 12 built from 1924 and used initially as reconnaissance aircraft, some later becoming basic trainers. These remained in service in the latter role until 1934.

UK

Airspeed Oxford Known to the RAF as the 'Ox-box', the Oxford was a military development of the Airspeed Envoy. Oxfords were in service by the outbreak of World War 2 as twin-engined advanced trainers. The Mk I version was powered by 375hp Armstrong Siddeley Cheetah X radials and had a maximum speed of 182mph.

Armstrong Whitworth AW16 Single-seat biplane fighter with maximum speed of 203mph. Three sold to China in 1932. Armament consisted of two machine guns and underwing racks for light fragmentation bombs. Developed into the AW35 Scimitar, of which four were operated by the Norwegian Army Air Service as fighters and later trainers.

Armstrong Whitworth Scimitar Biplane fighter, powered by one 640hp Armstrong Siddeley Panther

VII radial engine. Maximum speed 221mph. Four exported to Norway.

Armstrong Whitworth AW23 Prototype bomber, first flown in mid-1935. One built, used subsequently in refuelling tanker experiments by Flight Refuelling Limited.

Avro 504 Used after World War 1 as trainer; served until 1933 with RAF and until World War 2 in

Below: *Avro 504*

Belgium in its 'N' version, and elsewhere. Total of 8,340 built during and after World War 1.

Avro 548 Two-seat trainer. Small number used to train RAF reserve pilots in early 1920s.

Avro 621, 626 and 637 Tutor/Seatutor Avro 621 of 1929; several hundred built as trainers and exported. Avro 626 of 1930; 168 exported as trainers, plus a few of a variant to RAF and RNZAF. Eight Avro 637s sold to Kwangsi Air Force as armed patrol aircraft.

Avro Aldershot Single-engined biplane bomber. Two prototypes built in 1922 and 15 production Aldershot IIIs ordered in 1923. Entered RAF service in April 1924. Operational for two years. Three ambulance versions, known as Andovers, in service from 1924.

Avro Avian Two-seat light biplane trainer, used by a few air forces including those of Estonia and South Africa.

Avro Bison Four-seat carrier-borne spotter-reconnaissance biplane. 53 built for FAA, serving 1923-9. Powered by one 480hp Napier Lion II engine and with extremely deep fuselage housing an internal cabin for the observer/navigator and radio operator. Pilot and rear gunner in open cockpits. One forward-firing and one dorsal machine gun. Maximum speed 110mph.

Avro Cadet Smaller version of Avro Tutor, used by many air forces, including that of Australia. Approved in early 1930s for use by Reserve Training School.

Avro Prefect Adaptation of Avro Tutor for navigational training with Royal Air Force.

Airspeed Envoy Three military Envoys, each with one forward-firing machine gun and a dorsal gun turret, delivered to South African Air Force in 1936. Small number of Envoys acquired by RAF in 1939.

Avro Manchester (Type 679) Twin-engined medium-heavy bomber. Prototype first flew 25 July, 1939 and production aircraft entered service November 1940. About 200 built, remaining operational until June 1942.

Blackburn B-2 Appeared 1932 as trainer. Total of 36 built, six going to Portugal.

Blackburn Botha Reconnaissance and torpedo bomber monoplane. Botha Mk Is entered service October 1939, being withdrawn 18 months later. Used subsequently as navigation and gunner trainers until 1944.

Blackburn Blackburn Four-seat biplane developed with similar accommodation and for a similar role as the Avro Bison. 59 built for the FAA, serving 1923-31. Maximum speed 122mph.

Blackburn Iris Three-engined reconnaissance and coastal patrol flying-boat. Iris Mk I prototype first flew 1927. Four production Mk IIIs entered service 1931. Iris Mk IV followed by three Iris Mk V conversions of Mk IIIs. Remained in service until 1934.

Blackburn Kangaroo Twin-engined biplane bomber, developed from Blackburn GP seaplane of 1916. 20 Kangaroos built, most being delivered before end of war. Some sold in 1919 to civil airline operators.

Blackburn Lincock Lincock I fighter flew May 1928. Two Lincock IIIs sold to China and two to Japan.

Above: *Avro 621 Tutor*

Blackburn Perth Three-engined general reconnaissance flying-boat. Largest biplane flying-boat in service with RAF. Four Perths, serving with two RAF squadrons from 1934-7.

Blackburn Roc Two-seat naval fighter. First flown 23 December 1938; entered service with Fleet Air Arm February 1940.

Boulton Paul Defiant Two-seat fighter. Like the Roc, the Defiant had no forward-firing guns, but a gun turret behind pilot's cockpit. Prototype flew August 1937 and entered service 1940.

Bristol Beaufort Twin-engined torpedo bomber and reconnaissance aircraft. First prototype flew 15 October 1938, production Mk Is entering service with Coastal Command from December 1939.

Bristol Bombay Twin-engined bomber-transport monoplane. First flown 1935; entered service March 1939. About 50 built, serving as transports in Mediterranean area and Middle East. Some used on night bombing raids in North Africa.

Bristol M1C Monoplane Single-seat monoplane fighter. Prototype appeared 1916. 125 built for RFC, plus six for Chilean Air Force. Those with Chile served after war.

Bristol PTM Two-seat primary trainer, powered by a 120hp Cosmos Engineering Company Lucifer engine (later taken over by Bristol). 24 built, serving with a Reserve Training School and exported to Bulgaria, Chile and Hungary.

Bristol 1923 Fighter Single fighter purchased by Sweden, powered by a 425hp Bristol Jupiter IV engine.

Bristol Type 89/89A Two-seat trainers, powered by Bristol Jupiter IV or VI engines. 23 built, serving with Reserve Training Schools in Britain.

Bristol Boarhound II Development of unsuccessful Boarhound, built as possible Bristol Fighter replacement. Two refined Boarhound IIs, powered by Bristol Jupiter VI engines, purchased by Mexico in 1928.

Cierva C-30A Two-seat autogiro, powered by a 140hp Armstrong Siddeley Genet Major radial engine. 12 delivered to School of Army Co-operation at Odiham from 1934 as Rota Is, built under licence by Avro.

De Havilland DH9 Single-engined biplane bomber. Prototype flew 1917; total of 3,204 built in Britain. After war, DH9s still equipped several RAF squadrons and were in service in other countries, including Chile, Estonia, Greece, Latvia, Poland, Spain and South Africa, where they served until 1937. Powered by one 230hp Siddeley Puma engine, giving maximum speed of 111mph. One fixed forward-firing Vickers and one or two free-firing Lewis machine guns; up to 460lb of bombs.

De Havilland DH9J Version of DH9 with Jaguar engine, used in early 1920s to train RAF reserve pilots.

De Havilland Queen Bee Radio-controlled pilotless aircraft, of similar configuration to de Havilland Tiger Moth. Large number built for British services. In service from 1937.

De Havilland Fox Moth Biplane with accommodation for four passengers in enclosed cabin and pilot in open cockpit. Power provided by a Gipsy Major engine. Five operated in Brazil as navigational trainers.

De Havilland Dragon Six-to-eight passenger biplane, powered by two 130hp Gipsy Major 1 engines. Operated by Iraqi Air Force from 1933, armed with machine guns and capable of carrying light bombs. Other Dragons used by air forces of Denmark, Portugal, Ireland and Turkey.

De Havilland Leopard Moth Three-seat successor to Puss Moth. Small number in military service before outbreak of war, including with Portuguese Air Force.

De Havilland Hornet Moth Biplane with enclosed cabin for pilot and passenger side by side. Powered by Gipsy Major 1 engine. Four purchased by Air Ministry in 1938 as experimental trainers, fitted with twin floats instead of usual tailskid/wheel landing gear.

De Havilland Dragon Rapide Smaller version of DH86, powered by two 200hp de Havilland Gipsy Six engines. Military version, designated DH89M. Small number purchased for Spanish and Lithuanian air forces for armed patrol duties, supporting nose and dorsal machine guns and with underfuselage racks for light bombs.

De Havilland Dragonfly Five-seat biplane, similar in general appearance to Dragon Rapide. First flown 1935, powered by Gipsy Major 1 engines. Small number operated by air forces of Denmark and Sweden.

De Havilland Don Three-seat cantilever low-wing monoplane communications aircraft, first flown in 1937. 30 operated by the RAF, powered by 520hp de Havilland Gipsy King 1 engines.

De Havilland Moth Minor Two-seat cantilever low-wing trainer, with fixed landing gear. First flown 1937, powered by an 80hp de Havilland Gipsy Moth Minor engine. Operated before war at RAF and other flying clubs to train reserve pilots.

De Havilland DH60 Moth Two-seat biplane trainer, powered by either Aircraft Disposal Company Cirrus I, Cirrus II, Cirrus III or Armstrong Siddeley Genet I engine (60-90hp). Operated by Central Flying School and exported for military use to Australia, Canada, Chile, Italy, Ireland, Finland, Sweden, New Zealand and the USA. One Moth

seaplane of New Zealand Air Force carried on HMS *Dunedin* to Somoa in early 1930 where it performed reconnaissance duties.

De Havilland DH60G Gipsy Moth Version of Moth powered by de Havilland Gipsy I, II or III engine (100-120hp). Used as trainer, communications aircraft or for observation duties with air forces of Australia, Chile, China, Denmark, Great Britain, India, New Zealand and Portugal.

De Havilland DH60G Moth and Moth Major Version of the DH60 Moth fitted with de Havilland Gipsy III and later Gipsy Major engine. Capable of inverted flight. Military users included Spanish Air Force. Civil registered aircraft trained military pilots in several countries, including Austria and Germany.

De Havilland DH60M Moth Version of Gipsy Moth with fuselage constructed of steel tubes (instead of wood). Large number built for military service, including those delivered to RAF (including Central Flying School and Auxiliary squadrons) and to the air forces of Australia, Canada, China, Denmark, Iraq, Norway and South Africa.

De Havilland DH60T Purely military trainer version of DH60M Moth, powered by de Havilland Gipsy II engine. In service from 1931. Operated by air forces of Brazil, China, Egypt, Iraq and Sweden.

De Havilland Hercules Large airliner of 1926, powered by three Bristol Jupiter VI engines. Three retired civil aircraft operated by South African Air Force from 1934.

De Havilland Hawk Moth Four-seat braced high-wing monoplane, powered by a 240hp Armstrong Siddeley Lynx VIA engine. Three acquired by Royal Canadian Air Force in 1930-31.

De Havilland Puss Moth Three-seat braced high-wing monoplane, powered by a 120hp Gipsy III engine. Small number operated by the air forces of Canada and Iraq from 1931, while others went to China and some eventually went into RAF service.

De Havilland DH82 Tiger Moth One of the most famous training aircraft of 1919-39 period. Two-seat biplane, powered by either a Gipsy III or Gipsy Major 1 engine (120-145hp). Large number built for RAF and exported, and licence-built in Canada, New Zealand, Norway, Portugal and Sweden. Main difference from earlier Moths was use of swept wings. Some aircraft capable of weapons and photographic roles. Aircraft with Gipsy Major engine,

Below: *Tiger Moth*

plywood-covered rear upper fuselage and blind-flying cover for rear cockpit designated DH82A. Operated also by air forces of Australia, Brazil, Canada, Denmark, Iraq, New Zealand, Persia, South Africa, Spain and Uruguay.

Fairey IIIA Two-seat reconnaissance biplane. 50 built, few seeing active service before Armistice. Withdrawn from service 1919.

Fairey IIIB Bomber seaplane. 30 built, few entering service with RNAS before Armistice. Converted to IIIC in 1919.

Fairey IIIC Two-seat general purpose seaplane; 36 built, too late for service in World War 1. Operated in Russia in 1919 from HMS *Pegasus*. In service until 1921.

Naval Air Service 1921 (built by Short Bros). Put into production in America 1922 as F-5L, with Liberty engines, and served with US Navy.

Gloster Grouse Two-seat trainer designed in 1922.

Gloster Nightjar/Mars/Sparrowhawk Aircraft based on Nieuport Nighthawk and known as Gloster Mars series. Mars II single-seat fighter: 30 built 1922 for Japanese Navy as Sparrowhawk Is. Mars III two-seat trainer version of Sparrowhawk I: 10 built for Japanese Navy which called them Sparrowhawk IIs. Mars IV was modified Mars II. Mars VI was Nighthawk single-seat fighter for RAF, plus 25 for Greek Air Force. Mars X became Nightjar single-seat carrier-borne fighter for Fleet Air Arm: 22 built, replaced 1923.

Above: *Fairey IIIC*

Above: *Sparrowhawk I of the Japanese Navy*

Fairey Albacore Single-engined biplane torpedo bomber. Prototype flew 12 December 1938, production starting 1939. Entered service with FAA March 1940; total of 800 built by 1943.

Fairey Campania Two-seat reconnaissance seaplane. First British aircraft designed expressly for aircraft carrier operations. Appeared 1916 and 90 ordered, of which about two-thirds built. Used in 1919 for patrols against Bolsheviks.

Fairey Fantome Single-seat biplane fighter of 1935. Produced at a time when faster monoplane fighters were appearing. Never in service, apart from a few individual aircraft in Spain.

Fairey Long-Range Monoplane Shoulder-wing monoplane with fixed spatted landing-gear, powered by a 530hp Napier Lion engine. Two built for long-range record breaking flights by RAF. Initial aircraft accomplished first non-stop flight from UK to India in April 1929, covering 4,130 miles. Second aircraft accomplished first non-stop flight from UK to South Africa in February 1933, covering 5,309 miles in 57hr 25min.

Felixstowe F3 Reconnaissance flying-boat, developed from F2A. Production aircraft appeared 1917; about 100 built by end of war. After war orders reduced or cancelled, F3s remaining operational until September 1921.

Felixstowe F5 General reconnaissance biplane flying-boat. Standard flying-boat in RAF service after World War 1. 15 F5s served with Imperial Japanese

Handley Page HP43 and HP51 HP43 military bomber-transport developed from civil HP42 airliner, powered by three Bristol Pegasus engines. Prototype only built, supporting machine gun positions at nose and tail. First flown mid-1932. Fuselage used in HP51 monoplane development, first flown May 1935.

Handley Page O/400 Standard RAF heavy bomber of World War 1, serving with seven squadrons by October 1918. Remained in RAF service for a short time after the war, two squadrons serving in Egypt until 1920. Eight aircraft built in USA after war for US Army evaluation.

Handley Page V/1500 Four-engined biplane bomber. Prototype first flew May 1918, and production aircraft appeared October 1918. Few aircraft delivered by Armistice, most of those built arriving afterwards. In December 1918 one V/1500 set off on first through-flight from Britain to India, and later made one raid during the 1920 Afghan War.

Handley Page Clive A 17- to 23-seat troop transport version of the Hinaidi bomber, Clive II production aircraft entered RAF service in 1931.

Handley Page Halifax Four-engined heavy bomber. First prototype flew October 1939, and Halifax Mk Is entered service in November 1940.

Handley Page Hampden and Hereford Hampden medium bomber first flew in mid-1936 and featured the famous 'frying pan' fuselage. Delivery of Mk Is to RAF began in August 1938 and by the outbreak of war equipped eight squadrons. 1,270 Mk Is were built, each powered by two 1,000hp Bristol Pegasus XVIII radial engines, and armed with six .303in machine guns and up to 4,000lb of bombs. A further 160 were built in Canada. Napier Dagger-powered Herefords were also ordered, entering service after the outbreak of war.

Above: *Handley Page Hampden*

Hawker Dantorp Export version of Horsley torpedo bomber; two delivered to Denmark in 1933, one as a landplane and one as a seaplane. 800hp Armstrong Siddeley Leopard IIIA engine, giving maximum speed of 125mph and weight of 9,950lb. One flown non-stop from Copenhagen to Faroes in July 1934, a distance of about 1,000 miles.

Hawker Hardy Two-seat general-purpose biplane; basically a desert version of the Audax. 47 built and entered RAF service in 1935. Operated against Italian forces in 1940; the last used for communications duties in 1941.

Above: *Hawker Hardy*

Hawker Hartbees Two-seat ground support biplane. Developed from Hart, to meet South African Air Force requirement. First of four Hawker built

Hartbees flew August 1935, followed by 65 licence-built at Aircraft and Artillery Depot at Roberts Heights. Some aircraft given armour plating to protect crew from ground fire. Maximum speed 180mph (Kestrel engine). Weight 5,150lb. Remained in service, finally as trainers, until 1946.

Hawker Henley Two-seat cantilever low-wing monoplane target-tug with retractable landing gear, powered by a 1,030hp Rolls-Royce Merlin II engine. First flown March 1937 as high-performance light bomber. Became operational as target tug late 1939.

Hawker Tomtit Two-seat primary trainer of biplane configuration, powered by a 150hp Armstrong Siddeley Mongoose engine. Small number served with RAF from 1930, others going to Canada and New Zealand.

Martinsyde F4 Buzzard Single-seat biplane fighter. About 65 built by Armistice, but none had entered service with RAF. Two used by RAF Communications Wing in 1919 to carry dispatches between London and Paris for Peace Conference. Some sent to Eire, Japan and Spain. Others became civil racing aircraft.

Miles Hawk Trainer Two-seat cantilever low-wing trainer, powered by a 130hp de Havilland Gipsy Major engine. Operated at flying schools in UK and in India, Romania and Spain.

Miles Magister Development of Hawk Trainer and also known as Hawk Trainer Mk III. Blind flying equipment available. Entered RAF service in October 1937, becoming RAF's first monoplane trainer. By close of production, nearly 1,300 built. Also used abroad, including Egypt.

Miles Master Prototype Master first flew in 1938, as two-seat cantilever low-wing monoplane advanced trainer, with retractable landing gear. Early production examples delivered to RAF in spring 1939, powered by 715hp Rolls-Royce Kestrel XXX engines.

Miles Mentor Cantilever low-wing monoplane, with enclosed cabin. Entered RAF service in 1938 for radio training and communications duties. 45 delivered, powered by 200hp de Havilland Gipsy Six engines.

Miles Nighthawk Two/three-seat training and communications aircraft, of basically similar configuration to previously mentioned Mentor. Prototype built for RAF evaluation. Two acquired by Romanian Air Force in 1936.

Nieuport Nighthawk Single-seat biplane fighter, designed to meet 1918 RAF specification. In 1920 the design was taken over by Gloucestershire Aircraft Company where it became the Mars VI. Fitted with either a Bristol Jupiter III or Armstrong Siddeley Jaguar II engine, Nighthawk had a maximum speed of 150mph. Small number built for RAF and used for evaluation trials in Mesopotamia, and 25 with Jaguar engine for Greek Air Force.

Parnell Plover Single-seat carrier-borne biplane fighter, capable of operation as landplane or amphibian. 10 built 1923 and entered FAA service for a short period of time.

Percival Vega Gull Four-seat cantilever low-wing monoplane, powered by a 200hp de Havilland Gipsy Six engine. Used by RAF as communications aircraft in latter 1930s.

Royal Aircraft Factory SE5a Single-seat biplane fighter. Entered service from mid-1917; by October 1918 the SE5a equipped 16 RAF squadrons. Used after the war by few air forces, including those of Canada and Chile.

Saro Cloud High-wing monoplane amphibian, powered by two 340hp Armstrong Siddeley Serval engines mounted on pylons above wing. Small number used by RAF as pilot and navigator training aircraft from 1933.

Saro Lerwick Twin-engined maritime patrol monoplane flying-boat. Appeared autumn 1938 and entered service in December 1939. 21 built; declared obsolete 1942.

Short Rangoon Three-engined general reconnaissance biplane flying-boat. Prototype first flew 24 September 1930, and the type entered service with RAF in 1931. Six Rangoons were built, remaining in service until 1936.

Short 184 Two-seat torpedo-bomber and reconnaissance seaplane. Appeared 1915; over 650 built for RNAS, of which more than 300 were still in service October 1918. After the war, small numbers acquired by other countries, including Estonia, Greece and Japan.

Short Sarafand Very large biplane flying-boat, powered by six Rolls-Royce Buzzard engines mounted in tandem pairs. Only one built, capable of 1,450 miles range. Crew of 10. On RAF strength between 1933 and 1936.

Short Singapore I and II Singapore I twin-engined biplane flying-boat first flown 17 August 1926. Used by Alan Cobham for his 1927-8 round-Africa flight. Singapore II appeared 1930 but did not enter production. Four built as development aircraft, becoming first Singapore IIIs.

Short Stirling Four-engined heavy bomber. Prototype first flew May 1939. First production Mk I flew mid-1940 and the type began to enter service August 1940.

Above: *Short Stirling*

Short Sunderland Basically a military development of the 'C' class Empire flying-boat for maritime patrol and reconnaissance duties. 21 ordered in 1936. Prototype flew October 1937. Sunderland Mk 1s entered RAF service in mid-1938

(75 built). Later versions produced throughout World War 2. Mk 1 powered by four 915hp Bristol Pegasus XXII engines. Armed with 10 .303in machine guns and up to 2,000lb of bombs.

Above: *Short Sunderland*

Sopwith Camel Single-seat biplane fighter. In October 1918 32 RAF Squadrons were equipped with Camels. Others had been delivered to Canada, Belgium, Greece and the AEF. Camels were used by the Slavo-British forces in Russia, fighting the Bolsheviks.

Sopwith Dolphin Fighter and ground attack biplane, powered by 200hp or 300hp Hispano-Suiza engine. About 1,500 built, of which some 600 in RAF service by November 1918. Number remained operational after war.

Sopwith Dragon Single-seat biplane fighter, developed from the Snipe. Prototype appeared 1919 and several were produced, although the Dragon was not used operationally by the RAF.

Sopwith T1 Cuckoo Single-seat biplane torpedo-bomber. Prototype appeared June 1917, 90 production aircraft being delivered by Armistice. After war production continued for a short time and Cuckoos served with Royal Navy until early 1923. Some delivered to Japan.

Sopwith TF2 Salamander Single-seat ground-attack biplane, developed from Snipe. 37 delivered to RAF by Armistice, only a few reaching France. Production continued after war until 82 had been built, although none served with postwar RAF.

Vickers Type 143 Scout Single-seat biplane fighter, built for Bolivian Air Force. Six examples acquired by Bolivia 1930, seeing action in 1932 during the Gran Chaco War.

Vickers Valparaiso Similar to Vixen, but powered by a 470hp Napier Lion IA engine. Built in two production variants and licence-built in Portugal. British-built Valparaisos purchased by the air forces of Chile (Navy) and Portugal.

Vickers Varuna Similar to Vedette but larger and powered by two Lynx engines mounted in tractor configuration.

Vickers Vedette Three-seat biplane flying-boat, in early 1920s form powered by either a 200hp Wright

Whirlwind or Armstrong Siddeley Lynx pusher engine. Vedette VI amphibian of 1930s powered by a 300hp Whirlwind.

Vickers Vendace Two-seat biplane trainer, powered in Mk III variant by 300hp Hispano-Suiza 8 engine. Three purchased for Bolivian Air Force and operated in the first half of 1930s.

Vickers Venture Proposed armed reconnaissance biplane of similar configuration to Vixen for RAF. Six built for service evaluation.

Vickers Vespa Designed as army co-operation biplane for RAF. Six Mk IIIs purchased by Bolivia in late 1920s. User of most Vespas was Irish Air Corps, which acquired eight aircraft as Mk IV and Vs, powered by 490hp Armstrong Siddeley Jaguar VIC engines.

Vickers Vixen General-purpose biplane of 1925, powered by a 500hp Napier Lion V. 18 purchased for Chilean Air Force. Armament comprised two forward-firing and one rear-mounted machine gun.

Vickers Warwick Twin-engined monoplane bomber. First prototype flew August 1939, but production aircraft did not appear until 1942. Initial aircraft used as bombers, later versions for Air/Sea Rescue, transport and general reconnaissance duties.

Vickers Wellington Cantilever monoplane medium bomber. Mk I powered by two 1,000hp Bristol Pegasus XVIII radial engines. Maximum speed 265mph. Armed with two machine guns in nose and tail, one in ventral position and up to 4,500lb of bombs. Prototype flew 15 June 1936, and Mk Is entered RAF Bomber Command from 1938.

Wellington Mk I was followed by IA and IC versions. Main feature of the design was its geodetic construction, which allowed the bomber to withstand heavy punishment, so proving one of the outstanding aircraft of World War 2.

Vickers Wibault Scout Single-seat monoplane fighter, built for Chilean Air Force. 26 built, being delivered from 1926-7. Maximum speed 141mph.

Westland Lysander STOL army co-operation monoplane, built as a replacement for the Hawker Hector and Audax. Lysander Mk I entered RAF service in 1938, powered by one 890hp Bristol Mercury XII radial engine. Maximum speed 229mph. Armed with three .303in machine guns and could carry light bombs on stub wings fitted to undercarriage. By September 1939, Lysanders equipped seven squadrons. Became famous during World War 2 for agent dropping operations in Europe.

Westland Walrus Spotter-reconnaissance biplane, developed from DH9A. Small number operated by FAA and RAF in early 1920s.

Westland Wessex Four-passenger braced high-wing monoplane transport aircraft of early 1930s, powered by three Armstrong Siddeley Genet Major engines. Used by Egyptian Air Force as general purpose aircraft.

Westland Whirlwind Single-seat twin-engined long-range fighter and fighter-bomber. First flew 11 October 1938 but did not enter RAF service until June 1940.

USA

Atlantic (Fokker) FVII series Slightly modified Fokker FVII/3m trimotors built in US by Atlantic Aircraft Corporation for US Navy (subsequently becoming RA-1/2/3) and US Army Air Corps (as C-2/C-2A/C-7/C-7A), as 8-10 passenger transport aircraft, powered by three Wright J-5 or J-6 radial engines.

Bell P-39 Airacobra Single-seat monoplane fighter and fighter-bomber. Original-design prototype flew April 1938, later being modified into XP-39B and flying 25 November 1939. Pre-production aircraft ordered April 1939, the first flying late 1940, followed by large-scale wartime production.

Bellanca 28-110 Low-wing monoplane fighter-bomber. A number were ordered by China in 1938, each with five machine guns and up to 1,600lb of bombs.

Bellanca 77-140 Twin-engined monoplane bomber. Developed from transport aircraft of early 1930s, a few examples were sold to Colombia. Armament consisted of five guns and 2,300lb of bombs.

Bellanca C-27 US Army Air Corps 12-seat transport aircraft, derived from civil Airbus. Powered by a 550hp Pratt & Whitney Hornet engine. 14 purchased.

Berliner-Joyce P-16/PB-1 Two-seat biplane fighter, designed for US Army Air Corps. 25 aircraft built designated YP-16, subsequently changed to PB-1, and served with 1st Fighter Group from 1932.

Boeing B-17 Flying Fortress One of the most famous bombers of World War 2, operated by the USAAF throughout America's participation in the war and by the RAF. The prototype first flew on 28 July 1935, and was followed by Y1B-17 and Y1B-17A evaluation aircraft, which subsequently became B-17s and B-17As respectively. First production B-17B flew on 27 June 1939, powered by four 930hp Wright R-1820-51 Cyclone engines and poorly armed with five .30in machine guns and up to 8,000lb of bombs.

Above: *Boeing B-17B*

Boeing GA-1 Twin-engined ground-attack triplane. Designed and built in 1920, the prototype GAX was a heavily-armoured experimental aircraft manned by a pilot and four gunners. 10 production aircraft subsequently ordered.

Boeing NB-1 and NB-2 Two-seat biplanes of 1924, powered by a 180-220hp engines. More than 70 built for US Navy with wheel or float landing gears, used as pilot and rear gunner trainers.

Boeing PB Twin-engined biplane flying-boat. Built in 1925 for a trans-Pacific flight, the PB-1 served for two years with the US Navy before being re-engined as the XPB-2. 2,000lb of bombs could be carried.

Boeing TB-1 Single-engined three-seat biplane torpedo bomber. Three ordered by US Navy in May 1925, delivered April 1926. Able to operate with floats or as a landplane, the TB-1 carried a 1,740lb torpedo. Remained in service for several years.

Boeing Y1B-9 and Y1B-9A All-metal low-wing monoplane bomber developments of Boeing Monomail. Open cockpits provided for the crew. First flight of prototype made in April 1931. Effectively caused end of development of the Douglas YB-7, which had been the USAAC's first monoplane bomber. One Y1B-9 and five Y1B-9A evaluation aircraft produced with 650hp Curtiss V-1570-29 engines and armed with two machine guns and 2,200lb of bombs. Arrival of Martin B-10 halted development of Y1B-9A.

Brewster F2A Buffalo Monoplane fighter. Prototype first flew January 1938, and 54 F2A-1s ordered June 1938. Only 11 delivered to US Navy, others going for export. The F2A was the US Navy's first monoplane fighter and entered service June 1939. Total of 507 aircraft of all versions built for US Navy and other countries.

Brewster SBA/SBN Two-seat scout-bomber. Prototype began test flying in 1936. 30 built by the Naval Aircraft Factory as SBN-1s, deliveries starting November 1940.

Consolidated PB2Y Coronado Long-range four-engined patrol bomber or transport flying-boat. Prototype first flew 17 December 1937 and evaluated by US Navy from August. Six PB2Y-2s ordered March 1939 and entered service 1941. Many Coronados built subsequently.

Consolidated PT/NY series Two-seat trainers. US Army Air Service received over 450 production PT-1s, PT-3s, PT-3As and PT-11s and derivatives (a few observation aircraft designated O-17s were also built and used mainly by the National Guard). The US Navy received over 300 NY-1s, NY-2s, armed NY-2As, and NY-3s. The Navy aircraft could be operated as land or floatplanes.

Consolidated PY-1 Three-engined parasol-wing flying-boat. Consolidated given contract to build the XPY-1 in February 1928. Aircraft of similar design were also built by the Glenn L. Martin Company.

Curtiss A-18 Shrike Twin-engined attack aircraft of which 13 were ordered by USAAC in 1936 for evaluation. Max speed 239mph.

Curtiss B-2 Twin 600hp Curtiss Conqueror-engined biplane bomber of 1929, of which 12

Right: *Curtiss A-18 Shrike*

delivered to the USAAC after losing major orders to Keystone. Maximum speed 132mph. Six machine guns and up to 4,000lb of bombs.

Curtiss BT-32 Twin-engined biplane bomber of 1934. Developed from the Condor transport aircraft, the BT-32 was exported to China. Armament consisted of five guns and 3,968lb of bombs.

Curtiss F-5L Patrol flying-boat, developed from the Felixstowe F5 (qv). More than 200 built for US Navy, remaining operational until 1928. Powered by two Liberty 12A engines.

Curtiss F7C Single-seat carrier-based biplane fighter. Prototype flew 28 February 1927 and 17 production aircraft were ordered, deliveries starting December 1928. Most aircraft later transferred to US Marine Corps.

Curtiss H-16 America anti-submarine and maritime patrol flying-boat. H-16s were ordered by RNAS, deliveries starting early 1918, and by the US Navy. 33 US Navy aircraft were still operational in 1925.

Curtiss HS-2L Single-engined anti-submarine and escort flying-boat. Over 1,000 HS-2s were built during World War 1; 40 still in service in 1925.

Curtiss JN 'Jenny' two-seat trainer, used during World War 1. Hispano-engined variants remained in service in USA until 1927.

Above: *Curtiss JN (Jenny)*

Curtiss Fledgling Two-seat biplane trainer, powered by a 220/240hp Wright radial engine. 51 delivered to US Navy as N2C-1/2s, being operational throughout most of the 1930s.

Curtiss N-9 Two-seat biplane trainer, fitted with one central and two wingtip floats. Essentially a

floatplane version of Curtiss JN Jenny. Original version powered by a 100hp Curtiss OX-6 engine. Final variant, N-9H, powered by Wright-built 150hp Hispano-Suiza engine. N-9s remained operational until the mid-1920s.

Curtiss NC Patrol flying-boat. Curtiss built four NC flying-boats, the first flying 4 October 1918. NC-4 aircraft made the first air crossing of the Atlantic, starting 16 May 1919. Naval Aircraft Factory built six more from 1919-20, these serving until 1922.

Curtiss/Orenco Model D Single-seat biplane fighter. Designed by the Army Engineering Division, the first prototype appeared January 1919. 50 production aircraft built by Curtiss. This was the first fighter designed in the USA to go into production.

Curtiss P40 Warhawk Single-seat fighter. The XP-40, derived from the P-36A Hawk, first flew October 1938. Ordered into production 27 April 1939.

Curtiss PW-8 25 production PW-8 single-seat biplane fighters built for the USAAS and delivered from mid-1924, powered by 435hp Curtiss D-12 engines. Maximum speed 165mph. One flown by Lt Russell Maughan across America non-stop during daylight hours on 23 June 1924.

Curtiss R-6 Two-seat observation biplane used during World War 1. Some modified after war as experimental torpedo carriers.

Curtiss FC, F2C, F3C and F4C (TS series) Single-seat carrier-borne biplane fighters. Designed by the Naval Aircraft Factory, the Curtiss TS-1 appeared May 1922. Curtiss built 34, and the NAF built eight TS-1s, TS-2s and TS-3s. TS-1s were delivered from late 1922. In March 1923 these aircraft were redesignated FC-1, F2C-1 and F3C-1. Two further aircraft were built by Curtiss as F4C-1s.

Curtiss-Wright Condor Development of civil transport aircraft. Very small number in military service.

Curtiss-Wright CW-21 Demon Single-seat fighter. First flew January 1939 and 35 examples ordered by China. 24 improved CW-21Bs ordered by Netherlands East Indies 1940.

Dayton-Wright TA-3 and TW-3 Two-seat (side by side) biplane trainers. TA-3 powered by a 110hp Le Rhône rotary engine. 10 operated by US Army Air Corps from early 1920s. TW-3 powered by a Wright-built Hispano-Suiza engine. 20 purchased by USAAC after TA-3s.

Douglas B-18 Bolo Twin-engined monoplane bomber. Using the wings and tail of the DC-2, Douglas produced the DB-1 bomber. After trials in August 1935, a contract was placed for 133 examples, designated B-18. These were followed by 217 B-18As.

Douglas B-23 Dragon Twin-engined monoplane bomber. Developed from the B-18, the B-23 had a redesigned fuselage. The first aircraft, flown 27 July 1939, was one of 38 ordered for the USAAC.

Douglas DB-7 Twin-engined light bomber. Prototype flew December 1938. France ordered modified aircraft as DB-7s, and prototype of this version flew 17 August 1939. 108 aircraft reached France before its fall. Others served during war with other countries.

Douglas DT series Two-seat torpedo bomber.

Three examples ordered 1921 as DT-1s for US Navy competition. Douglas built 38 DT-2s and a number of DT-2Bs for Norway and Peru 1924-5. LWF built 20 DT-2s, of which some converted to SDW-1s by Dayton-Wright. DT-2 remained in service until 1926. NAF built six DT-4/5s in 1923. A DT-6 was also built.

Above: *Douglas DT-2*

Douglas O-2 and derivatives Series of two-seat Liberty-powered armed observation biplanes that were in service with the USAAC from the latter 1920s until the outbreak of war. Important developed versions became O-25, powered by a Conqueror engine, Pratt & Whitney Wasp-powered O-32 and Pratt & Whitney Hornet-powered O-38. The O-32s later converted into BT-2 two-seat trainers, plus some built as such, serving alongside earlier converted O-2s. Total of nearly 700 built, most observation examples armed with two or three Browning machine guns. Some had provision to carry bombs.

Douglas O-31s and derivatives Braced high-wing or parasol-wing observation monoplanes, used by US Army Air Corps from early 1930s. Final and main variant, the O-46A, powered by one 725hp Pratt & Whitney R-1535 engine. Armament comprised one forward-firing and one rear-mounted Browning machine gun. Total of 126 of all variants built.

Douglas C-1 Transport biplane of 1924, powered by one Liberty engine. 27 built in two versions for USAAC, in eight and nine-seat configurations (with two pilots).

Douglas C-33 Military transport version of Douglas DC-2, powered by two 750hp Wright Cyclone radial engines. 18 purchased by USAAC in 1936. US Navy also purchased five as R2D-1s.

Douglas TBD-1 Devastator Cantilever low-wing monoplane torpedo bomber, powered by one 900hp Pratt & Whitney R-1830-64 Twin Wasp radial engine. Max speed 206mph. Armed with one .30in and one .50in machine gun, one 21in torpedo or up to 1,000lb of bombs. 129 built for US Navy, entering service in late 1937. Used during early stages of Pacific War.

Douglas Dolphin military derivatives Shoulder-wing amphibian, first produced as commercial transport. First ordered by US Coast Guard as transport and search and rescue aircraft, designated RDs and powered by two 400hp Wright Whirlwind radial engines. Subsequent Coast Guard order for improved RD-4s. The USAAC ordered Dolphins as C-21 and C-26 seven and eight-seat transports, powered by Whirlwind and Pratt & Whitney Wasp Junior engines respectively. These and later aircraft subsequently converted into OA observation amphibians. US Navy also ordered similar transport aircraft, powered by Wasp engines. Type in service from 1931 until outbreak of war.

Douglas YB-7 Twin-engined monoplane bomber. After flying the prototype in 1930, Douglas built seven YB-7s for service testing.

Above: *Douglas YB-7*

Engineering Division XB-1A Two-seat biplane fighter of 1919, based on Bristol F2B Fighter, powered by a 300hp Wright H engine. 40 built for United States Army Air Service.

Fairchild C-8 Military version of Model 71 airliner, powered by a 410hp Pratt & Whitney Wasp engine. 14 built for USAAC and used during 1930s in seven-passenger transport or photographic roles.

Fleet PT-6 Two-seat biplane of 1928. 17 built for USAAC as basic trainers.

Ford Trimotor military derivatives 21 Trimotors used by USAAC, US Marine Corps and US Navy from 1927 as 15-passenger transports, powered by either three 235-300hp Wright or 450hp Pratt & Whitney Wasp engines.

Grumman F4F Wildcat Single-seat carrier-borne fighter. Prototype XF4F-2 flew 2 September 1937. New prototype built as XF4F-3, and order placed for production F4F-3s in August 1939. First production aircraft flew February 1940.

Grumman OA-9 and JRF-1 Military version of Goose high-wing monoplane amphibious flying-boat, used by USAAC and US naval services from 1938.

Huff-Daland TW-5/AT-1 Two-seat biplane trainer, powered by a 180hp Wright-built Hispano-Suiza engine. 15 purchased by USAAC, originally as TW-5s but thereafter as AT-1s.

Kellett autogyros Single two-seat KD-1 acquired by USAAC in 1935 as USAAC's first rotary-winged aircraft. Designated YG-1, joined by eight other Kellett autogyros before the outbreak of war, the seven YG-1Bs powered by 225hp Jacobs engines.

Keystone NK-1 Two-seat biplane trainer, powered by a 220hp Wright R-790 engine. 19 purchased by USAAC from 1930, sometimes known under the name of Pup.

Kinner XRK-1 Braced low-wing monoplane, with accommodation for four passengers in enclosed cabin. Three acquired by US Navy in 1936 as military examples of Envoy civil aircraft, powered by 340hp Kinner R-1044 engines.

Lockheed C-36, C-37, R20 and R-30 Six Lockheed Model 10 Electra airliners acquired by the USAAC and the US Navy and Coast Guard from 1936 as staff transport aircraft, powered by two 450hp Pratt & Whitney Wasp Junior engines.

Lockheed C-40, JO-1 and JO-2 Nineteen Lockheed Model 12A airliners acquired by the USAAC as C-40s and C-40As and by the US Navy and US Marine Corps as the JO-1 and JO-2.

Lockheed P-38 Lightning Twin-engined long-range fighter and fighter-bomber. XP-38 prototype flew 27 January 1939. Many built during war.

Lockheed Hudson Military development of Lockheed Model 14 commercial airliner. First of initial batch of 250 Hudson Is for RAF flown December 1938. More than 2,000 Hudsons eventually acquired by RAF and used mainly for maritime patrol duties. Hudson I powered by two 1,100hp Wright R-1820 engines. Max speed 246mph. Two or four .30in machine guns.

Loening OA and OL series Observation, ambulance and general duties aircraft. XCOA-1s flew mid-1924. More than 50 built for US Army as COA-1s, OA-1As, OA-1Bs, OA-1Cs and OA-2s. A further 120 built for US Navy as OL-1s, OL-2s, OL-3s, OL-4s, OL-6s, OL-8s, OL-8As and OL-9s.

Martin 167 Maryland Twin-engined light bomber. Delivered for US Army evaluation March 1939 as XA-22. France ordered first batch of 115 167Fs in January 1939, and first production aircraft flew August 1939.

Martin MB-1 Twin-engined four-seat biplane. First MB-1 flew August 1918. 14 were built as bombing, reconnaissance and transport aircraft. 12 similar aircraft bought by US Navy as TM-1 torpedo-bombers.

Martin PBM Mariner Twin-engined patrol bomber and transport flying-boat. XPBM-1 prototype first flew 18 February 1939. Deliveries to US Navy started 1940.

Martin P3M Twin-engined monoplane flying-boat. Prototype built by Consolidated Aircraft and delivered mid-1929. Nine production aircraft built by Martin as P3M-1s and P3M-2s.

Naval Aircraft Factory N3N Two-seat biplane basic trainer built in two major versions, the N3N-1 powered by a 220hp Wright J-5 and the N3N-3 powered by a 235hp Wright R-760 engine. Total of nearly 1,000 N3Ns built, serving with US Navy from 1936, on wheel or float landing gears.

North American BT-9 Cantilever low-wing monoplane basic trainer, powered by a 400hp Wright Whirlwind engine. Total of over 260 built, becoming operational with the USAAC from 1935.

North American NA-44 and NA-50 Single-engined light attack-bomber. Developed from NA-16 design, the NA-44 appeared 1938. Ordered by Brazil and Siam. NA-50 built 1939, and seven acquired by Peru 1939-40. Others ordered/built during war.

North American O-47 Cantilever low-wing monoplane observation aircraft, with retractable landing gear and powered by a 975hp Wright Cyclone engine. About 240 built, serving with the USAAC and reserve units from the late 1930s.

North American Texan General purpose trainer, used in vast numbers during and after World War 2. First ordered for USAAC in 1939.

Packard-Le Père LUSAC-11 and -21 Two-seat biplane fighters. LUSAC-11 designed by Capitaine Le Père. Two of the aircraft built by Packard reached France September 1918. After war, three LUSAC-21s were built with 420hp Bugatti engines.

Republic P-43 Lancer Single-seat fighter and reconnaissance monoplane. The prototype, designated AP-4, was built as a private venture. The USAAC ordered 13 YP-43s in March 1939 for service trials. Production orders placed 1940.

Ryan PT-16 Two-seat braced low-wing monoplane trainer powered by a 125hp Menasco L-365 engine. Evaluation PT-16s operated in 1939, prior to orders for later Ryan PT developments.

Seversky BT-8 Two-seat cantilever low-wing monoplane trainer, powered by a 450hp Pratt & Whitney Wasp Junior engine. Small number built for USAAC.

Sikorsky C-6, PS-3 and RS series USAAC and US Navy/Marine Corps versions of the commercial Sikorsky S-38 sesquiplane amphibian, each powered by two 450hp Pratt & Whitney Wasp engines. Small number used in transport and other roles from 1929.

Spartan Executive and Zeus Two-seat single-engined light-bombers. Appearing 1938, the Zeus was based on the Executive — a converted lightplane sold to China as a light bomber in early 1938 — and carried 250lb of bombs. A small number was sold to Mexico.

Stearman NS-1 and PT-13 Two-seat biplane basic trainers, of which many thousands were built (mostly during World War 2 as the Boeing-Stearman Kaydet). First ordered by US Navy in 1934 as NS-1, powered by a Wright J-5 radial engine. Refined 215hp Lycoming R-680-5-engined Stearman ordered by USAAC in 1936 as PT-13, followed by 220hp PT-13A and naval N2S-1 of 1940.

Thomas-Morse S-4 Designed originally as low-powered single-seat fighter during World War 1. Adopted as unarmed single-seat advanced trainer in 1917, designated S-4B, followed by mostly 80hp Le Rhône-powered armed S-4Cs. In limited use after the war.

Thomas-Morse O-19 Two-seat armed observation biplane, powered by a 450hp Pratt & Whitney Wasp engine. Over 170 built from 1928 for the USAAC.

Vought SB2U-1 and SB2U-2 Vindicator Monoplane scout and dive bomber, powered by one 750hp Pratt & Whitney R-1535 Twin Wasp Junior radial engine and armed with one forward-firing and one rear-mounted machine gun and up to 1,000lb of bombs. SB2U-1 entered US Navy service in 1937 and SB2U-2 entered US Marine Corps service in

Right: Vought SB2U-1

1938. France received a number from a batch ordered as V-156s. SB2U-3 USMC version ordered in 1939.

Vought FU-1 Single-seat land- or floatplane fighter trainer. Appeared January 1927. 20 built, operated mainly from the USS *Langley* during 1927-8. In late 1928 the remaining aircraft were converted to FU-2 two-seat trainers.

Vought VE-7 and VE-9 Single-engined biplanes. Between 1920 and 1924, 129 VE-7s were built for the US Navy. Used mainly as trainers but considerable number were built as VE-7SF single-seat fighters. A VE-7SF made the first take-off from a US Navy carrier, USS *Langley*, on 17 October 1922. Later VE-9 version used as observation aircraft.

Vultee V-11 and YA-19 V-11 was a monoplane attack bomber, powered by a Wright Cyclone radial engine, developed from the V-1A eight-passenger commercial airliner of 1934. Number produced for export to Brazil, China, Turkey and USSR. Also licence-built in USSR as BSL-1. A few similar YA-19s purchased by USAAC in 1938 for evaluation, powered by 1,200hp Pratt & Whitney Twin Wasp engines. Armament comprised six machine guns and up to 3,000lb of bombs.

Above: *Vultee V-11*

Waco XJW-1 US Navy designation of two Waco UBF three-seat biplanes used for 'hook-on' experiments with the airship USS *Macon* (see Curtiss Sparrowhawk).

Waco J2W-1 Four/five-seat cabin biplane, of which three purchased by US Coast Guard in 1936, derived from Waco Model C.

USSR

Beriev KOR-1 Single-engined reconnaissance and light bombing floatplane. KOR-1s entered service in 1938 and were used for catapult operations from warships, coastal reconnaissance and other duties.

Chetverikov MDR-6 Twin-engined patrol and reconnaissance flying-boat. Prototype first flew 1938 and series production began 1939. MDR-6s served in several versions from 1939 to mid-1950s.

Grigorovich IZ (TsKB-7) Single-seat low-wing monoplane fighter, powered by 450hp M-22 engine and armed with two underwing large-bore cannon and one fuselage-mounted machine gun.

Grigorovich PI-1 Single-seat low-wing monoplane fighter evolved from the IZ. Prototype appeared in 1934, armed with two 75mm APK cannon and one ShKAS machine gun. Production of the type was started, and from 1936 the 75mm cannon were replaced by two 20mm ShVAK cannon on production machines. The new armament made the type inferior to the Polikarpov fighters then being built and production of the PI-1 was terminated.

Grigorovich TSh-2 (TsKB-21) Two-seat ground attack biplane. First prototype flew in February 1931. Production aircraft, designated TSh-2s, appeared late 1931. Ten were built.

Kocherghin DI-6 Two-seat biplane fighter. The DI-6 appeared in 1934. Aircraft entered production in following year. Armament consisted of four forward machine guns and one rear-mounted. Maximum speed was 239mph.

Lavochkin LaGG-1 Single-seat monoplane fighter. First appeared as I-22 and made first flight 30 March 1939. Following some modification, it entered production in 1940 as the LaGG-1. Superseded by LaGG-3.

Lebed 12 Two-seat reconnaissance biplane. First flown 28 December 1915, the Lebed 12 entered service October 1916. By 1 March 1919 a total of well over 200 completed aircraft had been produced.

Petlyakov VI-100 (Pe-2) Twin-engined ground attack aircraft. Designed in 1938-9, this aircraft was originally designated VI-100, changed later to PB-100. Production began in June 1940 as the Pe-2.

Polikarpov I-1 Single-seat low-wing monoplane fighter. This was the first Soviet-designed fighter to enter production. The prototype, designated IL-400, first flew 23 August 1923. Production aircraft proved unstable.

Polikarpov I-17 Single-seat low-wing monoplane fighter. First prototype flew 1 September 1934, designated TsKB-15. An improved version followed

as the TsKB-19, and this entered limited production as the I-17-2.

Polikarpov U-2 (Po-2) Designed as a primary trainer and first flown in 1928. Also widely used as a civil transport and agricultural biplane. Well over 13,000 built and used during World War 2 as light attack and general purpose aircraft. Its replacement, the Shcherbakov Shche-2, was not successful and was used only for evacuation of partisans and casualties. U-2 powered by one 110hp M-11 engine. Maximum speed 91mph. Armament comprised one 7.62mm machine gun and up to 507lb of bombs or rockets.

Sukhoi Su-2 (ANT-51) Single-engined low-wing monoplane light bomber. Prototype, designated ANT-51, was tested in 1937 and was ordered into production as the BB-1 in 1940. In 1941 it was re-designated Su-2.

Tupolev MDR-2 (ANT-8) Five-seat twin-engined reconnaissance-bomber flying-boat. Prototype appeared in 1931 and the type entered production powered by two 650hp M-17 engines.

Tupolev MDR-4 (ANT-27) Three-engined reconnaissance-bomber flying-boat. 15 MDR-4s entered service April 1936. Maximum speed was 145mph at sea level.

Tupolev ANT-42 or TB-7 (Petlyakov Pe-8) Four-engined monoplane heavy bomber. The TB-7 (air force designation) first flew 27 December 1936. Production started at end of 1939 and the aircraft was redesignated Pe-8 in 1940. Production ended 1944.

Tupolev RD-DB-1 Military derivative of ANT-25, powered by one 860hp M-34 engine. Entered production in 1934 as a low-wing monoplane bomber with retractable undercarriage, but was very underpowered for its size and so proved slow and unsuccessful.

Above: *Tupolev RD-DB-1*

Yakovlev BB-22 (Yak-2) Twin-engined monoplane bomber and reconnaissance aircraft. The BB-22 was flight tested in 1939, reaching nearly 336mph. Production started 1940. Designation changed later to Yak-2.

Yugoslavia

Ikarus IK-2 Single-seat high-wing monoplane fighter. First IK-1 prototype flew April 1935 but crashed. Production of IK-2s totalled 12 aircraft, delivered late 1937. By outbreak of war only eight IK-2s still in service, used mainly for ground attack. Maximum speed was 266mph.

Rogozarski IK-3 Single-seat low-wing monoplane fighter. Prototype IK-3 first flew in the spring of

1938, and 12 production aircraft ordered. Deliveries started 1940.

SIM-XIV-H Twin-engined three-seat reconnaissance and anti-shipping seaplane. First aircraft flew February 1938, followed by 12 production aircraft. All served with Royal Yugoslav Navy. Maximum speed was 151mph and armament consisted of two 7.5mm guns, mines or bombs.

Index